T0243341

the

Diamond

cutter

20TH Anniversary Edition

The Buddha on Managing Your Business & Your Life

With 25% new wisdom for your life

the

Diamond

cutter

Geshe Michael Roach

Published in the United States by Diamond Cutter Press
Arizona, LLC.
www.diamondcutterpress.com

Reprinted by arrangement with Image, and imprint of Random
House, a division of Penguin Random House, LLC.

The original edition of the Work published in 2000 by Image.

English edition originally published in the United States by
Doubleday, New York, in 2000, and subsequently published in
trade paperback in the United States by Doubleday Religion, an
imprint of the Crown Publishing Group, a division of Penguin
Random House, Inc, New York, in 2009.

Library of Congress Cataloging-in-Publication Data
Roach, Michael, 1952–
    The diamond cutter: the Buddha on managing your business
and your life / Geshe Michael Roach.
            p.   cm.
    1. Business—Religious aspects—Buddhism.   2. Triptaka.
Sutrapitaka.   Prajñāpāramitā.   Vajracchedikā—Criticism, inter-
pretation, etc.   3. Roach, Michael, 1952–   4. Lamas—United
States—Biography. 5. Diamond cutting industry—New York—
History. I. Title.

BQ4570.B86 R63 2000
294.3'444—dc21   99-053059

ISBN 9781937114411

PRINTED IN THE UNITED STATES OF AMERICA

Cover design by Rosa van Grieken
Inside design by Donna Sinisgalli

Cover art:
Mandala of Amoghapasha
Rubin Museum of Art C2004.15.1 (HAR 65345)

contents

goal three—looking back, and
knowing it was worth it

20th Anniversary Edition
of The Diamond Cutter

In 2000, after 19 years in Manhattan helping to build Andin International Diamond from zero into one of the largest diamond jewelry companies in the world, I stepped back to do a silent retreat and give some thought about what I wanted to do with the rest of my life.

In the car driving up to the gate of the retreat center, I finished up the last edits to this book—*The Diamond Cutter: The Buddha on Managing Your Business & Your Life*—and handed the manuscript to my personal assistant. I was in retreat for the next three years, with no news from the outside world.

When I came out, one newspaper interviewed me about the World Trade Center tragedy, because I was one of the few people in the world who had never heard about it. Neither did I know if *The Diamond Cutter* had ever gone to print, or whether people liked it.

I'm happy to say that the book was a big hit! I've been on a plane from New York to London, and watched the person sitting next to me read the book, then suddenly look up and realize who I was; or in a taxi in Taipei, I've watched the driver stop at a red light and pull the Chinese-language version out from under his seat, to read a few sentences before the light turns green.

The Diamond Cutter has now been printed in more than 35 languages, and well over a million copies. More importantly, it has become sort of a "daily success guide" for a huge number of people in 75 of the major cities of the world.

The book has spawned the Diamond Cutter Institute (DCI), which as of this writing offers programs in business and personal success to over 35,000 participants every year, in some 20 countries. DCI, in turn, has given birth to SCIM (the Sedona College of International Management), which occupies an elegant and bustling facility in the USA and offers a four-year program in becoming a fully certified trainer of the DCI curriculum. Some 93 candidates from 19 different countries have already completed academic terms in the first three years of the program.

Ten years after we first published *The Diamond Cutter*, Trace Murphy—my erstwhile editor at what is now Penguin Random House, the world's largest trade publishing group—proposed that we publish a tenth-anniversary edition of the work, including a major new section about people who had used the book to help achieve business and personal success.

I was a bit dubious that anyone would be very interested in such a work, but went ahead and wrote out 39 wonderful success stories from many countries of the world, and added it to the book. Again, the reaction of the world audience was amazing, and sales of *The Diamond Cutter* climbed steadily for another 10 years.

To be honest, for that anniversary edition there were no significant points in *The Diamond Cutter* that I felt needed any changes at all: the book was meant, in a way, to address eternal human needs with eternally effective solutions, and it still does.

And so aside from a few words, you won't see any significant changes to the content of the original book here in the 20th anniversary edition. What was already here from the twenty years ago is enough for you to change the rest of your life into an amazing material and emotional success.

What I have added are two important sections at the back that will help you achieve these goals more quickly. The two new sections will, in my opinion, be as valuable to you as the original book itself.

The first of these is an essay called "Cutting Diamonds," which I wrote recently for the introduction of a book named *Sunlight on the Path to Freedom*. This is a full translation of what is easily the most important native commentary ever written to the original *Diamond Cutter Sutra*, from 25 centuries ago. The commentary was composed by Choney Lama Drakpa Shedrup (1675-1748), whose explanations I first used 20 years ago to tackle difficult points in this *Diamond Cutter* business book.

The story behind this essay is that—during the last ten years especially—I have spent more and more time every year circling the globe, presenting the ideas of the book you hold in your hands now to over a hundred thousand people, face to face.

And so naturally I have discovered new language and new techniques to convey the deep ideas of the book to fit the needs of very different people from very different countries. That is, I and the other DCI trainers have had to find words and expressions that are equally comfortable and available to all of our global audience—which has included Catholic lawmakers filling the halls of the Congress of Mexico; Arab nobility attending the world congress of diamond-producing countries in Dubai; influential oligarchs of the Russian oil and banking industries; crowds of thousands of people in the Muslim centers of Kazakhstan, Indonesia, and Malaysia; and officials of some of the biggest mega-corporations of China.

To meet this need, we have developed three special tools that we rely on constantly to convey the great ideas of *The Diamond Cutter* to normal people everywhere; these are called The Pen; The Four Steps; and The Two Husbands in the Kitchen.

When I first started doing business in Hong Kong many years ago, people there had a saying that if you couldn't become a millionaire after three years in Hong Kong, there was something wrong with you. I would venture to say something similar about anyone who learns these three success tools well, and doesn't quickly surprise themselves with unexpected and overwhelming success.

The second new section you will find here is called "Success: 5 Goals, 5 Continents." Looking back at most of the people whose life stories were featured in the 10th anniversary edition, I realize that they became a second generation of Diamond Cutter success that has now given birth to a third generation, whose stories you will find here in the 20th anniversary version.

I thought it would be very helpful to readers if we allowed this new generation to tell their story—not just about the success they have found with *The Diamond Cutter,* but also frankly about the difficulties they may have encountered as they tried to use its wisdom, and how they overcame these challenges.

In order not to make the book too long—now that there are tens of thousands of Diamond Cutter success stories around the world—I have chosen one of my favorite stories of success from each major area of our planet. I have tried to strike a balance between stories by females and males; business and family life; hard economics and successful inner peace.

In this regard, there was a common belief—when I first wrote *The Diamond Cutter*—that you could be either a successful businessperson or successful on the inside, as a deep and thoughtful person. But not both.

It is one of my greatest satisfactions in life that the book has contributed, in some small way, to the idea that we can be successful on the outside and on the inside as well—that these two go hand-in-hand. I hope that this new edition will help you make that precious journey yourself.

Geshe Michael Roach
February 2020

Rainbow House
Rimrock, Arizona US

The Buddha

and Business

During the seventeen years from 1981 to 1998, I had the honor of working with Ofer and Aya Azrielant, the owners of the Andin International Diamond Corporation, and the core staff of the company to build one of the world's largest diamond and jewelry firms. The business was started with a $50,000 loan and only three or four employees, including myself. By the time I left to devote full time to the training institute I had founded in New York, our sales were in excess of 100 million U.S. dollars per year, with over five hundred employees in offices around the world.

During my time in the diamond business, I led a double life. Seven years before joining the trade, I graduated from Princeton University with honors, having previously received the Presidential Scholar Medallion from the President of the United States at the White House, and the McConnell Scholarship Prize from Princeton's Woodrow Wilson School of International Affairs.

A grant from this school allowed me to travel to Asia, for study with Tibetan Lamas at the seat of His Holiness, the Dalai Lama. Thus began my education in the ancient wisdom of Tibet, which culminated in 1995, when I became the first American to complete the twenty years of rigorous study and examinations required to earn the ancient degree of *geshe*, or master of Buddhist learning. I had lived in Buddhist monasteries both in the United States and Asia since graduating from Princeton, and in 1983 taken the vows of a Buddhist monk.

Once I had gained a firm foundation in the training of a Buddhist monk, my principal teacher—whose name is Khen Rinpoche, or "Precious Abbot"—encouraged me to enter the world of business. He told me that, although the monastery was an ideal place for learning the great ideas of Buddhist wisdom, a busy American office would provide the perfect "laboratory" for actually testing these ideals in real life.

I resisted for some time, hesitant to leave the quiet of our small monastery, and nervous about the image of American businessmen in my mind: greedy, ruthless, uncaring. But one day, after hearing my teacher give an especially inspiring talk to some university students, I told him I would agree to his instructions and seek a job in business.

Some years earlier I had had something of a vision at the monastery during my daily meditations, and I knew from that time what business I would choose to work in: It would surely involve diamonds. I had no knowledge of these gemstones, and frankly no attraction whatsoever to jewelry; neither had any of my family ever been involved in the trade. So, like the innocent Candide, I began visiting one diamond shop after another, asking if anyone would be willing to accept me as a trainee.

Trying to join the diamond business this way is a little like attempting to sign up for the Mafia: the raw diamond trade is a highly secretive and closed society, traditionally restricted to family members. In those days, the Belgians controlled the larger diamonds—those of a carat or more; the Israelis cut most of the smaller stones; and the Hassidic Jews of New York's Diamond District on Forty-seventh Street handled the majority of the domestic American wholesale trade.

Remember that the entire inventory of even the largest diamond houses can be contained in a few small containers that look a lot like ordinary shoe boxes. And there is no way to detect a theft of millions of dollars of diamonds: you just put a handful or two in your pocket and walk out the door—there is nothing like a metal detector that can spot the stones. And so most firms hire only sons or nephews or cousins, never an odd Irish boy who wants to play with diamonds.

As I remember, I visited some fifteen different shops, asking for an entry-level position, and was summarily thrown out of each of them. An old watchmaker in a nearby town advised me to try taking some courses in diamond grading at the Gemological Institute of America in New York;

I'd be more likely to get work if I had a diploma, and might meet someone in the classes who could help me.

It was at the institute that I met Mr. Ofer Azrielant. He was also taking a class in grading very high-quality diamonds, known as "investment" or "certificate" stones. Distinguishing an extremely valuable certificate diamond from a fake or treated stone involves being able to spot tiny holes or other imperfections the size of a needle point, while dozens of dust motes land on the surface of the diamond, or on the lens of the microscope itself, to parade around and confuse things. So we were both there to learn how not to lose our shirts.

I was impressed immediately by Ofer's questions to the teacher, by how he examined and challenged every concept presented. I determined to try to get him to help me find a job or even hire me himself, and so struck up an acquaintance. A few weeks later—the day I finished my final exams in diamond grading at the New York labs of the GIA—I made up an excuse to get into his office and ask him for a job.

By great good luck he was at that moment just opening a branch office in America, having already founded a small firm in Israel, his home. So I talk my way into his office and beg him to teach me the diamond business: "I'll do anything you need, just give me a try. I'll straighten up the office, wash the windows, whatever you say."

And he says, "I don't have any money to hire you! But tell you what, I'll talk to the owner of this office—his name is Alex Rosenthal—and we'll see if he and I can split your pay between us. Then you can do errands and things for us both."

So I start as an errand boy, at seven dollars an hour, a Princeton graduate dragging through steamy New York summers and winter snowstorms on foot, uptown to the Diamond District, carrying nondescript canvas bags filled with gold and diamonds to be cast and set into rings. Ofer, his wife Aya, and a quiet, brilliant Yemeni jeweler named Alex Gal would sit around our single rented desk with me, sorting diamonds into grades, sketching new pieces, and calling around for customers.

Paychecks were few, often delayed while Ofer tried to talk his London friends into some more loans, but soon I had enough to buy my first business suit, which I wore every day for months. We often worked past midnight, and I would have a long trip back to my little room at a small monastery in the Asian Buddhist community of Howell, in New Jersey. In a few hours I would be up again and back on the bus to Manhattan.

After our business had grown a bit, we moved uptown closer to the jewelry district proper, and took the brave step of hiring a single jewelry craftsman, who sat alone in the big room that was our "factory," making our first diamond rings. Before long I was trusted enough to get my wish, to sit down with a parcel of loose diamonds and start sorting them into grades. Ofer and Aya asked me if I would take responsibility for the newly formed diamond purchasing division (which at the time consisted of myself and one other person). I was excited at the opportunity, and plunged into the project.

One rule my Tibetan Lama had given me about going to work in a normal business office was that I keep quiet about being a Buddhist. I was to wear my hair at normal length (rather than shaved), and dress in normal clothes. Whatever Buddhist principles I used in my work had to be applied quietly, without any announcement or fanfare. I was to be a Buddhist sage on the inside, and a normal American businessman on the outside.

And so I set about trying to run the division by Buddhist principles, without anyone knowing it. Early in the game I established an understanding with the Azrielants: I was responsible for managing every aspect of the Diamond Division and realizing a healthy profit on the stones; and in return I had complete authority over hiring and firing, over pay and raises, over the hours my people worked, and who took which responsibility. I only had to deliver the product on time, and with a good profit.

This book is the story of how I built the Diamond Division at Andin International, using principles culled from the ancient wisdom of Buddhism, from nothing into a worldwide operation generating many millions of dollars per year. I did not do so alone, nor were my views the only ones we followed, but I can say that the majority of the decisions and policies in our division during my tenure as vice president were driven by the principles you will find in this book.

What, in a nutshell, are these principles? We can divide them into three.

The first principle is that the business should be successful: that it should make money. There is a belief prevalent in America and other

Western countries that being successful, making money, is somehow wrong for people who are trying to lead a spiritual life. In Buddhism though it is not the money which is in itself wrong; in fact, a person with greater resources can do much more good in the world than one without. The question rather is *how* we make the money; whether we understand where it comes from and how to *make it continue to come*; and whether *we keep a healthy attitude about the money.*

The whole point then is to make money in a clean and honest way, to understand clearly where it comes from so it doesn't stop, and to maintain a healthy view toward it while we have it. As long as we do these things, making money is completely consistent with a spiritual way of life; in fact, it becomes part of a spiritual way of life.

The second principle is that we should enjoy the money; that is, we should learn how to keep our minds and bodies in good health while we make the money. The activity of creating wealth should not exhaust us so much physically or mentally that we cannot enjoy the wealth. A business-person who ruins his health doing business is defeating the very purpose of business.

The third principle is that you should be able to look back at your business, at the end, and honestly say that your years of doing business have had some meaning. The end of every business enterprise we engage in, and in fact the end of our lives, must come to every person who ever does business. And at the most important part of the business—at the end, when we are looking back on all we have achieved—we should see that we have conducted ourselves and our business in a way that had some lasting meaning, that left some good mark in our world.

To summarize, the goal of business, and of ancient Tibetan wisdom, and in fact of all human endeavor, is to enrich ourselves—to achieve prosperity, both outer and inner. We can enjoy this prosperity only if we maintain a high degree of physical and mental health. And over the length of our lives we must seek ways to make this prosperity meaningful in a larger sense.

This is the lesson of what we accomplished in the Diamond Division of Andin International, and it is a lesson which can be learned and applied by anyone, whatever his or her background or beliefs.

goal one

Making

the Money

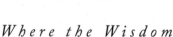

chapter 1

Where the Wisdom
Comes From

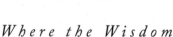

In the ancient language of India, this teaching is called the *Arya Vajra Chedaka Nama Prajnya Paramita Mahayana Sutra.*

In the language of Tibet, it is called the *Pakpa Sherab Kyi Paroltu Chinpa Dorje Chupa Shejawa Tekpa Chenpoy Do.*

In the English language, it is called *The Diamond Cutter, a High Ancient Book from the Way of Compassion, a Book which Teaches Perfect Wisdom.*

What makes this business book different from any other you have ever read? It's the source of what we have to say here: an ancient book of Buddhist wisdom called *The Diamond Cutter.* And the lines above are how the book starts out.

Hidden in *The Diamond Cutter* is the ancient wisdom that we used to help make Andin International a company with sales of over $100 million per year. It's good to know a little about this important book at the beginning, to recognize the role it has played throughout the history of the Eastern half of our world.

The Diamond Cutter is the oldest dated book in the world that was printed, rather than being written out by hand. The British Museum holds a copy that is dated A.D. 868, or about 600 years before the Gutenberg Bible was produced.

The Diamond Cutter is a written record of a teaching given by the Buddha over 2,500 years ago. In the beginning, it was passed down by word of mouth, and then—as writing first developed—it was inscribed onto long palm leaves. These were durable fronds of palm on which the words of the book were first scratched, using a needle. Then charcoal dust was rubbed into the scratches left by the needle. Books that were made this way are still to be found in southern Asia, and remain quite legible.

The loose palm leaves would be kept together in one of two ways. Sometimes a hole would be bored with an awl through the middle of the stack of leaves, and a string passed through to keep the pages together. Other books were kept wrapped in cloths.

The original *Diamond Cutter* was taught by the Buddha in Sanskrit, the ancient language of India, which we guess is about four thousand years old. When the book reached Tibet, about a thousand years ago, it was translated into Tibetan. Over the centuries in Tibet it has been carved onto woodblocks, and printed onto long strips of handmade paper by coating the block with ink and then pressing the paper with a roller against the block. These long strips of paper are stored in bright cloths of saffron or maroon, a throwback to the days of the palm leaves.

The Diamond Cutter also spread to other great countries of Asia, including China, Japan, Korea, and Mongolia. Over the last twenty-five centuries it has been reprinted in the languages of these countries countless times, and its wisdom passed down in an unbroken lineage, from the lips of the teachers of each generation to the ears of the students of the next. In Mongolia, the book was considered so important that every family would keep a copy carefully preserved on an altar in their home. Once or twice a year, the local Buddhist monks would be asked to come to the home and read the text out loud to the family, in order to impart the blessing of its wisdom.

The wisdom of *The Diamond Cutter* is not easily won. The original teaching, like so many teachings of the Buddha, is cloaked in highly mystical language that can only be revealed by a living teacher, using the great explanations that have been written over the centuries. In Tibetan we have three of these older explanations, ranging in age from about sixteen centuries old to a mere eleven hundred years.

More important, we have recently located another commentary on the work, one which is much more recent, and much more easy to understand. During the last twelve years, a group of colleagues and myself have been engaged in the Asian Classics Input Project, dedicated to preserving the ancient books of Tibetan wisdom. Over the past thousand years, these books have been kept in the great monasteries and libraries of Tibet herself, protected from war and invaders by the great natural wall of the Himalayan Mountains. This all changed with the invention of the airplane, and in 1950 Tibet was invaded by Communist China.

During the invasion and subsequent occupation—which continues today—over five thousand libraries and monastic colleges holding these great books were destroyed; only a handful of the books were carried out by refugees making the dangerous journey on foot over the Himalayas near Mount Everest. To get a feeling for the destruction, imagine that some powerful country has attacked the United States, and burned almost every single college and university, and all the books in all their libraries. Imagine that the only books left are those that have been carried out in their hands by refugees, journeying on foot for the several weeks or months it would take to walk to Mexico.

The Input Project has trained Tibetan refugees in camps in India to type these endangered books onto computer disks; they are then organized on CD-ROM or the Web, and distributed without charge to thousands of scholars around the world. So far we have saved about 150,000 pages of wood-block manuscripts this way, going to the far corners of the world to locate the books that never made it out of Tibet.

Deep in a dusty collection of manuscripts in St. Petersburg, Russia, we were fortunate enough to find a copy of a wonderful explanation of *The Diamond Cutter* brought back to Russia by early explorers who visited Tibet. This commentary is called *Sunlight on the Path to Freedom*, and it was written by a great Tibetan Lama named Choney Drakpa Shedrup, who lived from 1675 to 1748. Coincidentally, this Lama comes from the Tibetan monastery where I completed my own studies: Sera Mey. His nickname, over the centuries, has been "Choney Lama," or the "Lama from Choney," an area in east Tibet.

Throughout this book we will be using the original words of *The Diamond Cutter*, along with the text of *Sunlight on the Path to Freedom*. This is the first time that this important explanation has ever been translated into English. Along with the selections from these two great works we will include explanations that have been passed down orally throughout the last twenty-five centuries, as I received them from my own Lamas. Then finally we will add actual incidents from my own life in the arcane world of the international diamond business, to demonstrate how the secrets of this ancient wisdom can make your own work and life a more certain success.

chapter 2

What the Name

of the Book Means

༄༅། །རྒྱ་གར་སྐད་དུ། ཨཱུ་ད་བཛྲ་ཙྪེ་ད་ཀཱ་པྲ་ཛྙཱ་བྱ། དེ་བོད་སྐད་
དུ་བསྒྱུར་ན། ཨཱུ་ཙུ་ནི་འཕགས་པ། བཛྲ་ནི་རྡོ་རྗེ། ཙྪེ་ད་ཀ་ནི་གཅོད་པ།
པྲ་ཛྙཱ་ནི་ཤེས་རབ། པཱ་ར་ནི་ཕ་རོལ་དུ། ཨི་ཏ་ནི་ཕྱིན་པ། ནཱ་མ་ནི་
ཞེས་བྱ་བ། མ་ཧཱ་ནི་ཆེན་པོ། ཡཱ་ན་ནི་ཐེག་པ། སཱུ་ཏྲ་ནི་མདོ་ཞེས་
པར་འགྱུར་རོ།

The title of *The Diamond Cutter* itself contains a great degree of secret wisdom, and before we actually get into how to reach success with this wisdom, we might do well to discuss its meaning. We turn first to Choney Lama's own explanation of the long title:

> The root text here begins with the words, "In the ancient language of India, this teaching is called the Arya Vajra . . ." The equivalents for each of the Sanskrit words in the title are as follows. **Arya** means "high," and **vajra** means "diamond." **Chedaka** is for "cutter," while **prajnya** stands for "wisdom."
>
> **Param** means "to the other side," while **ita** means "gone"— the two together meaning "perfection." **Nama** means "called." **Maha** stands for "greater," referring to "compassion," and **yana** means "way." **Sutra** translates as "ancient book."

The most important word here, for explaining how to succeed in business and in life, is "diamond." Diamonds represent, in the ancient Tibetan way, a hidden potential in all things: This is usually referred to as "emptiness." A businessperson who is fully aware of this potential thereby understands the very key for attaining success, both in financial and personal terms. We will explain this potential with much more detail in the following chapter; for now, it's enough to know that the potential in all things resembles a diamond, in three important ways.

Pure diamond is, first of all, about the closest thing to an absolutely clear physical substance. Think of a large pane of glass; for example, the kind we use in a sliding glass door which leads to an outside patio. Viewed from the front, the glass looks completely clear—so clear that on occasion visiting neighbors have been known to walk through such panes and break them. Viewed down the length of the pane though, this and most other kinds of glass have a deep green color. This color represents the accumulative effect of a tiny bit of iron impurities spread throughout the glass, and is most obvious when looking through a thick mass of glass.

Pure diamond though is different. In the trade we grade the value of diamonds first by their *lack* of color—completely colorless diamonds being the most rare and valuable. A totally colorless diamond we rate as "D," itself sort of a historical mistake. When the modern system of diamond grading was being invented, many different competing systems already existed. The letter "A" was widely used to represent a very fine or colorless diamond, and then second-best stones were called "B," and so forth down the alphabet.

Unfortunately each company's idea of what "A" and "B" and so on represented was different, and of course this could lead to a lot of problems for customers. One firm's nearly colorless "B" could be another company's medium-yellow "B." So the designer of the new system just decided to start over farther down the alphabet—and he called the best or most colorless stone a "D."

Look through a windowpane made of a D-color diamond (if a diamond this big could ever exist) and it would look totally clear. Look *down the length* of a D-color diamond windowpane, and it would look *just as clear*. This is the nature of something which is totally pure or clear. If there were a wall of diamond several feet wide between you and another person, and if no light were reflecting from its surface, *you couldn't see the diamond at all.*

The hidden potential for success found in *The Diamond Cutter* is just like this pane of diamond glass. It is all around us, at all times; every object and person around us contains this potential. And it is this potential which, if harnessed, leads to certain personal and business success. The irony of our lives is that, even though this potential imbues every person and thing around us, it is invisible to us: We simply cannot see it. The purpose then of *The Diamond Cutter* is to teach us how to see this potential.

Diamond is significant in a second way. It is, very simply, the hardest thing in the universe. Nothing that exists can scratch a diamond, except another diamond: By one way of measuring hardness, called the Knoop scale, diamond is more than three times harder than the next hardest natural mineral—a ruby. And diamonds themselves can only scratch other diamonds when the diamond being scratched has a "soft" direction.

This in fact is how diamonds are "cut." Although a diamond cannot be scratched, it can be "cleaved" or split along a plane like a piece of wood when it's split by an ax. To cut a diamond, we take small leftover pieces from cutting another diamond—or else we take a piece of raw diamond stone which is not pure enough to make into a gemstone—and we split and crush the pieces into a powder.

This diamond powder is passed carefully through a series of fine sieves or iron mesh until it is very fine, and then stored in a small glass bottle. Next a large flat plate of heavy hardened steel is prepared by scoring: drawing narrow lines across the surface until a network of thin gouges has been created. The wheel is then covered with a fine oil. This is often mostly olive oil, although every cutter has his or her own secret recipe for just the right mix.

The steel plate is affixed to a shaft connected to a motor on a heavy table reinforced with strong steel struts. This is to avoid any kind of vibration when the wheel begins spinning, at hundreds of revolutions per minute. Diamond powder is then sprinkled onto the oil until it forms a gray paste.

The raw diamond often looks no more glamorous than a muddy pebble—a bit of clear crystal ice trapped under a mottled outer skin of dishwater brown or olive green. This skin, if you happen to be having a bad day, can actually extend through the whole stone—meaning you grind halfway down only to discover that the piece of rough diamond you paid so much for is completely worthless.

This pebble is fixed into a small cup called a "dop," and the dop is attached to a holder which looks like the arm suspended over an old record player. The stone is fixed into the dop with a special glue that will not get soft when the diamond heats up during cutting.

When I first apprenticed to a master cutter, Sam Shmuelof by name, the stone was glued in with a paste made of asbestos and water. As soon as the stone got hot, the asbestos would dry and contract, locking the diamond nicely into the dop. We made the paste by chewing on the asbestos—this was before anyone had realized that even a tiny bit of asbestos can cause cancer, and I remember one cutter who developed a large tumor near his throat this way.

The motor is switched on, and the wheel must be up and spinning without the slightest trace of vibration: Aligning the wheel with some of the older diamond cutting machines would take us hours. Then the cutter sits on a tall seat that looks like a baby's high chair, and bends over the wheel. He takes the holder with the raw stone stuck on it and touches it very lightly to the flying wheel.

Diamond is infinitely harder than steel, so if the cutter pushes down too hard on a raw stone with a pointed edge it will actually begin to cut through the wheel itself. You swing the stone gently across the wheel, and then flip the holder up to your eye. In your other hand is a cutter's magnifying glass, called a "loupe." An experienced cutter is swinging the stone up to his face, checking the progress of the "cutting" (actually grinding) of the diamond, and flipping the stone back down on the wheel in one smooth motion, several times a minute. It looks a little like a cheerleader swirling a baton.

When you flip the stone up to check it, you brush it against a towel draped across your shoulder; this removes the oil and diamond powder that have collected on its surface. Within a minute or two the wheel has ground a tiny flat spot into the diamond, and this will be your "window" to the interior of the stone. You peer into the window with your magnifying loupe to see if there are any spots or cracks inside, since you will be attempting to position these in such a way that they are ground off, or at least placed as innocuously as possible at the edge of the diamond, while the stone takes shape. A black spot at the sharp tip of a diamond, for example, will be mirrored in the bottom facets of the stone, giving the appearance of a whole family of spots where in fact there is only one—this makes the finished gem worth next to nothing.

This process of looking through the window and trying to imagine exactly how the finished gem will be oriented is much like planning a piece of marble for a sculpture, to take best advantage of natural areas of color and texture. Planning a large stone for cutting can involve polishing a number of windows into the skin, and then studying the stone for weeks or even months, plotting out geometric models that will get the absolute maximum size of stone from the rough.

The little black spots that you sometimes see inside a diamond are most often actually other little diamond crystals that have been caught inside a larger crystal as it grew. Diamonds are ordinary carbon that has been melted by the intense heat within a volcanic pipe, and then kept under extremely high pressure deep within the earth, which alters the raw carbon's atomic structure into that of diamond. Tiny diamonds can in fact be grown under quite different circumstances, and form for example at the precise point of impact when a meteorite with carbon in it strikes the Earth, blowing out a sizable crater with some tiny jewels at the center.

The cute little "diamonds within a diamond" can appear either as black spots or, if they are aligned along the proper axis, form an invisible pocket inside the rough stone. Either way, they are big trouble for the cutter. They create tiny areas of stress within the stone. When the stone comes down on the wheel and the cutter begins following his or her plan to fashion the edges or facets of the gem, the diamond almost seems to fight the process.

Despite the oil, the stone begins to scream against the steel, with the sound of a Fury. Diamond cutting shops in New York's Forty-seventh Street Diamond District are most often gray, dimly lit, open rooms on the upper floors of buildings channeling billions of dollars' worth of diamonds into the United States and out to the manufacturers of jewelry. Imagine row after row of cutters, each bent over their cutting wheel, forcing the flat sides of the diamond down into the steel wheel, each stone screaming like a very bad set of brakes. In the middle of this cyclone of noise sit the cutters, accustomed to the chaos, their eyes at peace, deep in concentration.

The friction between the stone and the wheel builds up so much heat that the rough diamond is soon glowing a deep fluorescent crimson that can give you a burn as nasty as any ember. As the heat hits the pocket of stress surrounding an inner inclusion, the whole stone can explode, flying off the wheel at high velocity, throwing little pieces throughout the entire room. If it is a large stone, you may be watching several hundred thousand dollars go up in bits of diamond sand.

Why is it significant that a diamond is the hardest material in the universe? Think about the idea of something which is the *most* anything: the tallest, the shortest, the longest, the biggest. Our minds struggle with the concept, because in fact there is nothing so tall that you could not add another inch; nothing so short that you could not snip off a bit of it.

The hidden potential that we have talked about is something which is truly absolute, in a way that no physical thing can be. It is the highest nature that a thing can have, it is the absolute truth of every person and object. The hardness of diamond is in nature the closest that any single object in the universe can come to an absolute: It has the greatest hardness there is. And so a diamond is significant in a second way—as a metaphor for that one thing which is truly absolute.

Now think back to those little bits of diamond sprinkled all over the floor of the cutting factory after a stone has burst off the wheel from within. They are reminders of the third important quality of diamonds. Every diamond is atomically quite simple: pure, unadulterated carbon. The carbon in a pencil lead and the carbon in a diamond are, in fact, exactly the same substance.

The atoms of carbon in pencil lead have bonded together in loosely joined plates, like sheets of shale rock or the layers of a fine pastry. As you draw the tip of a pencil across a piece of paper, these layers sheer off in plates, spread across the surface of the paper. You call it writing with a pencil.

The atoms of pure carbon in a diamond have bonded together in quite a different way, with a perfect symmetry in every direction that prevents any loose plates of material, making a diamond the hardest thing we know of. The interesting thing though is that every diamond, everywhere, is made of the same simple carbon bonded together in the same atomic structure. This means that every tiny sliver of diamond, down to a molecular level, is exactly the same internally as every other piece of diamond.

What's this got to do with the hidden potential of things? We said before that every single object in the universe—inanimate things like pebbles and planets, and animate things like ants and humans—has its own hidden potential, its own ultimate nature. The point here is that every one of these examples of the potential, every single instance of ultimate nature, is exactly the same as every other. In this sense again, the hidden potential of things—the one quality in things that can bring you both inner and external success—is like a diamond.

And so this is why the name of the book has the word "diamond." Diamonds are perfectly clear, almost invisible, and the hidden potential of everything around us is just as hard to see. They come very close to being something which is absolute—the hardest thing there is—and the hidden potential in things is their pure and absolute truth. Every sliver of diamond that exists anywhere in the universe is exactly the same stuff as every other one—pure 100 percent diamond—and it is true of the hidden potential of things too that every instance of the potential is just as pure, just as absolute a reality, as every other instance.

But now why do they call the book "The Diamond *Cutter*"? Some early translators of the work into English in fact left off the second part of the name, not understanding how crucial it was for the meaning of the book.

Here we have to mention, just briefly, that there are two ways of seeing the hidden potential in things, their ultimate nature. One way is to "see" this nature by reading explanations about it such as the one found in this book, and then sitting and thinking hard about the explanation until you understand the potential and can use it. The second way is to go into a deep state of meditation, and "see" the potential this time directly, in your mind's eye.

Seeing the potential this second way is much more powerful, although the potential can be used successfully by anyone who only understands the principle of it.

Someone who has seen this potential in a direct way understands, shortly afterward, that they have seen something which is ultimate. They search in their minds for something to which they can compare it. The closest thing in our normal world to this ultimate potential, the closest normal thing to being ultimately anything, is the diamond—that one thing which is hardest.

Although the diamond is the nearest thing in the everyday world to something ultimate, it cannot compare much at all to the hidden potential we have been talking about, and which we will describe more fully in the following chapters, for this potential is something truly ultimate. In this sense then the diamond is an entirely inadequate metaphor, and so it is "cut" or outdone by the power of what is really ultimate. And this is why this ancient book of wisdom is called *The Diamond Cutter*: It teaches about a kind of potential which is even more ultimate than the diamond, the hardest thing, the closest thing to an ultimate in the normal world around us.

If all this sounds a little difficult, don't worry. The very purpose of *The Diamond Cutter* is to help us through it. The secret of how things really work, the secret to achieving true and lasting success in our everyday lives and in our business endeavors, is something deep, and not easily seen without effort. But it is certainly worth the effort.

chapter 3

How the Diamond

Cutter Came to Be

༄༅། །འདི་སྐད་བདག་གིས་ཐོས་པ་དུས་གཅིག་ན། བཅོམ་ལྡན་
འདས་མཉན་དུ་ཡོད་པ་ན་རྒྱལ་བུ་རྒྱལ་བྱེད་ཀྱི་ཚལ་མགོན་མེད་ཟས་
སྦྱིན་གྱི་ཀུན་དགའ་ར་བ་ན་དགེ་སློང་སྟོང་ཉིས་བརྒྱ་ལྔ་བཅུའི་དགེ་སློང་
གི་དགེ་འདུན་ཆེན་པོ་དང་། བྱང་ཆུབ་སེམས་དཔའ་སེམས་དཔའ་ཆེན་
པོ་རབ་ཏུ་མང་པོ་དང་ཐབས་ཅིག་ཏུ་བཞུགས་ཏེ།

We are about to embark on an important journey into completely new territory, ideas about managing your business and your life that have literally never been described in a modern book of this kind. It may help a bit to hear something about where and when this wisdom was actually taught.

To begin we will turn to *The Diamond Cutter* itself. The time is over two thousand years ago, in ancient India. A rich man, a prince by the name of Siddharta, has been capturing the hearts of the country, much like a man named Jesus, who will not appear for another five centuries. He has grown up in the wealth and luxury of a palace, but after seeing people suffer—after seeing that it is inevitable that we must lose all the things and people in our lives that we hold most dear—he has left the palace on a solitary quest to find out what makes us suffer, and how we might stop it.

And he has reached a final understanding of these things, and begun to teach his path to the people. Many of them have left their homes to follow him, agreeing to live a simple way of life, the life of a monk, free of possessions, clear in their thinking because their minds are free of the burden of having to remember what and whom they own.

Many years later, a disciple recounts how *The Diamond Cutter* was first spoken. He refers to his teacher, the Buddha, as the "Conqueror":

> Once I heard the Buddha speak these words.
>
> The Conqueror was residing at Shravasti, in the park of Anata Pindada at the gardens of Prince Jetavan. In convocation with him was a great gathering of 1,250 monks who were disciples of the first level, as well as an immense number of disciples on the path of compassion—and they were also great and holy beings.

"Once I heard the Buddha speak these words" is a common beginning to an ancient book of wisdom, for many were written down long after the Buddha had already passed from this world. People in those days were quite good at memorizing, on the spot, the instructions given by a great teacher.

The word "once" here is loaded with meaning. It refers first to the extraordinary level of intelligence that simple people of ancient India possessed—the fact that they could learn something by heart even as it was spoken, and understand its deepest meanings. The word shows secondly that *The Diamond Cutter* was taught but once, signifying that the wisdom it contains—the knowledge of what really makes everything tick—is something rare and precious in this world.

Choney Lama, in his explanation of *The Diamond Cutter*, gives us more background on how and where this great teaching occurred. The boldface print here shows where he has inserted the words of the *Cutter* itself:

> In these words the scene of the teaching is set. The person we hear speaking is the one who put this teaching down into **words.**
>
> He says first that **he heard the Buddha speak** the teaching. **Once,** meaning at a certain time, **the Conqueror was residing at Shravasti, in the park of Anata Pindada at the gardens of Prince Jetavan. In convocation with him**—that is, together with him— **was a great gathering of 1,250 monks who were disciples of the**

first level, as well as an immense number of disciples on the path of compassion—and they were also great and holy beings.

Now in India there were six great cities, including the one known as "Shravasti." This particular city was located in the domain of King Prasena Ajita, and contained a particularly beautiful site—the exquisite gardens of one known as Prince Jetavan.

There came a time, several years after the Conqueror attained his enlightenment, when a certain householder by the name of Anata Pindada resolved that he would construct a large, wondrous temple where the Buddha and his followers could live on a regular basis. To this end he approached Prince Jetavan and purchased his gardens by paying him many thousands of gold coins, enough in fact to fill the gardens themselves.

Jetavan as well offered to the Conqueror a parcel of land that had been part of the quarters for the caretakers of the property. In these gardens Anata Pindada, availing himself of the abilities of Shariputra, directed artisans from the lands of both gods and men to construct an extraordinary park.

When the park was completed, the Conqueror—perceiving that Jetavan wished it—named the main temple after him. Anata Pindada, by the way, was a great being who had purposely taken a birth as someone who could act as the Teacher's sponsor. He had the power to see deposits of precious gems and metals deep under water or below the earth itself, and could utilize these riches whenever he wished.

The point of these opening lines from *The Diamond Cutter* is significant. The Buddha is about to give his teaching to a group of monks who have decided, much like the disciples of Jesus, to leave their normal occupations and devote their lives to learning his path. But the reason the teaching is happening at all is that powerful people, wealthy people, have appeared to make it possible.

The royalty of ancient India were the driving force in the economic and political life of their countries: They were nothing less than the exact equivalent of the business community in modern Western society. When we speak about the Buddha and Buddhist ideas nowadays, we tend to think of an odd-looking, oriental man with a bump on his head and—if we have seen one of those Chinese statues—a big smile and a big tummy. But think rather of a tall and graceful prince, traveling quietly through the country, speaking with knowledge, conviction, and compassion of ideas that every man or woman can use to succeed in life, and to make this life meaningful.

And think of his followers not just as shaved-head mendicants sitting on the ground cross-legged, chanting *om* at the wall. Perhaps the greatest masters of Buddhism in ancient times were the royalty, those with the drive and talent to manage entire countries and economies. There is for example a great Buddhist teaching called the "Kalachakra," or "Wheel of Time"—in the last few hundred years it has been passed down in special gatherings by each of the Dalai Lamas of Tibet. Yet in the beginning it was taught by the Buddha to ancient kings of India, to individuals of extraordinary insight and ability, who in turn taught it to yet other kings, for many generations.

The reason I bring this up here is to address a common misperception about Buddhism in particular, and about each person's inner spiritual life in general. Buddhism has always taught that there is a time and a place for taking on the life of a secluded monk, for living apart from the world in order to learn to serve the world. But serve the world we must, and to do so we must be in the world.

I was struck during my years in corporate life by the number of leading business figures who revealed to me the extraordinary depth of their own inner spiritual lives. I can think of one in particular, a diamond dealer from Bombay (recently renamed to the more proper Mumbai) by the name of Dhiru Shah. If you glanced at Mr. Shah getting off a plane at Kennedy Airport in New York, your first impression would be of a shortish brown man, bespectacled, with thinning hair and perhaps a shy smile. He would move through the crowd and pick up a small, worn suitcase, then take a cab to a modest hotel in Manhattan, where he would eat for his evening meal a few slices of homemade bread cooked by his wife Ketki and placed in his bag with loving care.

In truth though, Mr. Shah is one of the most powerful diamond buyers in the world, purchasing thousands of stones every day for Andin.

And he is, quite simply, one of the deepest spiritual persons I have ever met. Quietly, over the years, he has uncovered for me the wealth of his inner life.

Mr. Shah is a Jain, an ancient faith of India that had its birth in the same era as Buddhism did, over two thousand years ago. We have sat together in the silence of the evening on the cool floor of his neighborhood temple, a simple but exquisite structure of stone, on a quiet corner in the middle of the chaos of Bombay. Priests move quietly before the altar, in the cool darkness of the inner sanctum, their faces bright with the soft light of the small red lamps of oil they light before their god.

Women in soft flowing silken dresses enter in silence, and touch themselves to the ground in reverence, then sit again in silence to pray. Children whisper as they pass from statue to statue, looking up at a thousand holy beings. Businessmen drop their briefcases and shoes at the foot of the steps to the temple, and rise in devotion to the portal, to enter and sit for their own quiet communion with Mahavir.

You can sit there, in the temple, and be with your spirit; you can forget the time completely, forget what day it is or that you have to get up and go home, forget the thousand deals of the day, forget the Opera House.

The Opera House epitomizes the diamond business in India, where some half a million people labor in mud brick homes and multimillion-dollar high-rise offices to cut most of the world's diamonds and feed them to clients in America, Europe, the Middle East, and Japan. The Opera House is actually just two dilapidated old buildings, one of sixteen stories and the other of twenty-five stories, so named because of a dilapidated old opera house nearby, in the depths of Bombay.

To get into the buildings you drive in a dilapidated car to an incredibly crowded parking lot, and then push your way toward a concrete opening through a crowd of budding diamond dealers, yelling offers and counteroffers to each other and waving dilapidated paper parcels with a few tiny stones in them. Partners in a deal stand facing off against the buyers, pushing their fingers into the palms of each other's hands in an invisible sign language that indicates how high the price should go before the deal is made.

After struggling your way through the small fry you fight your way through the crowd trying to get into the only dilapidated elevator working today. (It's always a choice: Take the elevator and risk getting stuck for hours somewhere between floors when the electricity goes out again, or walk up about twenty flights of stairs and arrive with your fresh new shirt soaked with sweat from the Bombay heat and humidity.) Then it's opening an exotic combination of ancient Indian locks, digital motion detectors, and sophisticated sound sensors to get into the haven of the office.

Here things change. In the larger offices there'll be lots of marble on the floor, marble on the walls, marble throughout the bathroom, and finely carved antique masterpieces on marble pedestals, shipped back from the branch office in Belgium. The fixtures on the toilet might be gold-plated, and the toilet itself a wondrous combination of a Western seat sprouting porcelain wings on the side, so people can also climb up and crouch the old Indian way if they like.

Behind the inner locked doors are quiet air-conditioned rooms with long rows of young Indian ladies dressed in the flowing sarees worn by the women of India for the last few millennia. They sit quietly under soft fluorescent lights of a specified wavelength, and before each of them is a neat pile of diamonds that might be worth a hundred thousand dollars. Their arms reach out from under the folds of the sarees with a pair of special, fine-tipped tweezers—they pluck a diamond from the pile, bring it up to the jeweler's magnifying glass pressed against their eye with their other hand, and then flip the stone in a graceful arc across the pad of fine white paper, so that it lands in one of maybe five different smaller piles of diamonds, each representing a different grade and price.

The only sound in the room is the slight scrape of the tweezer against the paper, and the tiny patter of stones landing in the right piles. This scene is repeated in sorting rooms throughout the world, whether they be in New York, Belgium, Russia, Africa, Israel, Australia, Hong Kong, or Brazil.

We went once out to the countryside to see how the stones were actually cut. A great number of the diamonds are fashioned in people's homes, with the whole family helping out. The rough diamond pebbles go out daily from the great diamond houses of Bombay to the countryside, through a vast network of messengers carrying tiny satchels and traveling by train or bus or bicycle or footpath. The stones return daily in the same way, ending up in a sorting room somewhere, then in a tiny metal box guarded by a Brinks courier on the daily overnight flight to New York.

Navsari is a typical cutting town in Gujarat State, the area north of Bombay with the greatest concentration of diamond factories. Workers flood to Navsari from all over the country, hoping to get one of the more stable jobs you can find in India. They contract for say six months of work, usually up until one of the big religious holidays, like Divali. Then they collect their holiday bonus and head out of town the next day, back sometimes a thousand miles to see the wife and kids for a few weeks, and to invest their money in a neighbor's corn crop. Then they pack a small satchel and return to the factory for another six-month stint.

Buying diamonds in Navsari is like nowhere else in the world. Imagine trying to get through a mob covering an entire mile or two of dirt road in the middle of a small Indian town. Each screaming man in the mob is clutching a tiny folded scrap of paper, and in the paper is a small diamond or two, slightly bigger than the period at the end of this sentence. The stones are still covered in the cutting oil, leaving them a dull gray, and in the bright sunlight only a fool—or a highly trained Indian dealer—would attempt to buy a stone, unable to tell if it's pure white (expensive) or bright yellow (worthless).

Cars work their way through the solid mass of the crowd from both ends, horns blasting. The sun beats down on your head. Your shirt is covered in a fine dust turning to a brown paste as it mixes with your sweat. Street urchins on their hands and knees work through the crowd, literally crawling between the dealers' legs, hoping to find a tiny chip of diamond dropped accidentally on the ground, looking like chickens bobbing up and down as they scratch for grain.

The farthest flung lands of the diamond empire of India are found close to Bhavnagar, near the western coast and the Arabian Sea, where the deserts of Rajasthan and the pink sandstone city of the emerald dealers, Jaipur, begin. Dhiru Shah has taken me there on a rickety Indian airplane, and we are in a car on the way to the mountain of Palitana, holiest site of the Jains.

We stop at one last diamond factory, no more than a villa at the edge of the desert, drink tiny cups of thick spiced Indian tea, with children and the exotic women of the household peeking out from behind tiled walls and veils, to giggle and gawk at the first white person to pass that way in a long time. Leaving the house and the last factory is like leaving our lives behind, passing from business up through the foothills, to find our inner lives.

We spend the night in a modest hostel at the foot of the mountain, built by the diamonteers for their own kind to come to, whenever the sense of spiritual need comes to them. Dhiru takes me before dawn, silently, to a special courtyard where the path up the mountain begins. On the stone walls are carved the prayers of twenty-five centuries, and here we leave our shoes, for the walk up the stony path to the heights of the mountain must be done in bare feet, for respect of the holiness of the place.

We move with thousands of pilgrims in the dark before the light. The air is cool, and the indentations worn into the stone beneath us speak of millions of feet climbing the mountain this way every morning, for centuries. The climb takes hours, but they do not feel long, for we are surrounded by the thoughts and prayers of the others, as reassuring as the rock beneath our feet.

At long last we are at the top, stepping into a network of small temples and chapels and altars carved from the stone, darker inside than the dark outside. We simply move blindly ahead until it feels right, sit down wherever we have reached, and stay there in meditation on the cool stone. There is an undercurrent of near-silent chanting, but no light. You feel the breath and heartbeats of thousands around you, and the anticipation.

We are all facing east off the top of the mountain, looking over the Indian plain. And then the dark begins to change subtly, from behind closed eyes as we meditate; soon come the rose, and then the saffron shades, and so finally the golden bronze of the Indian sun as it rises. We stay, we all stay in meditation, each thinking of his own life, and how to spend that life when we return.

No one takes water or any other sustenance; it would seem almost a sacrilege upon this mountain. In time we rise, pay our respects to the temples, and begin the half-skipping walk down the mountain. The mood changes to one of festivity, the children laughing and running ahead. For the first time in your life you appreciate the miracle of shoes, as your raw feet begin to swell and crack. But it makes it all seem that much more of a gift.

Only then do I learn that Dhiru Shah, this happy dark little diamond dealer, spent years of his early life at the feet of spiritual masters on this same mountain; only later do I learn that on his visits to New York for international directors' meetings he is likely to be on a spiritual fast, praying in his small hotel room over the garish lights of Times Square, late into the night. His offices in Bombay radiate an intense family warmth; he cares for each person there like a son or daughter, helping out with the expenses of a marriage ceremony here and the cremation of a loved one there. With millions of dollars of deals floating around him all day, he takes absolute care never to use a single penny he is not properly entitled to.

At home his own family is just as well managed. For years while I worked closely with the Shahs they lived in a tiny apartment on the third floor of a small quiet building in a place called Vileparle. Mrs. Shah was wealthy even before they married, and Dhiru—with his son Vikram—has added to the wealth, so people around them would harass them constantly to get a larger place. The children were growing bigger, they said, and needed their own rooms. But the family went on just as they had for years, grandfather in his own comfortable room off to the side of the kitchen, respected and cared for by all; the rest of the family giggling and going out onto the balcony at bedtime, to set their beds under the stars side by side, to enjoy the night air and the smell of the flowering trees while they slept. Even when they finally finished a huge suite of rooms in an exclusive enclave of the city, they all ended up sleeping together in a small corner room. They are happy.

The point here is quite simple. People in America, including myself, have always had a very cynical view of those creatures we call "businessmen," and when I was growing up in the sixties it was almost an insult to refer to someone with the word. The stereotype is one of a wolf dressed in a sharp business suit, talking too fast, living only for money, and doing whatever he can to get it, oblivious of the needs of the people around him. But think about it.

The business world today is without question a vast pool of the most talented people in the country. They have drive and they have the ability to do what must be done to get something done, as no one else does. They churn out billions of dollars' worth of goods and services like clockwork, constantly improving products, constantly cutting down the time and money it takes to make them. Innovation and efficiency are a way of life, as in no other sector of our society.

Business people are thoughtful, resilient, thorough, and insightful. Those who are not do not survive, for business has its own purity, its own process of natural selection: No one will put up with you for very long, at any level in a company, if you do not produce. The ownership and management, and even more your own fellow workers, will expel you from their midst if you fail to pitch in and produce. I have seen this process happen often; it's like your body rejecting a foreign antibody.

The greatest businesspeople have a deep inner capacity—they hunger, as we all do, but perhaps more strongly—for a true spiritual life. They have seen more of the world than most of us; they know what it can give them, and what it cannot. They demand a logic in spiritual things; they demand that the method and the results be clear, as clear as the terms in any business deal. Often they have dropped out from an active spiritual life—not because they are greedy or lazy, but simply because no path has measured up to their demands. *The Diamond Cutter* was literally made for these people—talented, tough, and savvy.

Never accept the idea that, because you are in business, you don't have the opportunity or time or personal qualities which a true spiritual life demands, or that maintaining a deep inner life is somehow contradictory with leading a business career. The wisdom of *The Diamond Cutter* says that the very people who are attracted to business are exactly the ones who have the inner strength to grasp and carry out the deeper practices of the spirit.

This wisdom is good for people and, unabashedly, good for business as well. And this is perfectly consistent with the message of the Buddha. In America, it will be the business community that leads a quiet but certain revolution in how we conduct the business of our work, and our lives as well, using ancient wisdom for the goals of the modern world.

So in closing now see how the Buddha got up and went to work, on the day he spoke *The Diamond Cutter*.

In the morning then the Conqueror donned his monk's robes and outer shawl, took up his sage's bowl, and entered the great city of Shravasti in order to go from house to house, asking others for some small thing to eat, in the way of a Buddhist monk. And when he had gathered some food this way, he returned from the city, and then partook of it.

When he had finished eating, the Buddha put away his bowl and shawl, for he was following the practice of eating no evening meal, in order to keep his mind clear. He washed his feet and then seated himself on a cushion that had been set forth for him. He crossed his legs in the full-lotus position, straightened his back, and placed his thoughts into a state of contemplation.

And then a great number of monks advanced toward the Conqueror and, when they had reached his side, bowed and touched their heads to his feet. They circled him in respect three times, and then seated themselves to one side. At this point the younger monk Subhuti was with the same group of disciples, and took his seat with them.

Then the younger monk Subhuti rose from his cushion, and dropped the corner of his upper robe from one shoulder in a gesture of respect, and knelt with his right knee to the ground. He faced the Conqueror, joined his palms at his heart, and bowed. Then he beseeched the Conqueror in the following words:

O Conqueror, the Buddha—the One Gone Thus, the Destroyer of the Enemy of Hurtful Thoughts, the Totally Enlightened One—has given much beneficial instruction to those disciples on the path of compassion, to those who are great and holy beings. All the instruction that you, the Buddha, have ever given us has been of great help to us.

And the One Gone Thus, the Destroyer of the Enemy of Hurtful Thoughts, the Totally Enlightened One, has as well instructed these same disciples by granting them clear direction. Whatever clear direction you have granted, O Conqueror, has been a wondrous thing. It is, O Conqueror, a very wondrous thing.

And then Subhuti asked the following question:

O Conqueror, what of those who have entered well into the way of compassion? How should they live? How should they practice? How should they keep their thoughts?

Then the Conqueror spoke the following words, in reply to Subhuti's question:

O Subhuti, it is good, it is good. O Subhuti, thus it is, and thus is it: The One Thus Gone has indeed done benefit to those on the path of compassion, these great and holy beings, by granting them beneficial instruction. The One Thus Gone has indeed given clear direction to these disciples, by granting them the clearest of instruction.

And since it is so, O Subhuti, listen now to what I speak, and be sure that it stays firmly in your heart, for I shall reveal to you how it is that those who have entered well into the way of compassion should live, and how they should practice, and how they should keep their thoughts.

"Thus shall it be," replied the younger monk Subhuti, and he sat to listen as instructed by the Conqueror. The Conqueror too then began, with the following words . . .

chapter 4

The Hidden Potential

in All Things

ༀབཙམ་ལྡན་འདས་ལ་ཚེ་དང་ལྡན་པ་རབ་འབྱོར་གྱིས་འདི་སྐད་
ཅེས་གསོལ་ཏོ། །བཙམ་ལྡན་འདས། ཆོས་ཀྱི་རྣམ་གྲངས་འདིའི་མིང་
ཅི་ལགས། ཇི་ལྟར་གཟུང་བར་བགྱི། དེ་སྐད་ཅེས་གསོལ་པ་དང་།
བཙམ་ལྡན་འདས་ཀྱིས་ཚེ་དང་ལྡན་པ་རབ་འབྱོར་ལ་འདི་སྐད་ཅེས་
བཀའ་སྩལ་ཏོ། །རབ་འབྱོར། ཆོས་ཀྱི་རྣམ་གྲངས་འདི་ཤེས་རབ་ཀྱི་
ཕ་རོལ་ཏུ་ཕྱིན་པ་ཞེས་བྱ་སྟེ། འདི་དེ་ལྟར་ཟུངས་ཤིག

So now we're ready to get down to brass tacks. Admit it. You want to be good in business, you want to be a success in your life, but you also have a strong instinct that tells you life wouldn't be much unless it had a spiritual side to it. You would like to make a million and meditate too.

The fact is that, for real success in business, you're going to need some of the deep insights that come with a spiritual life. So you can have your cake and eat it too. In this chapter we will cover the potential in all things—something the Buddhists call "emptiness"—but please don't worry about the strange name now, or in fact try to figure it out too soon. It's not at all what the word implies, and it is, quite simply, the secret of every kind of success.

A good place to start would be a surprising exchange between the Buddha and his student Subhuti:

⁓ The younger monk Subhuti spoke the following words, with great respect, to the Conqueror:

O Conqueror, what is the name of this particular kind of teaching? How are we to think of it?

And the Conqueror answered him, saying:

O Subhuti, this is the teaching on "perfect wisdom," and this is how you should think of it.

Why is it so? Because, O Subhuti, the same perfect wisdom that the One Thus Gone teaches is perfect wisdom that could never exist.

And this, in fact, is why we can even call it "perfect wisdom."

Tell me, Subhuti, what do you think? Is there any teaching at all which One Thus Gone ever gives?

And Subhuti respectfully replied,

There is, O Conqueror, none; none at all. There never could be any teaching that the One Thus Gone could give.

With these words, *The Diamond Cutter* seems to be floating off into that world of nothing-makes-sense which Buddhism is unfortunately known for in our culture. But it's anything but.

Let's see what's being said here, and why, and then try to see how it could have any application at all in our business lives. Because it really does—the words here contain the real secrets to a totally successful life.

The conversation seems to amount to this—

SUBHUTI: What shall we call the book?

THE BUDDHA: Call it *Perfect Wisdom.*

SUBHUTI: How shall we think about the book?

THE BUDDHA: Think of it as perfect wisdom. And if you're wondering why, it's because the perfect wisdom I'm writing about is perfect wisdom that could never exist anyway—and that's exactly why I've decided to name the book *Perfect Wisdom*. By the way, Subhuti, were you thinking that the book was a book?

SUBHUTI: Not at all. We know you never write books.

The crux here, and the key to the hidden potential in all things, is the statement that "You can call the book a book, and you can think about the book as a book, because it never could have been a book." This statement has a very specific and very concrete meaning; it is not some kind of mumbo-jumbo, and contained in it is all you need to know to be successful both in your personal and your business life.

Let's take a very common example from business life to illustrate this idea of hidden potential. It's about real estate.

When we started out at Andin, we were renting a room or two in a larger office from a jewelry company down near the Empire State Building. Ofer and Aya, the owners, sat in a small room next to a slightly larger cubicle where Udi (the diamond man), Alex (the jewelry designer), Shirley (the computer lady), and I sat around a larger table. Diamonds were being sorted over on the edge of the table, with accounts being typed into a computer on the other corner. Meanwhile I sat on the phone at another corner trying to find out the names of the secretaries of the big jewelry buyers around town, so we could go directly to the person making the decisions.

The entire line consisted of about fifteen rings, photographed on a single page of paper that Ofer and Aya would run around and show people. It was fun working for them because they didn't know anything at all about business in America, and so paradoxically they were much more creative, since they weren't aware of all the things that couldn't ever work (which did), or all the things you absolutely weren't allowed to do (like wearing a Dallas Cowboys football jersey to a meeting with the executives of one of the largest department store chains in the world).

Ofer would come in and ask us crazy questions about America like,

"The calendar here says that tomorrow is Groundhog Day. Is that a national holiday? Are you guys supposed to get that day off? Are we supposed to pay you for that day?" And sometimes yes, we would tell him it was a *very important* holiday in America.

On the other hand they couldn't understand why anyone would want to go home before 11 P.M., and more often than not we worked until that hour and sometimes even later. My commute back to the monastery was nearly two hours each way, and so I would get home about 1 A.M., and be up again at 6 for the ride back into the city.

The diamonds and jewelry would come in from the factory in Israel and go straight to the customer; I think people thought we had our own manufacturing facilities but it often boiled down to running uptown to the Brinks Armored office at Fifth Avenue and Forty-seventh Street, tearing all the other labels off the box that had just come in from Tel Aviv, putting on one of our labels with the customer's name, and walking it to their office on the next floor up.

I remember one scary incident when I had to open a box like this up, to split it between two customers. Sitting inside the box I saw a huge pile of copper diamond rings. I ran back down to the thirties with the shipment, which set off a furious series of phone calls to the Middle East. The problem is that fourteen-karat gold can be made a lot of different ways. In the karat system for gold (as opposed to the *carat* system for diamonds), twenty-four karat represents pure gold; this is much too soft to use in jewelry, and with normal wear a twenty-four-karat ring would just fall apart. So we mix in other metals that help make it harder.

If the mix is one quarter other metals, the ring becomes eighteen karat, and so on—the legal karatages in this country are eighteen, fourteen, and ten karat. The metal that you add to make the ring harder also determines what color it will end up: if you add nickel, the gold takes on a lighter yellow color. If you add copper, it takes on a burnished red color. Combinations result in other shades. Americans tend to like medium to lighter yellows; Asians generally prefer the deep gold colors; and many Europeans prefer an almost copper color. Our shipment had been cast in the European color by mistake.

This is one of the memories I cherish most about the early years of our company: the entire gang of three or four of us rushing to a sweat shop downtown, a plating factory, and trying to get the owner in a rush to add another layer of yellow gold (expensive) on top of the reddish gold. I'm sitting with these future multimillionaires around a table with about fifteen Puerto Rican girls, Ofer and Aya are yelling instructions to each other in Hebrew, the girls are yelling in Spanish, nobody can understand why we want to plate gold with gold, and pretty soon we're all sitting shoulder-to-shoulder hunched over these diamond rings, painting them with special chemicals that will protect the parts that we don't want to turn out yellow.

Then we took a chance and started our own factory. This facility was just about the same; a room down the street in Manhattan with huge walls of iron bars stretching across a raw cement floor, along with our first real vault. Fond memories here too: Ripping up the carpet the night we left the old space and crawling around on our hands and knees, scouring for tiny diamond chips we had dropped over the last few months of work (there were a few hundred). An employee locking herself in the new vault all night by accident, and her husband wondering how late we could possibly be working. Me sweating in the one suit I owned (it was wool) during the steamy New York summer, because my Lama had insisted that I always look the part—I was to wear it every day, and was never supposed to take the coat off, nor loosen the tie.

After I think about six months at our baby factory it was time to make a decision about moving elsewhere. Should we take the risk of moving up to the Diamond District or not? What if we rented a big space and the orders slowed down? What if we rented a small space and big orders came in—how could we ever fill them?

So we took about half of a small floor in a shabby building just outside the main district—a compromise between the risk of a bigger place and the safety of a cheaper rent. I was alone in a chair in the "diamond department" (a smallish room); sometimes I worked in the "systems department" (a very small room that doubled as a waiting room); or else in the vault (a small, stand-up affair that would fit two workers a little like two mummies in a sarcophagus). The factory was a bigger room with one lonely polisher in the corner.

Within a year or so we had doubled in sales (this happened nearly every year for about ten years), and the risky amount of large space had become a liability. We were literally elbow to elbow; there was a joke that you would get an inch of desk space for every thousand dollars of salary, and so in those days I was up to about fifteen inches. We couldn't take the raw diamond suppliers inside for security reasons, and so we would make deals standing out in the hallway between the foyer (called a "man trap") and the waiting room, so other diamond dealers wouldn't hear the prices we were giving the first. Imagine standing in a small, dimly lit hallway with a small piece of paper in your hands filled with thousands of tiny diamonds, trying to yell over the noise of a factory behind you, but trying not to be heard by the people sitting in front of you, calculating composite purchase totals for differing grades, and interest rates, and sliding payment arrangements as your opponent does the same. It often felt like a duel between swordsmen, held in a closet.

A "man trap," by the way, is a special area in diamond houses where a visitor from the outside gets buzzed inside the front door, checked by camera or through bulletproof glass as the first door closes, and then buzzed on past the second door, into the actual company premises. An electric mechanism prevents both doors from being open at the same time. This can lead to some interesting situations when you're the last man out at night and have already passed the inner door, but forgotten your key to the outside door.

When we got to this stage, we took the safe step of paying off the party with the other half of the floor. When the whole floor got down to about twenty inches of desk space again, we took another floor, and joined them with a staircase. We got down again to twenty inches, doubling in sales all the time, and took the next floor we could get—which unfortunately was two floors away.

By the next time we needed more space, there was absolutely no way we could get anyone to move off another floor. We checked the building immediately next door, one with fewer floors, but could find nothing there. So we took a floor two doors away, high enough to clear the building between, and hung all these totally illegal network wires through the air over the shorter building to hook up the computers. It looked like those laundry lines you see strung between tenement buildings in Brooklyn, but this time between steel and glass towers in the heart of Manhattan.

Now we were in the awkward situation of traveling a lot up and down the street with large parcels of diamonds—and also rubies, sapphires, amethysts, and a dozen other gems—just to work between sorting rooms in different buildings. It was dangerous, and the Diamond District had begun to expand out to our area, rents rising all the time. We had to make a decision about how to house our business, which by this time was many millions of dollars per year, and about a hundred employees. And so we come back to the question of real estate, and the hidden potential of things.

There is a certain level of businessperson in New York who *must* get *The Wall Street Journal* every morning. Read it or not (and I have a feeling very few people really do), it's important in many firms to be seen with a copy tucked under your arm as you cheerily dash up the steps into the front doors in the morning. Better still is to make sure that a copy is delivered to your room every day—shoved under your office door around nine o'clock in such a way that part of the name *Wall Street Journal* is still clearly visible from the hallway. The nine o'clock thing, by the way, is so that the newspaper can sit there until you saunter in around nine-thirty. Every lesser employee who passes your door before that time will see the *Journal* still there, evidence positive that you have not yet reached the office—and they will be reminded that you are the boss, and need not punch in by 9:05.

The few times I did read *The Wall Street Journal*, it was always a very curious experience. On the first page, over toward the right (because the area to the left is all taken up by the summary of the national and world news), there would be an enthusiastic article about a businessperson, somebody like George Soros, who had taken major risks with an investment and scored big time. He would be hailed as a "visionary," someone whose insight was far ahead of the rest of the market, someone who had the courage and self-confidence to forge ahead to new plateaus of profit while lesser-minded and more conservative businesspeople lagged behind.

On about page four of the *Journal* there would be an article about a business that was floundering because the management had gotten old and stuck in their ways; all the vice presidents had been shooed out by the board and the CEO traded in for a new one. A week or a month later I would open the *Journal* again (actually I used to swipe a copy out from under the door of another VP, and replace it before he got in). On page one there would be an article lauding a firm that had stuck by its tried and proven methods year after year, and made big profits this quarter. They were a "blue chip" company captained by a leader with the wisdom to stick to the principles of the past. Then around page four there would be a highly critical article about a foolish capitalist who had taken imprudent risks with his company's equity.

It struck me that the names of the risk-taking geniuses in one month would be the names of the risk-taking fools several months later. And the names of the conservative fools one month would be the names of the conservative geniuses later on. Or maybe the risk-taking genius would continue to fly, or the conservative fool would continue to drop. Anyway, nobody seemed to notice that *almost randomly different results seemed to be following from exactly the same actions, taken by one and the same individuals or companies.*

How does this apply to real estate; how does this reveal some "hidden potential"? Imagine the questions that our firm was asking when we were contemplating getting our own building, after years of uncertainty over whether to rent or not to rent, to expand or not to expand. Should we take this giant step or not?

At this point businesspeople each begin their own calculations, the assessment of pluses and minuses. A big new building will impress our customers, lending an impression of strength both to them and to our suppliers. Or maybe they will perceive that we have expanded beyond our capacity—maybe the customers will be afraid that we'll have to raise prices to cover the new expenses, and maybe the suppliers will think that they have sold their stones to us too cheap—that we are acquiring the new building at their expense.

Maybe the move away from the Diamond District will make it harder, and riskier, for gemstone suppliers to bring us goods when we need them. Maybe the money we save on rent will allow us to pay them higher prices, and we'll attract more dealers, and make more money.

Maybe the move to the new location will make it harder for employees to get to work, maybe the extra half hour on the subway will impel good people to quit and look for work closer to the Diamond District. Or maybe people will like the quieter area of our new home, West

Greenwich Village—the quaint shops and restaurants with much bigger plates of food than midtown.

Maybe the value of the property will shoot up after we move there, and tack on more largesse to the owners' return on investment. Or maybe New York real estate will go through another sudden downward paroxysm, and stick us with high mortgage payments.

Maybe the economies of scale, of doing all the manufacturing in one building, will allow us to lower our prices and make a killing in the market. Maybe the expense of maintaining a large manufacturing facility, even during slow times, will gradually strangle us.

Those of you who have been in business long enough, and who are really honest with yourselves, know that things could easily go either way at this point. If you buy the building and all goes well, you're a genius—it was a great deal. If you buy the building and things go badly, you're a risk-taking idiot. If you don't buy the building and things go well, or if you don't buy and things don't go well—oh well, you know what they'll call you. And you know you're the same person either way.

This leads us, very gently but surely, to the hidden potential of things.

A real estate deal like Andin International's acquisition of a large nine-story building on the West Side of Manhattan is a good example of hidden potential, or what the Buddhists call "emptiness."

The important point to understand here is that there is, within the building and the acquisition of the building, all sorts of hidden potential to be a good thing or a bad thing, all at the same time.

If we acquire the building and suddenly the value of real estate in New York goes down (which I'm afraid is exactly what happened when we bought our building), then the acquisition of the building is a bad thing—for our owners, Ofer and Aya.

If we acquire the building and suddenly all the managers have more office space than they had before, then the acquisition is a good thing—for the managers.

If we acquire the building and all the employees from New Jersey have to commute an extra half hour, it's a bad thing—for them. But it's a good thing for all the people from Brooklyn, who save time on their commute.

If we purchase the building and it gives our suppliers the impression that we're strong financially, then it's a good thing—for us. If it gives them the impression that we're making a killing off them, then it's a bad thing for us.

But what if we take away the "for us" and "for them"? What if we try to evaluate whether the building, or the acquisition of the building, is *in itself* a good thing or a bad thing? The obvious answer, if you think about it for even an instant, is that, *in itself,* acquiring the building is neither a good thing nor a bad thing—it just depends on who's looking. It appears good to some people who benefit from it, and it appears bad to other people who are hurt by it. But there is no *innate* goodness or badness about the purchase of the building—it has no such quality in and of itself, it is *empty* of any such quality.

And this is exactly the meaning of emptiness: Things could go either way, there is no "thing" about the building in and of itself, it all depends on how we perceive it. This is the hidden potential in things.

Everything in the world, by the way, is the same. Is a trip to the dentist for a root canal operation *in and of itself* a bad thing? Well, if it were, then it would have to appear bad to everyone. But think about it— regardless of how very bad it seems to us, the root canal operation can appear to be something good to other people: An unscrupulous dentist might perceive it as a very good opportunity to make his kid's college tuition for the quarter; for the assistant appointments secretary it might represent enough new business to assure her continued employment; for the dental supplies salesman it might represent a chance to sell another box of syringes. Not even a painful procedure like this has any *innate* quality of being a good thing or a bad thing. In and of itself, independent of how different people are perceiving it, it has no such nature; it is neutral or blank or empty. In short, it has "emptiness," and this—according to the deepest books of ancient Tibetan wisdom—is its hidden and ultimate potential.

The people around us are the same: Think about the people at your workplace who irritate you the most. They seem to have a quality or nature of being irritating, from their own side. "Irritating-ness" seems to be emanating or flowing *from* them *toward* you. Think about it though. *Someone* (perhaps another employee, perhaps someone in their family, a wife or a child) finds them very loving and lovable people. When they look at the same individuals, when they see them in the room even as you see them, doing or saying the exact same things, they see something good.

Apparently there is no "irritating-ness" flowing from these people to them—which very simply proves that this is not a quality *within* the people themselves. They *have* no such quality within themselves, or it would show itself to others; they are, rather, like blank screens, neutral, and different people see different things in them. This is a very simple and undeniable proof of emptiness, or hidden potential. And everything else in the world is the same.

Now, by the way, we can go back and understand what the Buddha said about the book: "You can call the book a book, and you can think about the book as a book, because it never could have been a book." In terms of acquiring a building, "You can say that acquiring the building is a good thing, and you can think about acquiring the building as a good thing, because acquiring the building never could have been a good thing [or a bad thing] *all by itself:* that is, from its own side, independent of how we see it."

So what's all this got to do with business? How can this hidden potential be the key to success in both our personal lives and our businesses? For this we have to know how the principles behind using the potential work.

chapter 5

Principles for Using

the Potential

༄༅། །བཙོན་ལྷུན་འདས་ཀྱིས་བགལ་སྐུལ་པ། རབ་འབྱོར། བྱང་
ཆུབ་སེམས་དཔའ་གང་ལ་ལ་ཞིག་འདི་སྐད་དུ། བདག་གིས་ཞིང་
བཀོད་པ་རྣམས་བསྒྲུབ་པར་བྱའོ། །ཞིས་ཟེར་ན། དེ་ནི། མི་བདེན་
པར་སྨྲ་བའོ།

In the last chapter we spoke about the hidden potential in all things—
what the Buddhists have always called "emptiness." We saw, clearly, that
nothing that ever happens to us is a good thing or a bad thing *from its own
side*, because—if it were—then everyone else would experience it that way
as well. For example, our irritating person at work would strike everyone
else in exactly the same way, if his or her "irritating-ness" were something
inside that was flowing out of that individual and flying across the room to
us. In reality though there is almost always *someone* who finds the person
to be good and lovable.

The fact that this is the case has two important implications:

1) This person has no quality, within him, of being irritating or
   nice. He himself, from his own side, is "blank" or "neutral" or
   "empty."
2) The reason that we personally experience this person as being
   irritating must be coming from somewhere else.

So where is it coming from? The answer to this question lies in certain principles behind unlocking the hidden potential in things, principles for using the potential to succeed in our business and in our personal lives. Here's what the Buddha has to say in *The Diamond Cutter* about making a perfect business and a perfect life—a perfect world, or paradise.

> And then the Conqueror said:
>
> Suppose, O Subhuti, that some disciple on the path of compassion were to say, "I am working to create a perfect world." They would not be speaking the truth.

The great master Choney Lama explains these cryptic lines in the following way:

> The Buddha wishes to indicate that, in order for a person to reach the highest state of being we spoke of earlier, he or she must first create a perfect world in which to reach this highest state. Therefore **the Conqueror** says to **Subhuti**,
>
> **Suppose some disciple on the path of compassion were to say** or think to themselves **"I am working to create a perfect world."** And suppose they believed, at the same time, that perfect worlds could exist from their own sides, and that the creation of these worlds could come from its own side. In such a case **they would not be speaking the truth**.

The Buddha goes on to explain himself in the next lines of *The Diamond Cutter*:

> Why is it so? Because the Ones Thus Gone have stated that these perfect worlds, these "perfect worlds" that we work to make, could never even exist. And this is exactly why we can call them "perfect worlds."

Here you can think of a "perfect world" as a "perfect business." The first point here is that it would be wrong to say that the perfect business could ever exist from its own side. A book, a building purchase, or a pain-in-the-butt who sits next to you at work—none of them, nothing, comes from its own side. None of them is a bad thing to happen, or a good thing to happen, from its own side—because if it were, then everyone would experience it that way.

But people don't. So these things are blank, or neutral, or what the Buddhists call "empty." And yet we do experience some things as good things, and we do experience other things as bad things. If it's not coming from the things themselves, then where is it coming from? If we could solve this puzzle, then perhaps we could *make things happen the way we want them to.*

It's pretty obvious with just a few moments of reflection that the way we see things is *coming from ourselves.* Whether we experience another person at work as irritating or inspiring is a matter of our own perceptions, which is proved by the fact that other people at work see the individual in different, even opposite, ways.

How is it that things are coming from ourselves? And how can we use this phenomenon to our advantage?

I think the most important thing to talk about first is how these things *don't* come from ourselves. It's easy to say that the way we see other people and things is something coming from our own minds, from our own perceptions, but one thing that's painfully obvious is that this *doesn't* mean we can control the way we see things just by wishing it. There's not a businessperson in the world who *wanted* to fail, who wanted to go bankrupt and feel the pain of disillusioned employees, unpaid suppliers, disappointed spouse and children.

It may somehow be true that our perception of a bankruptcy is coming from our own minds, but that doesn't mean that the bankruptcy will go away just by wishing it to go away. Whatever is making us see things one way or the other is *forcing* us to see them that way, despite ourselves, despite what we want in the present.

From here we have to go on to the Buddhist idea of imprints in the mind, the true meaning of the word *karma.* But since there are so many misconceptions about this word floating around, let's stick to talking about "mental imprints."

Think of your mind as a videotape recorder. Your eyes and ears and all the rest are the lenses that you see out of. Almost all the knobs and switches that determine the quality of the recording are tied to intention—to what you want to happen, and why. So how does a recording get made? How are the imprints for business success or failure impressed into our minds?

Let's talk first about the whole idea of a mental imprint. Think of the mind as a very sensitive piece of putty: Whenever it gets exposed to anything, that thing makes an imprint on the putty. But the putty has some other amazing qualities. First of all, it is totally clear and ineffable—it's not at all like our bodies, not at all something made of flesh and blood and bone.

Buddhism doesn't accept the idea that the brain *is* the mind, although part of the mind may reside, in some senses, around the vicinity of the brain. But the mind also extends to the end of your hand: You can be aware of someone touching your finger, and it is your mind that is aware. If, moreover, I ask you if there are any interesting goodies in your refrigerator at home, your mind's eye goes there—your memory pulls up a few things that are probably still there from this morning, and so your consciousness, through the media of reason and memory, has in a sense traveled far beyond the physical bounds of your immediate world, beyond your physical body, and gone elsewhere. And if I say think of the stars or beyond, where then is your mind?

Mind-putty has another interesting quality: Think of it as one long piece pulled out like a spaghetti noodle from the first moment of your life to the last (and maybe longer both ways than that, but we won't get into that now). In other words, it extends over time. Imprints made on the mind in first grade, imprints for your ABC's, are carried over to second grade, and that's why you can read whole words by then, and now too.

We in the West aren't much used to talking about learning as "purposely planting imprints," but if you think about it that's exactly why we send our children to school: We are hoping that the teacher in the first grade will have the skill to plant a few imprints in Johnny's mind, and we are hoping that these imprints will still be there when he gets to medical school, so we won't have to depend on Social Security alone. We do accept the whole idea of mental imprints, although we think precious little about how the whole process works—for example, how come our brains don't get bigger as we get older, while they get filled up with all that stuff?

Let's talk about the kinds of imprints that force us to see otherwise "blank" or "neutral" (or "empty") things as good or bad. (By the way, by now I'm sure you've read enough here about this "emptiness" thing that you realize it has nothing to do with "meaninglessness" or "black holes" or trying to think about nothing, or anything of the like. It just means that the good or bad things that happen to us don't happen like that from their own side.)

These imprints for "good" or "bad" experiences are planted in three different ways: They happen whenever we do something, or say something, or even when we think something. Our built-in VCR, the mind, is turned on all the time—one level of the mind is constantly recording everything we sense through the lenses of our eyes or ears and the rest, including thoughts themselves. When you see yourself helping out an employee who's having a hard time, a good imprint is made in your mind. When you see yourself telling a little lie to a customer or a supplier, a bad imprint is made in your mind.

The intention knob on the camera is the most important factor in deciding how strongly the imprint is made. If you're helping the employee out not because you care about him much, but rather because his problem is affecting your production and your profits, then the good imprint planted in your mind is next to nothing. If you're helping him out because you're aware that the problem is really making him unhappy, then the good imprint is a lot stronger. And if you're helping him out because you recognize that the line between "you" and "me" is artificial, and that what hurts one of us hurts all of us—in short, because you see yourself fighting our common enemy, of human unhappiness—then the imprint is in fact one of the most powerful you can plant.

There are other settings that count too. First there are emotions. If, for example, you tell your white lie to the supplier out of strong feelings of anger, then the bad imprint made on your mind is that much stronger.

Next is what we call "proper identification." If you overcharge a cus-

tomer through an honest mistake, say by misreading the price on a computer screen, then the bad imprint made is much weaker than if you had
understood clearly that the price was wrong.

The condition or circumstances surrounding the person toward whom
you perform an action also plays a large role in determining how strong
the imprint will be.

About two or three years into the business of trading in large parcels
of polished diamonds, I thought to myself that I would appreciate the diamonds more if I understood how they were cut. So I set out to knock on
the doors of the hidden little cutting shops way above the street-level diamond hawkers on Forty-seventh Street, trying to find someone who
would teach me.

I sought out one of the more famous cutters around; he was working as I remember at the time on the largest cut diamond in the world,
a "fancy" canary yellow stone of over four hundred carats that was bought
by the Zales jewelry chain. He said I could come over and watch sometimes, but that was about it. ("Fancy," by the way, is a name for naturally
colored diamonds like bright yellows or browns, or a blue like the Hope
Diamond.)

I stumbled across some South African cutters and spent a few days
with them, but the place was just too rowdy. There was also the problem
that I had to find someone who was willing to teach me pretty late at
night, since we were still working crazy hours building the Andin business.
And so I ran into Sam Shmuelof.

"Shmuel," as we called him, is another one of those true gentlemen in
the diamond trade. His wife Rachel was my right-hand man at Andin,
and the reason for much of the success of our division. He agreed to teach
me at night and on Sundays: One of the reasons that so many diamond
dealers in New York are Orthodox Jews is that the trade respects Shabbat,
the Sabbath, and no one on Forty-seventh Street is pressured to work on
Saturdays if he or she is religious.

The first time I stepped into the diamond cutting shop it was something like Dante being led into the realms of hell by Virgil. Shmuel took
me by the arm to a nearly invisible doorway between two marble-sheathed
skyscrapers on "The Street," Forty-seventh, of course, and led me to a tiny
elevator. It struggled up for about ten floors and let out to a dimly lit,

narrow corridor with narrow doors on each side. Each door was a strange combination of peeling paint and a worn-out look, but was dressed up with shiny new, heavy, and exotic locks and bolts. Most of the doors had five or six cheap handwritten little signs on them, which I later learned were the different "aliases" that a one-man operation of a small diamond merchant, say somebody with a name like "Bennie Ashtar," might work under:

"Ashtar International Diamond Corporation"
(that would be a small shoe box filled with odd diamonds
that he'd cut over the last few months,
along with a few really ugly, unsalable stones
someone had left him years before
to fulfill a bad debt)

"Ben-Ash Worldwide Jewelry Manufacturing Facility"
(that would be a few odd earrings he'd once made with a
few of his stones because he'd heard that jewelry manufacturers
make more money than diamond men,
and make their money a lot easier,
although of course he wasn't able to sell any anyway)

"Simzev Diamond Cutting and Repair International Factory"
(that would be the real business,
consisting of a single table with a diamond cutting
wheel, invariably named after the kids,
Simon and Ze'eva; but everybody would call
it Bennie's Cutting Shop anyway)

"Benjamin Rare and Exotic Gemstone, Limited"
(that would be the two kilos of "pink ice,"
or pink synthetic cubic zirconium,
that he got talked into buying back in '93
when it was the fad for six months,
but Bennie held it for seven months hoping the price
would keep going up,

and now his insurance agent is complaining
that the bag takes up too much space
in the safe and he should just throw them out)

As we approach the strange hallway we begin to hear a high-pitched whine that gets louder and louder, something like approaching a huge cavern in which millions of mosquitoes have been trapped, milling around madly. The door is just a huge metal contraption of gunmetal gray, with no numbers or signs at all on it. In the very corner of the ceiling, far above the door, a security camera pokes its snout down to us.

Shmuel pushes the buzzer, and we wait.

No answer.

He pushes again, and again, and finally there's a yell through the door: "Ya, who izh it?" (The security cameras are always broken anyway, you see, and no one has the time or desire to fix them.)

"Shmuel!"

"Okay, okay," and you hear bolt after bolt being opened, and then a few chains, and then finally the door creaks open.

Noise blasts out at you and envelops your head and ears—all the screeches and siren wails and jackhammer blasts that you encounter on a half-hour walk down a street in New York, but compressed into a few seconds. Shmuel leads the way through the first stares of the shop owner— "He's okay, he's with me"—and pulls me through the man trap (also broken) into the shop proper.

A head or two on the edge of the cyclone of pure noise pops up and checks the scene—no robbery, and no potential customer—then drops right back to judging whether a micron too much diamond has been sliced off by the wheel while the head was up.

There are about five long tables running like ribs across the room. Each table has embedded in it three or four spinning metal wheels, and facing each wheel is a cutter on a high seat, bent over his stone. The seats are offset on either side to save precious office footage in some of the most expensive real estate in the world—so that each cutter is just a few feet down from the next, facing the last. For the ten to fourteen hours a day you spend on the bench, all you really see is the face of the guy across, and hopefully he's fun to talk to.

The light in the diamond factories is like nowhere else. As the brownish skin of the rough diamond is ground off to reveal the crystal mirror facet, tiny particles of the diamond flake off and mix with the fine oil on the face of the metal cutting wheel. The incredibly high speed of the wheel throws tiny drops of diamond fairy dust and oil into the air; this gooey stuff floats to the nearest wall or person and deposits itself there.

So every inch of the place is gray, dull gray. The walls are gray, the floor is gray, the light fixtures are gray, the hands and faces are gray, gray shirts and pants and shoes and even windows. You could be a thousand feet underground or on the fortieth story of some shining glass New York skyscraper (which a lot of shops are), but you would never know the difference from the gray dimness trying to fight its way in through the windows. Seeing the exquisite gems that emerge from these dark netherworlds never failed to impress me, like watching a pink lotus in a pond near our monastery in India, rising from the only thing that can sustain it—a mash of mud and debris. The metaphor is cherished by Buddhists—*Can we be like the lotus? Can we swallow the pain and confusion of life, and thrive on it, and use it to become one of those rare jewels of the world—a truly compassionate person?*

Shmuel gives me a few essential pointers on getting started, and then sits me down on a creaky high chair facing Natan on one side and Jorges on the other. Natan is an Hassidic Jew from Brooklyn; he comes to work every day in a special bus, women sitting on one side and men on the other, separated by a curtain, each side doing their prayers as the old yellow school bus works its way across the Brooklyn Bridge up through Chinatown to the District. Natan is lucky, he has a regular contract for a large jewelry manufacturer to cut quarters (twenty-five-point stones, or a quarter of a carat). This normally wouldn't be a paying proposition—his labor would be close to or more than the cost of the finished stone—but they are dealing in fine goods, and he's giving them a good price for the steady quantity. So if he works really hard he can make a living.

Jorges is a whole different world. He is one of the Puerto Rican craftsmen in the diamond polishing trade: proud and volatile, sometimes going out on a binge and not showing up for a few days, sometimes disappearing back to Puerto Rico for a few weeks and suddenly appearing back at work as if he had just gone out for a coffee. But the touch! Nobody has hands like these, flickering across the wheel like a dragonfly, creating true masterpieces from the toughest piece of rough. He is trusted with the best raw stones in the world, and in his steady hands now a twelve-carat stone burns crimson against the crying iron wheel. Once cut, it will fetch over fifty thousand dollars.

Shmuel takes a trusty old diamond holder from the exotic collection of tools stuck into holes around the edge of his bench; it is perhaps the one he learned on himself, a true antique from the early days of diamond cutting. Attached to the end of the arm, which is made of fine hardwood, is a thick copper neck with a ball of lead on the end. We heat up one edge of the ball on a little alcohol lamp that he keeps at his elbow, until the lead is soft. Then with a quick motion he sticks the rough stone into the lead, and tamps it down with a few quick taps from the fingernail side.

The perfect atomic structure of a diamond makes it not only one of the clearest substances in the universe but also one of the best conductors of heat and electricity. A tiny square of diamond placed under a sensitive electrical connection—say a tiny switch in a satellite—ensures that it will never overheat and fail because the diamond draws off the heat like no other substance can. And in fact diamonds are to be found in many of NASA's best productions. I remember a large stone that they ordered from a nearby firm—it had to be nearly flawless, and a good size in diameter. It was cut into a disk shape and used to cover the outside lens of a camera on a satellite sent to Mars—for a diamond is impervious to almost any kind of acid or other corrosion. They even cut a second stone like this as a backup in case something happened to the first; I can't even imagine what it cost them. So anyway, Shmuel has to move fast, because a diamond carries heat even better than metals like gold or silver and can give you a nasty little burn.

For my first stone, Shmuel has entrusted me with a hefty piece of "boart," meaning one of nature's failed diamond creations. This is where the diamond material hasn't quite crystallized properly, and instead of looking like ice the inside of the stone resembles a cloudy Jell-O of army-tank green. The only thing these stones are generally good for is to be crushed into the powder used on the wheel, or else as sort of a plane to even out the iron wheel where it has been "scored" or gouged by an unruly diamond with an unexpected hard direction. The raw stone weighs a couple of carats but is worth less than ten dollars, so we have nothing to lose if I cut every angle wrong.

And the angles must be perfect. Diamond has the highest degree of refraction of any naturally occurring substance in the universe, which again is due to its perfect atomic structure. "Refraction" refers to the material's ability to allow light in, deflect it from one facet or internal mirror across to the facing one, and then back out to the eye of the beholder. If the angle of the bottom or the point of diamond is too narrow, then light will be refracted out the back or sides of the stone, giving the diamond a dull appearance even to an untrained eye. If the bottom is cut too flat, then light simply passes through from top to bottom, the way it would through the flat bottom of a drinking glass—and the stone has no scintillation. One of the most difficult skills for the apprentice to learn then is to hit the angle of the bottom facets just right: that is, forty and three-quarters degrees, and hopefully not even half a degree more or less.

Now Shmuel, being a master teacher, isn't even going to let me use a modern dop with an automatic angle setting: I'm to start off with nothing more than a round pebble of diamond stuck in lead at the end of a copper stick. To get the angle, I bend the copper and hold the arm down to the wheel. A few microns of diamond scrape off, and then I have to whip the stone back up to my jeweler's magnifier (the loupe) and check the angle with an odd tool that looks like an iron butterfly. The focal distance of the loupe is about an inch, which means that my face has to be stuck into the palm of my hand about half the day. I'm to use the crown of my nose to keep the loupe fingers steady—no human hand unsupported is stable enough to keep a microscopic inclusion from jiggling around while you check the inside of the stone for carbon spots, sort of like locking yourself in a small closet with a microscope and looking for fleas while there's an earthquake going on.

It takes me about half an hour to realize I'm not looking at inclusions in the stone, but rather the pores in the skin of my finger off on the other side of the stone. Holding up the degree gauge and the loupe and the dop with the stone, trying to keep my fingers from shaking, looking up at the light at the right angle, holding my breath and trying not to listen to the screech of the cutting wheels around me is a bit overwhelming. Out of one corner of my eye I'm watching the clock as it crawls toward quitting time, going slower and slower the closer it gets.

There's a little commotion and I see Jorges, or rather Jorges' rear end (he was a bit chubby), as he crawls around on his hands and knees with his nose to the floor. This, I later learned, is a common posture in the diamond business when someone drops a stone. There's nothing like it—a whole roomful of adults, many of them fashionable millionaires, crawling around on their hands and knees, grabbing every little ball of fuzz off the floor and tearing it apart carefully to try to find a stone that's popped off the wheel or out of someone's diamond tweezers. At diamond grading school we weren't allowed to go home until the errant stone was found, which one day kept us after class for three hours—a pretty good-sized brilliant had shot across the room and landed in the corner of the teacher's lectern, never making it to the floor, of which we had covered every inch, over and over.

Anyway, Jorges is crawling around sort of quietly and then a little louder, cursing softly in Spanish, and then Natan is on the floor, and Jorges gives Shmuel a bit of a desperate look that means, "We have a problem here. Can you get down here and help me out?" Within a few minutes every man in the shop is down on the floor, a few hundred thousand dollars' worth of diamonds suspended over the speeding wheels waiting to be cut, while the brotherhood of the diamonteers asserts itself. A man has lost a stone, a twelve-carater, the largest stone to visit the shop for a good while.

We searched far into the night. First every possible scrap of floor space, and then the windowsills (the windows, luckily, had not been opened for years, so there was no fear that the stone had flown down into the hands of some lucky stone dealer—which has happened many a time in the past on Forty-seventh Street). Then everyone's shirt pocket (a favorite hiding place); then cuffs of pants; then shoes; then socks; then under the belt, in the pants, in the underwear, in bags and boxes and cracks and crevices. We even checked everybody's head who had hair (where small stones will often stick)—but no luck. Then we went over everything one more time, and then again. It was almost dawn before we gave up, stumped to the last man, for everyone had stayed to help.

This incident is an example of how the imprint on the mind can be impressed in an especially strong way, when something kind or unkind is done to someone who is in great need. In the diamond trade there are insurance policies you can take out to cover accidents like this, but almost nobody can afford them. It would have taken Jorges the entire year to pay back the cost of the stone, and you can be sure he would have paid it back—for this is the code of the cutters. Every man who set aside his own work to help look for the missing diamond was attending to someone in great need; if we stop and take care to help such a person, or else ignore their need, then the imprint (good or bad, respectively) is much stronger.

The next morning, by the way, the owner of the cutting shop got a call from the cutter in the office next door, down the hall. Had we lost a large stone? He had found it on the floor in his bookkeeper's corner. This was my initiation into the absolute honesty of almost every single individual in the raw diamond trade—and I was deeply impressed. We figured out that the stone had ricocheted off the metal corner of the cutting bench, flown flat across the floor, dived under a tiny crack in the molding, made it through a gap under the wall, and emerged from a matching crack in the molding on the other side. Jorges, needless to say, was rather grateful.

Not only is an imprint stronger when you do something toward a person who is in great need, it is in a similar way enhanced when you act toward someone who has been very helpful to you, or someone who is of exceptional personal character. It is one thing to flippantly fire an employee who has been with the firm only a short time, and made no significant contribution; it is quite another thing to let go a long-term worker who has helped build the company only because the person is about to reach the length of service required for special retirement benefits. It is one thing to pay your phone bill late; it is quite another thing to break an oral agreement with a person who has entrusted you with an expensive parcel of diamonds out of the goodness of her heart.

And the stone business has these agreements. The entire wholesale trade in diamonds has traditionally worked off the concept of The Mazal. *Mazal* is an abbreviation of the Yiddish expression *mazel un b'rachah*, meaning "Enjoy it in good health." Among diamonteers the word means, "It's a deal." The majority of the diamond business at its highest levels works completely off the concept of this *mazal*, or verbal commitment to a deal. Millions of dollars of stones are bought and sold by phone, sometimes between people who have never met each other face to face, with the single word *mazal*. Once the *mazal* escapes from your mouth, then you have made a commitment to honor the deal, at whatever cost.

Keeping *mazal* is the heart of the diamond business. Breaking *mazal* is unheard of. When seller and buyer, after a tough negotiation, both say *mazal*, then the deal is written in stone, if only in their hearts. There are no contracts, there are no signatures. You will pay the amount that you promised, on the day you agreed to, because you have said *mazal*.

You can imagine then that the impression or imprint in your mind is much stronger when you have disregarded the spirit of *mazal*, or acted against a person of exceptional personal character. An example of this is what we call "switching," a violation of the "memo" system, another sacred tradition of the diamond craft.

Suppose Dealer A sends a parcel or small paper package of three hundred loose one-carat diamonds to Dealer B on "memo," or consignment. Dealer B gets several days to look over the stones carefully and decide whether to buy all of them, some of them, or none of them. If he decides to buy all the stones, he will definitely expect some kind of discount on the overall cost of the parcel, and the exact amount of this reduced price will be the object of a heated negotiation that could go back and forth for weeks.

If Dealer B decides to buy only some of the stones offered by Dealer A in the parcel, then Dealer A is by tradition entitled to ask for a higher individual price on each of the stones Dealer B decides to keep. This is because the value of the best stone in the package is normally much higher than the value of the ugliest duckling in the same paper; so when you "cream" or take the best stones, you're expected to pay a little more for them.

Now if Dealer B is an unscrupulous person he can call Dealer A after a few days and say, "I just got around to checking the goods you sent me— and I really can't believe that you'd offer me such *drek*. Send your guard over right away and take them back; I'd be ashamed to put such junk in my jewelry."

(*Drek*, by the way, is Yiddish for "garbage." If you're hassling an

Indian dealer you substitute the word *karab*. If he's Russian, you say *musor*. Anyway, you get the idea. When you're buying stones *from* someone else, they're always "garbage." When you're selling stones *to* someone else—even if they're the same "garbage" stones that someone else offered you this morning—they're always a *mitzia*, or an "unbelievable steal.")

During the few days, though, Dealer B *has* been checking Dealer A's diamonds, and quite carefully. He's picked out one or two of the most valuable stones and replaced them with a few of his own diamonds of lower quality, but with exactly the same weight. Now diamonds are like snowflakes: no two are exactly the same, and nobody but nobody can remember exactly what every stone in his inventory looks like, especially if the stock is something like Andin's—say a quarter of a million diamonds. Chances are that no one will notice the switch.

We did develop tricks by the way to detect whether we were the victims of such deception. Because you can't scratch a diamond, it's not as easy as just taking a pin and writing your initials on your stones. Fine-tuned lasers though have been developed in the trade that allow you to burn a tiny identification number into the side of a diamond, if you really want to. (It's so expensive that it's only worth it for what we call "certificate" or more valuable goods.) We also found ways of using X-rays to detect fakes and substitutes, and were able to check thousands of stones at a time in a little mobile X-ray unit stored in a van that could be driven to different locations.

Anyway, in actual practice, the rare dealer who indulges in switching sooner or later makes an obvious mistake in his cheating (dishonesty and stupidity often appearing in the same mind, like diamonds and garnets, a red gem that alerts prospectors to the possible presence of diamonds). Word spreads around the world in a day or two, and suddenly "No, we don't have those particular goods today" is all the dealer hears when he calls for a parcel.

The point here is that Dealer B has violated the sacred trust of Dealer A: He has hurt a person who trusted him, he has trampled on the honor system represented by *mazal*, and this again makes the imprint of his action much stronger in his own mind.

The particular *style* with which you do something good or bad also affects how powerfully the imprint is pressed into the putty called your mind. Say you not only fail to pay a supplier on time but give them a run-around on top of it. Some famous ones I've heard in the business are:

> "The check was mailed out last week;
> you know those New York mails!"

> "Our accounts payable manager has moved to
> another office in the building;
> no, we don't have his extension number yet."

> "We changed our accounting software,
> and checks can only be printed on every other Friday."

> "I know the terms were ninety days,
> but we thought it meant ninety days
> after we finished sorting the diamonds into
> different grades"
> (which can take weeks).

> "Even huge companies like Coca-Cola take a few
> extra days; what's the big problem?"
> (Except that you say this after you're already
> two months late.)

> "We're really tied up now;
> your check'll be ready in a day or two;
> what if you come over then, after lunch?"
> (Which is to say, our accounting
> department has been instructed to hand you
> the check on a Friday ten minutes after
> the bank closes, so we can get another
> three days of interest on the funds.)

Of course the most famous approach is simple evasion; take all the phones in the accounting department off the hook, or (if you're really feeling sadistic) install a recording with a very sweet voice that says, "Your call is important to us! Please hold another few seconds while our representatives serve other valued clients!" Loop this recording around every thirty seconds or so, add some really offensive music in the background, and you've made the imprint of the negative action *much stronger* than it would have been otherwise, just because of the *style* you've used.

The final factor that affects how imprints are planted in your mind has to do with the conclusion of the thought, word, or action, which is to say, do you feel glad about having done it? Would you do it again? Do you take ownership of it? If so, then the imprint is that much stronger—whether for good or for bad.

These then are the principles of mental imprints. Our minds are like a very sensitive piece of film, and whatever we expose them to—in particular, whatever good or bad we see ourselves doing to others—makes a definite imprint or impression; the track of a dove or a wolf in fresh snow, a track that stays long after.

How do these imprints affect our lives? Can we use them? Can we make the things happen the way we want them to? To understand this, we have to tie the principles of the potential to the potential itself.

⌒

How to Use the

Potential Yourself

༄༅། །བཙོམ་ལྡན་འདས་ཀྱིས་བཀའ་སྩལ་པ། རབ་འབྱོར། འདི་
 རྟེ་སྐྱེས་དུ་སེམས། རིགས་ཀྱི་བུའམ། རིགས་ཀྱི་བུ་མོ་གང་ལ་ལ་
ཞིག་གིས་སྟོང་གསུམ་གྱི་སྟོང་ཆེན་པོའི་འཇིག་རྟེན་གྱི་ཁམས་འདི་རིན་
པོ་ཆེ་སྣ་བདུན་གྱིས་རབ་ཏུ་གང་བར་བྱས་ཏེ་སྦྱིན་པ་བྱིན་ན། རིགས་ཀྱི་
བུའམ། རིགས་ཀྱི་བུ་མོ་དེ་གཞི་དེ་ལས་བསོད་ནམས་ཀྱི་ཕུང་པོ་མང་
དུ་བསྐྱེད་དམ།

Now we have all the parts to the puzzle, everything you need to know to use the deep knowledge of ancient Tibet in your own life and endeavors. We just have to tie it together.

We have seen first of all that everything has a hidden potential, a kind of fluidity about what it could be. No person we meet is irritating from their own side, because there's always someone there who finds them quite charming; no matter how they seem to us, it's not something that's coming from them. So where is it coming from? Obviously it's somehow coming from us, from our own minds.

So can we simply decide that, if everything is coming from our own minds, we will choose to see everything bad that happens to us as good? Every bad deal as a good deal? You know it doesn't work that way. You can't buy a house or send the kids to college on wishes alone. Apparently whatever makes us see things one way or another is doing so in a compulsory way; that is, whatever makes us see something good happening to us or something bad happening to us is *forcing* us to see these things as we do.

Now this is all because of those mental imprints that we talked about above, and the art of Buddhist wisdom is to turn them around to your own advantage. To do this, you have to know how the imprints work on you. Let's go back to *The Diamond Cutter* itself for some advice.

~ And the Conqueror said:

> O Subhuti, what do you think? Suppose some son or daughter of noble family were to take all the inhabited planets of this great galaxy, a galaxy with a thousand thousands of a thousand planets, and cover them with the seven kinds of jewels, and present them as a gift to someone. Would that son or daughter create many great mountains of goodness from such a deed? ~

The Buddha is going somewhere difficult; perhaps it's best if we bring Choney Lama along with us for each verse. Here is his explanation of what's come so far:

> With this next section of the sutra, the Buddha wishes to demonstrate a certain fact. In the sections above we have spoken about the act of reaching the highest state of being, and the act of teaching these things to others, and so on.
>
> Neither of these acts, nor in fact any other object in the universe, exists in and of itself. Nonetheless, they do exist in our perceptions. And so it is true that anyone who performs the deed of giving does create goodness thereby. But any person who studies the principles behind these things, anyone who thinks hard on them, and then meditates on them, creates infinitely greater goodness.
>
> To convey this point, **the Conqueror** asks **Subhuti** the question beginning with "What do you think? Suppose some son or daughter of noble family were to take all the inhabited planets of**

this great galaxy, a galaxy with a thousand thousands of a thousand planets . . ."

The galaxy mentioned here is described in the *Treasure House of Higher Knowledge* as follows:

> What we call a "first-order" galaxy
> Is a thousand inhabited planets,
> Each consisting of its own four continents,
> With a central mountain system
> And special beings in one realm,
> With the "World of the Pure" atop it.
>
> A thousand of these galaxies
> We call a "second-order" one,
> And a thousand of these then make
> A galaxy of the "third order."

"Suppose further," continues the Buddha, "that this son or daughter of noble family were to cover these planets with the seven kinds of jewels: with gold, silver, crystal, lapis, emerald, *karketana* stone, and crimson pearl. And say then that they offered these planets to someone. Would they create many great mountains of goodness from such a deed, from giving just such a gift?"

Back to *The Diamond Cutter*:

And Subhuti replied,

> O Conqueror, many great mountains of goodness would it be. Yes many, O Conqueror, would it be. This son or daughter of noble family would indeed create many great mountains of goodness from such a deed. And why would it be so? Because, O Conqueror, these same great mountains of goodness are great mountains of goodness that could

never exist. And for this very reason do the Ones Thus Gone speak of "great mountains of goodness, great mountains of goodness." ⌒

This verse too Choney Lama explains—

In response, **Subhuti replies:**

It would be many great mountains of goodness—and these great mountains of goodness are mountains of goodness that we could establish as existing only in our perceptions, only in the way that a dream or an illusion exists: **these same great mountains of goodness though** could **never exist** as mountains that existed in and of themselves. **The Ones Thus Gone** as well **speak** in a nominal sense **of** "**great mountains of goodness, great mountains of goodness**"—applying the name to them.

This section is meant to demonstrate a number of different points. Black and white actions that you have committed before now, and those which you are going to commit later, are such that the ones in the past have stopped, and the ones in the future are yet to come.

Therefore they are nonexistent; but we would also have to agree that in a more general sense they do exist. We would also have to agree that they are connected to the mind stream of the person who committed them, and that they produce their appropriate consequences for this person. These and other difficult issues are raised in the words above.

The Diamond Cutter continues:

⌒ And then the Conqueror said:

O Subhuti, suppose some son or daughter of noble family were to take all the planets of this great galaxy, a galaxy with a thousand thousands of a thousand inhabited planets, and cover them all with the seven kinds of jewels, and offer them to someone.

Suppose on the other hand that this son or daughter held but a single verse of four lines from this particular teaching, and explained it to others, and taught it correctly. By undertaking this second action, the person would create many more of those great mountains of goodness than with the former: the goodness would be infinite, beyond all measure at all.

Choney Lama explains these last verses in the following words:

We should first say something about the word **"verse"** here. Although this ancient book—in its Tibetan translation—is not written in verse, the idea is that one could put it into verse in the original Sanskrit. The word **"hold"** refers to "holding in the mind," or memorizing. It can also apply to holding a volume in one's hand and, in either case, to reciting the text out loud.

The phrase **"explain it correctly"** is said to mean speaking out the words of the book and explaining them well. The phrase **"teach it correctly"** is said to refer to teaching the meaning of the sutra well—and this after all is the most important point.

Suppose now that **someone held** this ancient book, and did the other things mentioned with it, rather than performing the other good deed that was mentioned before. A **person** like **this would** then create great mountains of goodness that were ever more infinite, and beyond all measuring at all.

So we've seen that every event that ever happens to us is, in a sense, "neutral" or "empty." The content that we see in it—that is, whether we experience it as something pleasant or unpleasant—is not something that is coming from its own side. Rather, it seems to be coming from our side, though not—apparently—in a way we can control at the moment.

Herein lies the secret of the mental imprints. They are planted in the mind as we described above: through the gates of our own awareness of ourselves, as we do anything to help or hurt another. The strength with which they are planted depends on the various factors we have outlined, including our intentions, the strength of our emotions; how well we recognize what we are doing; the style with which we act; the degree to which we "own" our actions afterward; and certain details of the person toward whom we have acted—someone in great need, someone who has been very helpful to us, or someone of exceptional personal character.

What remains is to discuss how these imprints determine what we perceive around us. According to the ancient books of Buddhism, the "VCR" or camera of our mind records about sixty-five discrete images or imprints during the space of a single finger snap. These imprints enter, you could say, a place in our subconscious. Here they remain for days or years or decades, reproducing themselves every millisecond as separate moments of the mind itself blink in and out of existence, moving by in a row like the frames of a movie, giving us the illusion of continuity.

Like seeds of the natural world, seeds within the stream of the mind continue to grow after they have been planted, and they grow, as in nature, in an exponential way. The magnitude of a mental imprint planted on the first of the month has doubled by the second, and then quadrupled by the third—and by the fifth of the month is sixteen times its original strength.

The principle here is nothing surprising, if you think about it. Consider the weight or mass of a single acorn, measured in grams, as opposed to the weight of the resulting oak tree—literally, a ton of trunk per gram of seed. The ancient wisdom of Tibet says that mental seeds behave no differently, and this too makes sense, if you consider something like the "mass" of the federal bureaucracy of the entire United States, as opposed to the tiny inkling of a new government in the country's founders' minds back in the 1700s—the seed that it all came from. You can imagine the first moment as a child in which you understood the meaning of money, and see now how much of the last twenty years of your life and thoughts has been occupied in its pursuit.

What we are talking about here is an idea that the Tibetans call *ke-nyen chenpo*: great potential for profit, and great risk of loss, both in the same package. Even very minor or careless acts toward others plant seeds in our minds that can, by the time they flower, grow into immense experiences. How then do these seeds flower? What are the rules at work here?

Our minds are like a vast repository of thousands upon thousands of mental imprints. They are queued up to take off like planes on the runway of an airport. The stronger imprints—according to the principles we talked about above—get to take off first, with fainter imprints lagging far behind but building up steam every minute they remain on the runway of the mind. Whenever we do another action toward others that plants an imprint more powerful than one of the existing ones, this imprint moves up in the queue, like a plane that the control tower has called ahead of the others.

When the imprint plane takes off—that is, when the impression in the mind comes up to the conscious mind—it colors (nay, even *determines*) our entire perception of whatever event we are undergoing at the moment. A collection of four moving flesh-colored cylinders attached to a larger tank shape presents itself before you, and an imprint comes up to the conscious mind which demands that you interpret this new data as a "person."

A pink oval shape appears in the middle of an egg shape at the top of the tank shape. In quick succession, a cylindrical red shiny shape appears within the oval shape and begins to wag back and forth. Decibel levels begin to change rapidly in the environs of the cylinder, along with syllables and vowels mixed in a certain way. Simultaneously, a negative imprint planted in past days rises into the conscious mind, demanding that you interpret this new data as "the boss, yelling at me." And so on.

There are four rules that govern how imprints from the past "flower" in the mind, thereby forcing you to see things around you happen the way they do:

> **1. The general content of the experience forced on you by the imprint must match the general content of the original imprinting.**

Which is to say, an imprint planted in your mind through a negative action—by something you did that hurt someone else—can only force you to perceive something as an unpleasant experience in result. And an imprint planted by undertaking some positive action—by something done to help someone else—can only force you to perceive something as a pleasant experience in result. To put it simply, a negative action can lead only to negative results, and a positive action can lead only to positive results. We would say Jesus had this idea in mind when He said that grapes could never grow from thorns, nor figs from thistles.

> **2. The strength of the imprint continually expands during its time in the subconscious; that is, until it flowers and forces us to undergo some experience, be it good or bad.**

We've already talked about this phenomenon, the point being that even very small or hardly intentional actions can trigger immense future perceptions.

> **3. No experience of any kind ever happens unless the imprint that triggers it has been planted first.**

The point here is that *every* experience we undergo is triggered by a previous imprint: Nothing around us—not people or things or events themselves, nor even our own thoughts—occurs without the cause of an imprint in our own mind coming up to our consciousness and making us perceive it.

> **4. Once an imprint is planted in the mind, it must lead to an experience: no imprint is ever wasted.**

Rule number four is something like the converse of number three; that is, while it is true that no experience of any kind ever happens unless there is a previous imprint that causes it, it is equally true that—once an imprint is planted—it *must* lead to an experience. Imprints are never wasted; they *always* have an effect, they *always* cause us to perceive something.

The second rule here, by the way, is where the quotation from *The Diamond Cutter* at the opening of this chapter comes in. And this, of all the points in this book, is the single most important one for business and personal success:

> Even a relatively minor action, if undertaken with a con-
> scious awareness of how imprints make us see an other-
> wise "neutral" or "empty" world as we do, will lead to
> *tremendous* results.

To illustrate this truth, the Buddha is telling his disciple Subhuti that it would be better just to lay hands on *The Diamond Cutter*, and have some inkling of its contents, than give another person an entire planet, or even a billion entire planets, covered with precious jewels. This is because a person who even comes close to understanding how imprints make us see our world as we do can then go about creating, consciously, a perfect life and a perfect world. The more we understand the process, the more per-fectly and powerfully the seeds of even insignificant acts and words and thoughts are planted in the mind, and the more powerful their results in fashioning the world around and within us.

All we have to do now is identify the kinds of goals we seek, and then use rule number one to identify the particular imprints that would make us see them. We call these the "correlations," meaning you can work back from a particular desirable result and identify the particular imprints that would make you see it.

In the majority of cases, the specific imprints in the mind that you need to create a given result in your life or business are quite nearly the opposite of what human nature tends to dictate. Suppose, for example, that your company is struggling in the marketplace, and cash flow has become a problem. The natural instinct of almost any person or corpora-tion in this position is to cut back. Corporate giving is an immediate victim, followed by blatant perks like business-class airline seats for shorter management trips.

Then go the items that are halfway between a perk and salary, say a car service home for employees who stay late. Next go the holiday bonuses; then raises are shaved; raises stop completely; and the knife goes to the benefits—"We've found an even better HMO plan" is a management announcement in a troubled company that's bound to make experienced employees nervous, since it usually signifies some kind of maneuver to cut existing benefits. These gradual levels of cutting also cut into the morale of

the firm, from top to bottom, setting off a general lack of charity in every
sense of the word:

> "Cash is tight, so we're going to have to defer your raise a few
> months."

> "Why should I stay late on this project? They won't even give me
> a raise."

> "Let's defer the raises again; no one is performing."

> "Why should I try to save the company money if they keep defer-
> ring the raises?"

> "We've cut expenses to the bone, but the cash flow just seems to
> get worse."

And so on. It's important, therefore, to be wary of your *natural* reaction to a problem: It may simply perpetuate the problem. In Tibetan this
phenomenon is known as *korwa*, or a "self-perpetuating circle of trouble."
Money's tight in your company so you begin to take actions that deny
others the help they need; and you begin to talk about cuts; and, most
important of all, your own thinking shifts from one of creation and creativity to one of defense and entrenchment.

Each of these reactions plants new imprints in your mind, negative
imprints. Every time you deny funds or help to those who depend on you
*you plant an imprint that will make you see yourself and your own business
denied the same funds and help.* This phenomenon escalates because of the
second rule of imprints: the way in which their power grows, the longer
they spend in the subconscious. Then when this sets off a new wave of
financial problems you react with an even stronger attitude of stinginess,
creating a third wave. The cumulative result is the downward spiral seen so
often in struggling companies.

The apparent implication of what we've said so far is that we should
avoid cuts and stingy thinking as a reaction to financial pressures. This
though has to be qualified. We said above that there were three different

ways of planting an imprint: through actions, words, and thoughts themselves. By far the most important of these is the third; that is, the deepest imprints are created by attitudes alone.

The point is that, as a reaction to financial pressures (either corporate or personal), one must above all avoid a stingy *state of mind*. It may well be true that there are no funds available to provide the perks that were handed out before, and you may in fact have to stop the perks because there is no money for them right now, but it is vital *not to think cheap*, not to lose creativity, not to lose a truly generous outlook within the new limitations of your financial situation.

If you descend to a cheap state of mind, denying others what you actually could—even in your current finances—well afford, then you create powerful imprints that will actually affect whether or not you are able to bounce back.

There's another vital point that we should mention right at this juncture. We *are not* in this system of ancient wisdom talking about how an attitude might *color* your perceptions of your financial situation. We are, rather, setting forth the details of a process *which actually determines the reality around you*. We are not talking about how you feel about not being able to make your payments. We are talking about *how you feel* actually *determining* whether or not you can make your payments. The premise here is profound, and bluntly unprecedented in other systems of how to run a business: *Money itself is created by maintaining a generous state of mind.*

Look at any given market situation.

Diamonds, flatly stated, are worth just about nothing. The ugly little deformed ones, brown and black pieces of boart or industrial diamonds no more fashionable than gravel, play a mighty role in the economy of the world. Things like the engine blocks of automobiles and important parts of an airliner must be fashioned with carbon steel, hardened to the point where it can shave and shape steel itself to the precision that is absolutely required for these objects to work. Carbon steel itself though must be sharpened, and diamond is the single best sharpening agent in the world.

For this reason, diamond used to be counted with the likes of uranium and plutonium as a strategic mineral, absolutely necessary for modern industry. The United States Government for many years stockpiled industrial diamonds in the event that a war or similar catastrophe would prevent the country from getting the supplies it needed, which at that time were concentrated in river-bottom deposits found only in a handful of African nations.

During the Cold War, the United States even took steps to assure that the supplies of these diamonds to Eastern Bloc countries like the Soviet Union *would* be disrupted. Ironically, this forced the Russians into searching the length and breadth of their empire to find their own diamond pipes.

Diamond pipes are huge carrot-shaped affairs that can range from several feet to hundreds of yards across where they break the surface of the earth. As we work the pipes for diamond ore, digging hundreds and thousands of feet deeper and deeper, the pipe generally gets progressively narrower and more difficult to mine. The pipes are actually tubes where ancient lava has driven up from the core of the earth to the open air, carrying with it nascent diamonds. These tubes are filled with a greenish ore named kimberlite; you might have to dig out an entire ton of this stuff to find the amount of diamond you could put on a pencil eraser, and so (contrary to popular belief) diamonds really are rather costly things to produce.

The positioning of pipes around the planet is one of the proofs of the theory that the continents of the world were once all joined together, and that the present oceans between them represent cracks or fissures created when the continents drifted apart. The classic pipes, as many people know, are located in South Africa. Here, for example—in the middle of some fields owned by the de Beer brothers, a pair of impoverished Boer farmers—was discovered the famed DeBeers pipe, which along with the Kimberley Mine on the same property, has produced millions of carats of diamonds since the brothers sold the land for a song around 1870. It is this mine that lent its name to the famed DeBeers diamond cartel, a powerful and unrelenting organization that has controlled much of the international raw diamond business for more than a hundred years.

An interesting thing happens over the couple of million years it takes for the cone-shaped pimple created by a diamond pipe eruption to flatten out, until it's on a level with the surrounding land. Rain, wind, and the effects of heat and freezing gradually wear the cone down. Raw diamonds break out of the "blue rock" or ore and begin to roll in rivulets of water, and then streams and rivers, down toward the ocean.

Diamonds are one of the heaviest of all minerals, on a level with gold itself, and since they are much harder than common stone they tend to dig little pockets for themselves out of the bedrock below a river. Some of the stones inevitably break loose again and make their way to the sea itself. Only the purest of the diamonds—those without even the tiniest cracks or fractures—survive the trip, which takes aeons. Perhaps the most fabled discovery of diamonds was on the west coast of Africa, where the Orange River empties out to the Atlantic Ocean.

As stones from diamond pipes rolled down the Orange and out to sea, strong ocean currents over the centuries pushed the stones back up onto the beach, where the highest quality diamonds of all were lying around like spilled popcorn for the German explorers who discovered them in 1908. One of my favorite photos is that of prospectors crawling on their hands and knees across this beach, later called the *Sperrgebeit* or "Forbidden Zone," simply picking up huge perfect crystals.

Anyway, there are areas of Brazil where the bottoms of the rivers teem with diamonds, places like the basin of the Jequitinhonha River near Diamantina, a quaint little town with a Swiss look in the modern state of Minas Gerais. But there are no diamond pipes in this country where the stones could possibly have come from. Ditto for some other alluvial or river deposits in western India, a country which produced the first great stones of history—masterpieces like the Koh-i-noor and the Orloff—long before the African deposits were discovered.

Take a map of the world, grab the bottom ends of South America and India, and squash them back to where they used to be—tucked up against South Africa on either side—and it's clear where the river diamonds have come from: huge pipes on the bottom edge of Africa that were worn down, stones spilling out into the rivers of Brazil and the Deccan Plateau of India before their respective continents wandered off from the motherland.

The geology of the land around the great diamond pipes of South Africa is similar in many respects to that of Siberia, and this fact was noted by the great Russian geologist Vladimir Sobolev during the years when American monkey business made it hard for the Soviet Union to get the supplies of African diamonds that they needed for industry. Under Sobolev's direction, teams of geologists were sent out into the vast coldness of the Siberian tundra to search for diamond pipes.

Unfortunately there were, at the time, few tools for locating diamond pipes aerially or otherwise. You pretty much had to be standing on the top of a pipe to tell the blue ground was there, and to add to your troubles it might be lying under several yards of plain old dirt that had collected there over the centuries. Diamond-business legend says that a woman geologist was wandering around the frozen wastes of Siberia, looking for Sobolev's dream pipes, and one day went out hunting to see if she could find some fresh meat to spice up her comrades' diet.

Her eye caught a motion in the distance—a red fox, disappearing into some brush. She raises the rifle, finds the fox in her telescopic lens, and through great good fortune is able to hold her trigger finger; for the side of the fox's coat is smeared with a blue stain, just the color of the ore in a diamond pipe. She tracks the fox to its lair, which descends into a pipe that will be the first great discovery of Russian diamonds: the Mir or "Peace" mine.

Over forty years later, the Russians have become one of the greatest forces in the diamond world, with new pipes spread over the vast hinterland of the frozen north. Here there are whole cities of mine workers, living on platforms suspended above the permafrost by a great system of pilings sunk deep into the frozen ground. And air conditioners must continually blow freezing air into the empty space between these towns and the tundra below, to prevent the ice from melting, and the town from sinking beneath a slush of half-frozen mud.

When the first Russian stones began to pour out onto the world diamond markets, it struck a wave of terror in the hearts of diamonteers around the globe. I had studied Russian at Princeton, and helped out with some of the research by the De Beers Industrial Division people near London, to try to keep abreast of what the Russians were up to. I had a devouring interest in all things diamond, ever since the experience back in 1975, and wanted to know everything about the business; so I volunteered to translate articles about diamonds from various Russian scientific journals.

We were very concerned because we knew that the Russians had already figured out how to produce a perfect diamond in a laboratory; this had been pioneered earlier by scientists at General Electric in the United

States, utilizing huge, bizarre pistons to keep tiny bits of graphite (pencil carbon) under high pressure for long periods of time, simultaneously heating the whole concoction up to the point where it resembled the processes going on deep within the earth, as real diamonds form in the original pipes.

Fortunately, the amount of electricity needed to keep this process going for the time it took to make a one-carat rough diamond was something on the order of the juice needed to keep a small city lit for hours; it was much more expensive to make a stone this way than to try to pluck it out of the haystack of a ton of blue ground, and so common wisdom said that it would never pay to make the stones at home. The diamond business was supposed to be safe from the threat of the perfect fake: a synthetic or laboratory-grown diamond that was in every way as pure and pretty as the real thing.

Perhaps the Russians though had figured out a way to make the production of synthetic diamonds cheap—it seemed to be the only way to explain the sudden appearance of vast quantities of raw material from Siberia, given one important fact about diamond mining. According to the technology we knew, huge amounts of water were required for processing the raw diamonds—for releasing them from the blue ground. This had traditionally been done by crushing the ore down to rocks of a certain size by using great gears (which, incidentally, almost always assured that the occasional really huge diamond would get broken into smaller pieces).

The finer ore was then mixed with water and spilled in a huge mush across the face of a broad table covered with a thick oil paste like axle grease. Again, diamonds, with their perfect atomic structure, tend to adhere to a grease-covered surface like no other mineral can. The slurry of water and diamond ore tumbled across the grease; the diamonds would stick; and the rest would spill off the side. The axle grease was then scraped off the table, collected into a huge container, and heated to a liquid so that the raw diamonds collected at the bottom.

But we knew it was impossible to trap and store this amount of water in landlocked places at the edge of the Arctic Circle—it would simply freeze as soon as it made contact with the open air. Detailed information about the diamond industry in the Soviet Union of those days—diamonds being absolutely necessary for the production of things like cars and airplanes, missiles and tanks—was considered a state secret, and a person who revealed this information was liable for the death penalty.

We had no way of knowing that there were indeed real mines in natural pipes below the Siberian ice, and that the Russians had developed a clever new way of separating the diamonds from the chaff. You see, most diamonds give off a faint glow when exposed to X-rays: they fluoresce, some so strongly that mere sunlight sets them off (thus giving rise to the myth of a "blue-white" diamond). The crushed ore was spread across a table peppered with tiny holes, each with a powerful air jet below it. X-rays were passed over the ore in a wave, and sensors spotted the stones that glowed. This set off one of the air jets, which popped the stone neatly into a special tank with a glass tray at the bottom for collecting the diamonds. And of course there was a *very good* lock to hold the tray in, and a guard sitting nearby, to keep the treasure safe.

Ignorant of this development, those diamonteers in the know were very fearful that the Russians had managed a breakthrough that would make large quantities of man-made diamonds a reality. This, we knew, might well set off the collapse of what we in the diamond business call the Overhang.

The Overhang is an expression used to describe the total number of polished diamonds that have accumulated in the world especially in the last sixty years or so, as the middle class in developed countries has come into the kind of money needed to buy a diamond ring as a symbol of engagement to be married—and as the discovery of new, viable diamond pipes around the world has assured increased supplies to keep up with the growth of this middle class.

Think about it. Once a diamond has been won from the blue ground and fashioned into a brilliant stone with fifty-eight blazing facets, its place in the family genealogy is assured. Nobody gets rid of a diamond; it is passed on from generation to generation with love and care. Stones may be remounted perhaps into different rings or pendants or other jewelry pieces as fashions change, and then entrusted to daughters or granddaughters. Being the hardest things in the universe, diamonds tend to hang around just about forever. The Tibetan wise men make a joke that a diamond is the kind of thing that sooner or later will always be forced to go out looking for a new owner, after the previous owner gets old and dies. Diamonds are forever—but we're not, it seems.

Regular old jewelry diamonds (as opposed to their industrial super-man brothers) don't have any real value at all: Let's face it, there are lots of glass beads that are just as pretty, or maybe more, and diamonds will always cost only whatever someone is willing to pay for them on any given day. The value of the huge store of diamonds in the hands of the public at this moment—what we call the Overhang—is only a perception of value, of consumer confidence in the continued rarity of diamonds.

If the Russians had developed a truly inexpensive synthetic—a real diamond made in the laboratory—it meant the collapse of the Overhang: an avalanche of the accumulated diamonds of the world onto the market from private parties, as they panicked and tried to get at least a few dollars from Grandmom's ring before diamonds became as common as candy. It was, potentially, a diamond dealer's nightmare—one which fortunately never came true.

Which brings us back to the question of markets, an especially sensitive issue in the loose diamond business. A company like Andin might be offering several thousand different jewelry designs at any given moment. Each design takes a slightly different configuration of diamonds; say, a one-carater in the middle of a bracelet, with a few quarter-caraters off to the side, and enough diamond chips sprinkled around to get the piece up to the legal minimum for a two-carat finished piece.

Now you never know what order is going to come in on any particular day from a firm like J. C. Penney or Macy's, two of our larger customers. Somebody like Penney's might suddenly order a thousand pieces of the bracelet just described, and demand that it be *in the stores* within fifteen days or so. The buyers of the Diamond Division of the company then begin a delicate game of poker: a version of "playing chicken," a game that was popular in my hometown when I was a teenager. Two crazy kids in cars drive at each other full speed, head on, until one of them "chickens out" and turns his car away.

We have to give the market the impression that we don't need the stones at all, or don't need them very much, so the price doesn't go crazy. And the market has to hold back its supplies until it's sure we're at our most desperate, and will pay the highest price to get the goods today. If either party waits a day too long though the whole game is over: the diamonds go back to being worth nothing, either because the order has been filled, or because it has become too expensive to honor.

With all the different styles of jewelry a diamond firm must offer its customers nowadays, it's flatly impossible to keep an inventory of the many diamonds you might need at any given time. Yesterday the company maybe didn't need a single stone of the particular sizes and qualities that the bracelet requires; now we need about twenty thousand of them, on short notice.

This kind of quantity would never be available on any single one of the world's markets; we'll have to alert our people around the globe to start picking up major parcels of goods quietly, before the word gets out that we need these particular diamonds. If it does, the "value" will jump—and we have already committed to Penney's for a fixed price on the jewelry: There's no room to raise the price to them.

Here is a very real example of the power of the hidden potential, and of mental imprints. I've seen it a thousand times, and you can believe it's real. One buyer, the one in New York named Kishan, gets a "feeling" about the order; he makes one phone call to a specific dealer, out of dozens with offices in the city.

By coincidence, this one office has just gotten in a big shipment of these particular stones from the Hong Kong branch. In fact, the uncle in Antwerp has a substantial payment to make to DeBeers for some rough in London next week. And that other jewelry company up on Forty-ninth Street has just called in saying that their cash flow is tight because *they* haven't gotten paid yet by such-and-such a department store chain. So anyway, you can have the stones this afternoon, a couple of thousand of them, for a very good price.

Another buyer in another city, on another continent—our friend Dhiru in Bombay—makes his phone calls too. There aren't any easy goods available, but small parcels start rolling in from the dealers around town every few hours. With a lot of work and some tough bargaining, he'll soon have enough purchases to supply his share of the order. The home office in New York though will have already spent most of its available cash flow on the easy goods picked up in New York, and so on top of the extra work he'll have to wait a bit extra to get paid.

A third buyer, say Yoram in Tel Aviv, starts with a few calls to his regular suppliers. But the time difference internationally means that the branch offices in New York have already alerted their Israeli counterparts that Andin is after these particular stones. Suddenly the price has firmed up, and the more he calls around, the more desperate he sounds to the dealers—thus triggering another price hike, since they can smell he's got an order with a short delivery date: Sooner or later he will have to break down and pay whatever he has to, to get the goods on time.

So buyer number three will come in late and over price on the order; he'll get paid way late, and we don't even have to mention what's going to happen to his annual bonus when the J. C. Penney buyer calls up the owner, Ofer, at his home over the weekend to find out why there are no bracelets in the stores, two days after the ad campaign for the piece has hit the streets.

The crucial question to ask here is: What accounts for the difference in the three markets on any given day? Why did the New York office pick up goods so easily? Was the buyer more skilled? Was there something about the strategy he used? Were there more stones of this size available? Was it just dumb luck? The principle of hidden potential and mental imprints says: no way.

A market for any given commodity in any given city on any particular day is just another example of a thing which is neither good nor bad from its own side. If it were, then every dealer and buyer in the city that day would be having the same easy time or hard time moving goods. But you know that's not the way it works. Some dealers will say it was an "okay day" (this is a code word in the diamond business for an *incredibly good* day—nobody wants to admit to anyone else that they're doing really well, or everybody in town will raise their prices to him within the week). Some dealers will say it was the worst day of the year, and they'll be right.

Therefore the market is "neutral," or—in Buddhist terms—empty. It is neither good nor bad from its own side; it is only either of these in the perceptions of the particular diamond dealer, on this particular day. Whether the markets are kind to us or cruel to us seems—at the end of the day, or at the end of an extended business career in any kind of market— almost random. The truth though is that the market will appear kind, *and the market will therefore be kind,* to any dealer who has the right mental imprints coming up to his conscious mind at any given moment.

Two dealers can be looking for the same diamonds from the same companies in the same market on the same day and have completely different results. It's not that there are two different worlds and markets going on out there at the same time on the given day. It's that the two dealers are being forced, each one by the imprints already in his mind, to see the market in two radically different ways. And these two ways are both very real. One dealer will make his orders, and the other will not.

This brings us down then to the whole crux of this book: How do we use this fact for success in our lives and business? The answer is obvious. We just have to figure out which imprint it is that we can plant in our minds to see, later on, the market as we want to see it: profitable. And this depends primarily on maintaining certain states of mind, maintaining certain standards of behavior, and knowing how to call on the power of what we call an "act of truth."

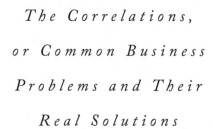

The Correlations,

or Common Business

Problems and Their

Real Solutions

At the end of the last chapter we talked about the "emptiness" of markets. Three buyers go on the market to get several thousand diamonds of a specific size and quality. One gets a "feeling," makes a call or two, and succeeds with ease. One has to make more calls and work harder, but comes through in the end. One basically fails to get the goods. The buyers in our example were in different cities, but it could have been a single city, no matter.

According to ancient Tibetan thinking, the "feelings" or "instincts" that successful businesspeople get that guide them through the dark forest of deals and markets is a direct flowering of a mental imprint—this then gives you some idea of what it feels like when a strong imprint comes up to the consciousness. These kinds of people are presented with a business problem and suddenly see, quite clearly, the right thing to do. No hesitation, no question in their minds.

People call them "brilliant" or "insightful" or "guys with the magic touch"; nothing's more fun than to be one of these people—someone who rips up the market, a baseball player who consistently hits home runs and says that the ball looks as big to him as a watermelon just before he whacks it. But nothing's more frustrating than *to have been* the guy with the right instincts and not feel them anymore—much worse than not having felt them in the first place. In either case, it would be nice to know how to get these instincts to happen to us on a regular basis.

Here we return to *The Diamond Cutter* for some insight on the instincts:

> Suppose, O Subhuti, that any particular person reaches even just a single moment of insight and belief into the words of an ancient book that teaches what this one does. The One Thus Gone, O Subhuti, knows a person like this. The One Thus Gone, O Subhuti, sees a person like this. Such a person, O Subhuti, has created, and they have safely gathered into themselves, a mountain of goodness far beyond all measuring.

Where do instincts come from? In the last chapter we mentioned the "correlations," meaning the types of actions or thoughts that "correlate" or lead to certain imprints, which lead themselves to the specific results we seek in our business and our lives. Now it's time to identify these actions, for if we truly understand the process—if we act with a knowledge of how imprints and the potential behind them work—then we can "gather into ourselves" a vast energy to make our business go the way we want it to. People acting with this knowledge tend to draw the attention of others acting this way, and then their success snowballs.

Perhaps the most famous proclamation ever to come out of the mouth of a Buddhist wise man about these correlations is the following, by an Indian master named Nagarjuna, some eighteen centuries ago. The verses are from his *String of Precious Jewels*; they speak first of the most desirable imprints we can plant in our minds:

> I'll tell you briefly the fine qualities
> Of those on the path of compassion:
> Giving, and ethics, patience, and effort,
> Concentrating, wisdom, compassion and such.

> Giving is giving away what you have,
> And ethics is doing good to others.
> Patience is giving up feelings of anger,
> And effort is joy that increases all good.

> Concentration's one-pointed, free of bad thoughts,
> And wisdom decides what truth really is.
> Compassion's a kind of high intelligence
> Mixed deep with a love for all living kind.

The next verse then gives the correlations themselves:

> Giving brings wealth, a good world comes from ethics;
> Patience brings beauty, eminence comes from effort.
> Concentration brings peace, and from wisdom comes freedom;
> Compassion achieves everything we all wish for.

We'll throw in the last verse too, which lays out the ultimate result of cultivating these imprints:

> A person who takes all seven of these
> And perfects them together will reach
> That place of inconceivable knowledge,
> No less than the world's protector.

These verses are perhaps the most famous brief list (there are other places where hundreds of imprints and their results are discussed) of the correlations between specific actions, their imprints, and what they make you see. We can summarize them as follows:

1) In order to see yourself do well in business and prosper financially, plant imprints for this in your subconscious by maintaining a generous state of mind.

2) In order to see yourself in a world which is just generally a very happy place, plant imprints for this in your subconscious by maintaining a very ethical way of life.

3) In order to see yourself as physically healthy and attractive, plant imprints for this in your subconscious by refusing ever to get angry.

4) In order to see yourself as a leader in both your personal life and in business, plant imprints for this in your subconscious by taking joy in constructive and helpful actions.

5) In order to see yourself able to focus your mind steadily, plant imprints for this in your subconscious by practicing deep states of concentration, or meditation.

6) In order to see yourself freed from a world where things don't work the way you want them to, plant imprints for this in your subconscious by learning the principles of hidden potential and mental imprints.

7) In order to see yourself get all you ever wished for, and see others get all they ever wished for as well, plant imprints for this in your subconscious by cultivating an attitude of compassion toward others.

I know by this point you're starting to wonder how all of this noble-sounding stuff applies to real life. So I'll describe an actual situation for you so you can get a sense of how the principles of potential and imprints are running the show in your own office.

Say I've been at Andin International for a number of years, applying the principles we've described so far: I've been purposely doing exactly those things which plant the imprints in my mind that will lead me to see success around me.

I walk in the front door of our new building on the west side of Manhattan: It has pleasing granite slabs facing the front of the structure, and crystalline glass doors opening onto the foyer. A gust of cold wind from the Hudson River snaps at me as I open the door, and I get a friendly nod at the security booth from John Vaccaro, a tough ex-subway cop known for the way he can get a parcel of diamonds from one building to another safely, even under the eyes of one of the Colombian gangs that hangs out on Forty-seventh Street, waiting for a careless diamond man to let his guard down.

Each of these objects and people in the scene we've just described has the same hidden potential—each one is in a way fluid, eligible to be something positive or something negative. I happen to like the granite slabs on the building: they shine in the morning light off the river, and give our building a look of respectability. To a window washer up on a catwalk on the ninth floor, the same granite slabs represent a potentially life-threatening danger, and he or she would much rather we had ordinary brick on the outside.

For me, the way I see the granite is a result of a good imprint that I put into my mind earlier—now what kind would it be? Here we get into something very deep—correlations between imprints and what we see that are beyond the ken of normal people. They have been written down though in the ancient books by great meditative masters of the long distant past. The imprint for this particular feature, the smoothness of the granite, happens to be speaking gently to others.

Now the window washer sees the same granite as something dangerous, and the imprint for this comes, understandably, from failing to respect life in the past. Now to the Western mind, entirely unused to this way of thinking only because of our own cultural myths and biases, this explanation itself seems like a myth. But again this was exactly the argument that Jesus Christ, in our own cultural background, was making for ethical living when He insisted that a good result cannot come from an unethical action, any more than a sweet fruit can come from the seeds for thistles or thorns.

Buddhist writings go on to explain the exact dynamic behind this truth, which is precisely the law that governs imprints and what they make us see on otherwise "empty" or neutral objects like a granite block. It is, in short, a brilliant and effective method for making things happen the way we want—and the extraordinary success of our Diamond Division at Andin International is eloquent proof of its truth. As the Buddha himself said, you can always just give it a try for a while to see how it works for you. The worst thing that can happen is that you're especially kind and generous to others for a bit.

When we say that the window washer has failed to respect life, and that this is why he or she sees the granite as something potentially dangerous, remember we're not saying that the person must have planted this imprint in his or her mind through some single, horrible, life-threatening act to others. As we mentioned before, all imprints grow in strength exponentially during the time they spend in the subconscious. What makes a business fail—what causes cash flow to slowly choke off and employees to leak away to competitors over the period of a year or two—*is normally the accumulated effect of many minor negative actions and thoughts,* small white lies and small bursts of negative emotions like stinginess, modest imprints that have grown into huge, twisted oak trees: the very reality of a large business gone sour.

It's *extremely important* here too to realize that we are not talking about some kind of social or psychological phenomenon, where you lie to others and so they lie to you, or you are cheap to others and so they are cheap to you. This is what we would call an "apparent" correlation between an action and a result, and it's not at all the point of this book.

There is no such thing as a person lying to you simply as a result of your lying to them; it must always be explained *through the process* of an imprint being made on your mind, and then the imprint flowering—you *see* a person lying to you because you have placed an imprint in your mind previously which flowers and *makes you see* a person lying to you. There is no such thing as a person out there, all on his own, who just happens to start lying to you. *Nobody* can *ever* lie to you unless you have, unwittingly or uncontrollably, planted an imprint in your own mind by telling a lie yourself. It's not really a question of how you act determining how things seem to you. Rather, *the things themselves* are being produced by your imprints—the world around you, the people around you, and even the way you are yourself, all of these things are a creation of your own past actions, words, and thoughts—good or bad done to others.

Keep this in mind then while we list some typical correlations from real business life. This is not some fairy tale that your first-grade teacher told you—"Step on a bug, Johnny, and you'll be a bug yourself some day and get stepped on." These are, rather, cognitive truths with a firm foundation in the actual experiences and wisdom of eminent individuals who have, over the last two and a half thousand years, tested and used them successfully. In short, they work—and they work without fail.

Wise men of Tibet have said that, whenever these laws don't seem to work, it's because you're not actually following them; and I think you'll find this true if you're honest with yourself. The laws must be observed over a period of time—and with complete self-honesty and a sensitive understanding of the principles we have set out above—in order to bring the business success we have promised. To try them out for a while and then give up on them would be like stopping an exercise program after three days because it hasn't given you bulging muscles yet.

For these principles to produce the business and personal success you hope for, they must be followed with about the same intensity and perseverance needed to become a good piano player or a very competent golfer, and that's not easy. Nothing less will work, and if you can't give it this kind of effort you can set this book down right now. These correlations, by the way, are derived directly from two of the most important books of wisdom ever produced in Asia: *The Great Book on the Steps of the Path*, by the Tibetan master Tsongkapa the Great (1357–1419 A.D.); and *The Crown of Knives*, by the Indian wise man Dharma Rakshita (about 1000 A.D.).

Typical Business Problems and Their Real Solutions, according to the Wisdom of The Diamond Cutter

Business problem #1: Company finances are unstable, in a state of constant flux.

Solution: Be more willing to share your profits with those who have helped you produce them, and be very strict about never making a single penny through any improper action. Remember, the *amount* you share with those around you is not what determines the strength of the imprint; rather, it is your *willingness* to share whatever you have made, even if it's not a lot.

Business problem #2: Capital investments like manufacturing equipment, computers, or vehicles tend to become quickly outmoded or unreliable.

Solution: Stop being envious of other businesspeople and their businesses; concentrate on making your own company innovative, creative, and fun, and don't be unhappy about the success of others.

Business problem #3: Your position in the company is unstable, you seem to be losing your authority.

Solution: Be very careful never to treat others around you with arrogance; come down to their level, sit with the troops, listen to those who work with you.

Business problem #4: You find yourself unable to enjoy the money and things you've worked so hard for.

Solution: Never begrudge others the results of their own efforts; stop comparing yourself to others, just enjoy what you have: Be your own person and appreciate what you have yourself.

Business problem #5: No matter how big or interesting your business gets, you always have the feeling that it's not enough; you feel driven by a sense of dissatisfaction.

Solution: Same as the very last one.

Business problem #6: The employees and management around you always seem to be fighting with one another.

Solution: Be really careful never to engage in the kind of talk that has, as either its expressed or implicit aim, splitting up other people. This talk, by the way, could be true or untrue, so long as your primary intent is to cause two other people to end up farther from each other than they were before you opened your mouth. "Did you hear what she said about you?"

"Do you know what he really thinks about your last project?" You know how it goes.

By the way, remember that we are not necessarily talking about an imprint that was made in the last week or month; it could be a lot older, and surely got bigger the longer it was in your subconscious. The point here is that you *may no longer be exhibiting the kind of behavior which planted the imprint that is giving you trouble.* No matter; the fix is the same. You must assiduously avoid repeating this kind of behavior, even in very minor ways. You, *in particular,* because you are plagued *by this particular problem,* must be even more careful than other people to avoid indulging in divisive talk.

Did you notice, by the way, that the solution has *almost nothing to do* with going to these other people and trying to talk them into being nice to one another? This is the incredibly profound key to this approach: The fact that they are fighting *in your presence, in your world,* is something you have to experience because of an imprint *in your mind.* You fix your life, and your business, and your world by fixing yourself.

Business problem #7: You always tend to have problems with your business partners; you fall out with them over and over, no matter how often you change them.

Solution: Exactly the same as with the previous problem.

Business problem # 8: You find yourself second-guessing your own decisions; you are developing an inability to be decisive in business matters.

Solution: This particular problem comes from two rather disparate causes: failing to care for your employees and the other management around you; and representing yourself as something to your customers and suppliers that you are in truth not at all. Avoiding this one is very difficult in today's business world of smoke and mirrors, but if you are able to represent yourself exactly as you are—in short, if you're able to maintain a high degree of integrity—then your own mind and business decisions will be crisp, decisive, and effective.

Remember, it *is not* a question of your customers slowly finding out that you are a straight shooter and then believing you more in the future. *The imprint from straight shooting* rises up to your conscious mind and actually creates a reality around you in which people are honest, your decisions are made fast and clear, and money comes easily.

Some people think that this kind of reality is less than their old "real" reality, but in fact this is the way it's always been. A car that hits you on the street may be only the result of an old imprint from hurting someone else coming up to your conscious mind, but—hey—it'll break your legs just the same. Get used to it. This is how things really happen, and you can ride it out.

Business problem #9: You want to make a purchase of another company; you see a business opportunity that's sure-fire but which is going to need some cash, and you're having trouble raising it.

Solution: Quite simple. Stop being such a cheapskate in your business dealings and your personal life. Give, give, give to others; make sure deals are win-win for both sides. Again, it's not the amount of money involved, it's maintaining—all day long—a truly generous, creative, flowing state of mind that wants to see everybody prosper. Ben Franklin was perhaps the greatest statesman, scientist, and businessperson in America's history—and his response to competition was to invite all his competitors to join a new society called a Chamber of Commerce, dedicated to finding ways to work together to *expand markets*, and make everybody involved richer.

This kind of *thinking* by itself creates powerful imprints in all the people involved, by the way. A group of businesspeople can, by acting in cooperation with one another, create imprints in each of their minds to see a common reality such as an expanding market. No problem. It's *not*, incidentally, that imprints can be shared or transferred to another person—they can't. Rather, a group of people acting in a concerted charitable way create imprints that flower as a shared experience such as a successful company or a more prosperous nation. And this in fact is why some countries are more affluent than others—but that's a little big for us to talk about here. Anyway, if you think about the principle you can get some pretty amazing understandings about wealth on a global scale.

Business problem #10: External failures, what they call "acts of God"—natural problems like bad weather or city infrastructure problems or power shortages—are hurting your business.

Solution: Be very careful to keep your promises, especially commitments you have made to stick to certain principles in how you conduct your business dealings and your personal life.

The mind rebels at the thought that even external forces like the weather or how traffic flows in a city could be the result of our own patterns of behavior; but according to the laws of this ancient wisdom this is exactly where they come from. Remember, these events are "empty," or "neutral" or "blank." Somebody will get into the city smoothly by some route, even on the worst traffic days for the other routes; and when it snows or rains too much, somebody will make a killing (ski slope operators, umbrella makers).

Whether any given event impacts on you in a positive or negative way is *not* something which is coming from the event itself; it is obviously, if you think about it even for a minute, something that's coming from your perceptions. And these perceptions don't just come out of thin air. Rather, they are forced on you by your own past patterns of behavior, in such a way that the *content* of the past behavior (infidelity to your own standards) resembles the external result it produces (fickle weather and unreliable infrastructures).

Business problem #11: You find yourself unable to concentrate or keep your mind focused when faced with a challenging business situation or decision.

Solution: Spend some time each day putting your mind, peacefully and in a concentrated way, on the larger questions of life. Would you be doing right now what you are doing right now if you knew you were going to die tonight? Are your priorities in order? Are there bigger questions about the way you live life that you are perhaps hiding from, by throwing yourself into longer hours and bigger deals?

Step back and look at your life, and at what's important. The imprint from spending some time this way every day comes up into the conscious mind as a fierce ability to concentrate. Which brings us to a very important point: It's not just outer events and the people around you that are created by the flowering of these old imprints in your mind—*the very way in which you experience your own mind and thoughts* is as well the result of past behavior and imprints, breaking through to the conscious mind in their proper sequence.

Business problem #12: You find yourself unable to grasp broad business concepts, or market patterns, or dynamics like whole manufacturing processes or systems.

Solution: Face up to the deficiencies in your own broad viewpoints about why greater things in the world happen. Let's face it: There are only three basic explanations for why all this stuff is happening in the world, things like global warming or wars in certain countries this month or the facts of life and death themselves—for why we're here, how we got here, why things happen this way.

You can't ignore the question of why the world works the way it does and expect to understand the question of why your business works the way it does (or doesn't). And this is not a question of beliefs or religious orientation or anything of the like, any more than the reason an atom bomb explodes is something that depends on whether you are Irish or Tasmanian.

Explanation number one: Things come from nothing, everything's just random, there are no patterns or logic at all to how and why things happen. This is the scientific "big-bang" approach. "Everything happens from something else, and scientific method depends upon the consistency of cause and effect. Except for important things like the beginning of everything, which just popped up out of nothing." You are here because something blew up a *long, long time ago*: Certain electrons hit other electrons and they formed certain atoms that glumped up into all kinds of molecules and they stuck together enough to make a gas that spun around and got hard because other little whatcha-ma-call-its hit it and matter formed and a little piece became the sun and a little spot became the earth and the sea formed and some little critter crawled out and lost a few legs and your grandmom and grandfather happened somewhere there and, well, everything is just random. If you are laughing by now then you are laughing at the very foundations of the way your culture views the world, and it really is funny.

Explanation number two: The world around you, everything in it, is the result of the conscious effort of a very powerful being basically beyond our immediate experience. This explanation does not account for where the being itself came from in the first place (some *other* big being's conscious effort?). Nor does it account for the inexplicable cruelty of so much of our lives—the fact that small children die in horrible fires that race through the upper stories of tenement buildings; the fact that some people live their entire time on this planet trapped in loneliness and anxiety; the fact that whatever we work for, and whomever we ever love in this life, must be torn from us.

Explanation number three: The very principles we have discussed here. Nothing is random, nothing is accident, and we have no one outside ourselves to blame for our own world. Things occur to us in exact accord with how we treat those around us, not by the decision of any outside person but in exact compliance with a moral law which is as sure and as undeniable and merciless as gravity itself. At any rate, a few hours of honest reflection, every few days or so, about where you really believe this whole world and its people and events could have come from do wonders for being able to conceptualize larger patterns in markets and business processes, all of which makes you a much more successful person.

Business problem #13: Rents are too high! Can't find a building to put that new branch location in.

Solution: Make sure that you help others find places to stay when they need them. Again it might seem an oversimplification to say that refusing a bed to Aunt Martha when she came into town over the holidays could have anything to do with the failure of your multimillion-dollar branch to find a home, but it fits the rules we have laid out here perfectly. A small imprint is placed in the subconscious, it grows there over time, and then comes up to the conscious mind to make you see a corresponding lack of needed space. Don't just dismiss it as silly, try it out and see what happens! But remember, we're talking about a concerted effort to find space for others who need it, along with a continual intellectual review of the principles laid out here: The imprints are *much more* powerful when you do them knowing what you're doing.

Business problem #14: Companies and individuals in your business world whom you consider especially reputable and capable seem hesitant to connect with you.

Solution: This particular imprint is planted by choosing associates poorly. Typically in business we tend to hook up with those who can be of greatest help to us financially—those who can provide serious backing or other needed assets, particular skills or contacts—and under the duress of our particular needs we might overlook some pretty evident problems in potential partners as far as their character, honesty, or other similar traits.

In the end though a partner who is lacking in integrity will always hurt the business, while those with strong integrity will, eventually, help the business build into a strong financial success. We distinguish here, by the way, between tough, honest bargaining and dishonesty: the chairman of Andin, Ofer, was one of the toughest negotiators you would ever want to meet. I remember one of the early office managers in the company coming to ask me if I could go in her stead to his office for her annual review. I was a bit taken aback by the suggestion, and asked her why on earth she would want me to do so.

"Because he always gives me a lousy raise; and he is so persuasive that by the time I leave his office I'm agreeing with him fully why I don't deserve a penny more!"

The point here though is, *although he negotiated like a tiger,* I never knew Ofer to renege on fulfilling what he had agreed to. And I think this has had a lot to do with Andin's success.

Business problem #15: The competition is ruthless, and always seems to get the upper hand when you go head to head with it.

Solution: One of the main causes for this particular phenomenon is speaking harshly to others. The ancient books have an interesting way of explaining just what makes something that you say harsh. They divide harsh words into two types: those that are in themselves unpleasant words, and those that are pleasant but intended to be harsh. And so while berating an employee in front of several of her fellows obviously plants this kind of imprint; so does a seemingly innocent "Loved the Sears presentation!" to a salesman who you know has just returned from the Sears buyer's office with his tail between his legs, and nary an order. Avoid either form of rough talk, consistently, over an extended period of time, keeping in mind just how many imprints you are *avoiding* planting in your own head—then sit back and watch the competition roll over.

Business problem #16: Over and over, when you get deep into a deal with anybody, he or she seems to turn around and stab you in the back.

Solution: The imprint for this situation is planted in our minds by a very specific attitude toward others: When we see someone else fail in any activity—whether it's a fellow employee who accidentally spills some coffee on herself, or a competitor who loses a few million dollars in a customer bankruptcy—we feel some small, private feelings of satisfaction or smugness over that person's trouble. This particular quirk of the human mind is so common that the ancient books of Tibet list it among the top ten mental troublemakers. We seem to have the habit of taking an unhealthy interest in the woes of others around us; at its worst, you can see this in the public obsession with the troubles of famous people.

To prevent this imprint, try to feel empathy with anyone who's having a problem, even a competitor. It's a lot more fun to have friendly competition between creative, spirited companies that are playing fair with each other—where the CEO's of the respective firms maybe even go out for dinner with each other once in a while—than to laugh at a man when he's down. Remember too the maxim, "Be good to people on the way up; you might meet them again on the way down."

This is a word to the wise, especially for you younger executives: respect everyone—fellow manager, lowest employee, your fiercest competitor. I have seen literally dozens of executives who ended up working under the very people whom they used to torment when they had the upper hand, and you can imagine how they are treated.

Business problem #17: You think up a major project, design it down to the last detail, work hard to get it up and running, and then it simply flops.

Solution: This again is due to a very special imprint: not understanding the way that things really work. You see, it's not just the failure to understand the principles we've talked about here that screws you up: Every time you do undertake a project with some active wrong idea about how things work—like thinking that if you work hard enough and put in enough extra hours everything should work out right—then you plant an imprint in your mind *to continue to misunderstand how things work*, and to continue to fail.

It's not capital—lots of projects with sufficient capital flop. It's not people—lots of projects with good people working on them flop. It's not the market—somebody out there in the same market is doing a project that's working fine. It's not how hard you work—some people put in practically no hours at all, and seem to succeed, while other people work overtime and weekends and fail all the same. The key to success is rather a state of mind, a state of understanding the principles we've put forth here. Projects done with this *knowledge*, in this state of knowing, work. Period. And thinking straight plants imprints that will come up into the conscious mind as—thinking straight again!

Business problem #18: People around you don't step forward to help you out when you most need it.

Solution: This again is a result of taking some kind of unhealthy pleasure in other people's problems. At best, try to step into every situation where you could help out—whether it's offering an aspirin to someone at the next desk who's having a headache, or pitching in on the last late night of preparing a presentation for a major customer. At the very least, keep a close watch on your mind and refuse to indulge in that morbid fascination with other people's problems.

Business problem #19: You find yourself unable to control your temper; you get angry at employees, suppliers, customers, the weather, the phone, and just about anything else.

Solution: Anger of this type is an interesting problem in the world of potentials and imprints. It is a *result*, again, of wishing problems on others—or at least not being unhappy at all to see certain people have a problem. This by the way is a very common phenomenon toward those whom we dislike, and if you think about it is one of the unkindest things about the human mind. Why should we wish trouble on anyone, even those who wish trouble upon us? Trouble in our lives, trouble in our businesses and our families, is a common enemy to us all. It is like AIDS or cancer, a suffering that does no good to anyone, a blight on our world.

If we really want to succeed, on any level, on every level, we must seek to stamp out unhappiness in its every form, and within any mind—even in those of people who compete with us for the next promotion, or in the marketplace.

Business problem #20: The market and business atmosphere is chaotic; it seems to go up and down without any sense or logic.

Solution: Once more, this kind of chaos is a result of a chaotic intention, of wishing failure on others. Disorder on a global level, on a market level, on a business level (whether your own or your competitor's), and on a personal level is just another form of unhappiness for whomever is in the midst of it—and we have to reach a point where we wish ill on no one. The imprint planted in your mind from wishing well for all those around you, even for those with whom you are in competition, creates a market which is stable—an economy that is growing consistently and feeds every player more than he or she could ever want.

The implication of this view of economies is profound: It's not true that there are limited resources, and that only a certain number of people can be wealthy at any given time. Think of the new, additional wealth created by the invention of the personal computer; think of the additional wealth generated by the invention of the telephone; think of the potential for additional global wealth inherent in vast networks of personal and corporate computers—whether it be the Web or something similar to come.

According to the view of potential and imprints, this new wealth is the result of new imprints, in the minds of everyone affected, coming up to their conscious minds and creating the perception of new sources of wealth for large groups of people. Limited resources for growing numbers of people is an event with its own causes; if the imprints had been different, it might just as well have been resources that grow at the same speed, or a little faster, than the population. We have to be visionary enough to create vast new wealth, not restrict ourselves and our future to what has existed up to now.

Business problem #21: Corruption is a problem in your business; in its regulation by government, in the way companies interact, in the way individual employees behave.

Solution: Again, the solution is a very pleasant one: *Consciously take joy in the successes of everyone around you*—little successes, big successes, success by your firm or success by the competition. Admire a job well done, no matter who does it, and refuse to give in to the base emotion of jealousy over another person's happiness. Life is precious short; you and your competitors will be dead and forgotten before you can blink an eye, and a good streak of happiness is precious rare.

When someone in your firm does a good job or gets recognized for an important contribution, stop them in the hallway and take the opportunity to enhance your own happiness by sharing the success *with* them, rather than begrudging one of those good moments in life that comes all too rarely, and ends all too swiftly, anyway.

When a competitor comes out with a great new idea, stop him at a trade show or charity dinner and express sincere admiration and pleasure in his achievement. *The mental imprint planted by this kind of behavior* will rise up into your conscious mind as *the next great idea in the market!* And that's a lot more fun than sitting home unhappy about the good things that have happened to others.

Business problem #22: As your corporate career moves on through the years, you notice small health problems cropping up and steadily starting to become more serious.

Solution: There's a very specific and satisfying solution to this problem. Go through the company with a new eye: walk from corridor to corridor and peek in on each department. Try to locate any condition that might be impacting negatively on any employee's health. Is the lighting good enough? Are the desks and chairs set up with a sensitive eye toward people's comfort and health? Are you honestly respecting all the guidelines for fire and occupational safety, or just putting up whatever signs the government is especially tough about? Do you take the time to assure that your managers and employees are protected from overworking, not just from the overwork that you lay on them, but from the overwork they tend to impose on themselves? The imprint from caring for others in this way flowers in the conscious mind as improved personal health.

Again this is not something that's going to happen in a day. Remember the comparison to learning to play piano, or to mastering golf.

Your concern for the welfare of those around you in your firm has to reach a point where it's a natural part of your life—it has to come to you as automatically as a well-practiced song on the piano, hands gliding across the keys of their own accord, unwatched—in order for your own health to be affected.

Business problem #23: The market strategies that used to work for you don't succeed anymore.

Solution: If you've been in business any length of time you know how this goes. You break into your industry with a new idea or a new product. The money rolls in. Your only big problem is how to handle all the orders, how to train new staff as the company grows by leaps and bounds. You're on top of the world, you can't do anything wrong, and you wonder why all the companies that have been around before you can't get it right.

A year or two goes by, and then one day your most important customer shows you the breakdown of his company's orders by supplier—and you're number two. You don't even recognize the name of the company's number-one firm. You send out people to the stores to buy some of that firm's product, whatever it may be, and try to find out how your competitor's doing it. You think you see something there that you can do, and you mass the troops in the company with a firm talk about what happened to Coke when they let Pepsi get a foothold. Then you send each director out to do what he or she does best; the directors know the score, they know what to do, they march out to do what they've always done, and you all believe it's going to work the same as it always has.

Days and weeks go by and—for the first time—it's like marching on a long muddy country road. First one trusted source of success, and then another, fails to come through as it always has in the past. At some point there is the first real moral crisis in the company—the moment when it dawns on people that things have changed, and that for some reason the old magic doesn't come as easy as it used to.

At this point you can blame a lot of things. The market has gotten more competitive. There aren't any more easy breakthroughs to be made in your particular product category, the way there were when you first got into the market. A few key people who really used to make things work aren't around anymore, or factories from such and such a foreign country are dumping nowadays. You know the excuses, you've been through it a thousand times.

Here it's vital to realize that you haven't identified *why* your old strategies aren't working anymore; all you've done is to state *how* they aren't working. The real question is not what factors have arisen to threaten your traditional approach; it's *why* these factors at this particular time are now *able* to threaten your business. And this again is the result of an imprint in your own mind, something planted there in the past, and just now coming up to the forefront of your perceptions. Get this: It's not that business strategies themselves change in their effectiveness. Sometimes a strategy works for years, sometimes it works for months, sometimes it doesn't work at all. Sometimes it's smart to change strategies, sometimes it's smart to leave them alone. It's not outer conditions that are changing. It's your own perceptions. Your strategies will continue to come in and out of style in your world for exactly as long as you fail to see what's really changing: your own perceptions.

At any rate, the imprint which causes your perceptions to change— that is, the imprint which actually explains *why* you see your traditional strategies threatened—is nothing more complicated than some form of deceit, some kind of dishonesty in the way you make your money. Again, we're not saying necessarily that you've been selling fire extinguishers that will never work, and that you know will never work, or anything as perfidious as that. The imprints which get us in trouble, again, are the small ones—the minor ones—that we plant continually throughout the day. A small exaggeration to a potential customer in order to nail down the first order; a small white lie to an existing customer about why their order is late; a bit of an adjustment on the balance sheet to the bank that floated your last project. Avoid this kind of small-change ethics, avoid even the slightest stretch of your integrity, and you'll find that your traditional business approach continues to work just fine.

Business problem #24: You find yourself feeling down more often, whether or not the business is doing well. You start to get little bouts of depression or self-doubt.

Solution: This phenomenon as well has a very direct and simple fix. Examine how you work with the people who work for you. Are there any circumstances in which you are encouraging them to fudge a bit in some way? Do you have any policies, stated or unstated, that would lead an employee to think that you condone any kind of negative or dishonest behavior, whether it be toward a customer, or a supplier, an employee, or even a competitor?

It never failed to amaze me, in the diamond business, when an employer would encourage an employee to cheat a customer or a competitor on their behalf. We would occasionally run into companies where the owner had trained his people how to mislead customers, or prepare false reports for auditors, or even fudge on things like the weight of some stones. We had one supplier who for weeks supplied us parcels of stones bubble-wrapped in plastic, in such a way that it was very difficult to check the weight of the stones properly without mixing them all together.

He had offered to supply us with rubies prematched into sets of stones that could easily be dropped, for example, into a bracelet that required five marquise or boat-shaped gems set up in a row. Normally the labor of assuring that the five stones were all exactly the same hue, and had exactly the same outline, was particularly intense, and required a highly trained "matcher" with an excellent eye for color. This sort of vision, the ability to distinguish fine shades of color, is something that doesn't much last beyond the age of forty in most people—color perception deteriorates gradually quite long before that, and so a truly experienced matching expert is something hard to find.

Anyway, we were grateful for the offer of receiving sets of matched stones, and thought it would be a good deal for the supplier since we would favor him whenever it came time to fill a largish order. We didn't consider at first the fact that we wouldn't be able to weigh the stones properly after they were pressed into plastic, but as a matter of course checked a few weights at random.

The deception was going on in a very clever way: The weight of *every* single set of stones was overstated by exactly the same percentage, a minor but very profitable percentage in a business where 1 or 2 percent on a sale may be your entire profit. You see, the amount of money that changes hands in any deal involving thousands of stones is so large, and is moving so fast, that saving even one percentage point may make you twice as profitable by the end of the year. So the deception was spread over thousands of sets of stones, rather than taking the risk of grossly overstating the weight of a few sets.

We kept mum to see if the supplier would continue, and he did. We quietly kept very good records of the overstated weights, and carefully stored each plastic sheet with the hundreds of rubies pressed into it. In the end we invited the supplier over to review the weights with us and adjust his invoices, then proceeded gradually to cut his orders to nothing.

The point here though is the stupidity of teaching dishonesty to the people who work for you; the naïveté of a person who really believes that someone whom he has taught to cheat *for* him won't, in good time, *cheat him too*. In later years, this particular supplier had major problems with internal theft, losing tens of thousands of dollars on any given day. And the owners, two brothers, became noticeably less happy each year— struggling with personal problems, bad marriages, and the like.

This kind of sadness or depression is a direct result of an imprint planted in your mind by encouraging those who work for you to have less than total integrity in all their dealings on your behalf. And a kind of confidence and joy in your work comes when you support integrity in every employee in your firm, from top to bottom.

Business problem #25: The people around you, whether fellow employees or managers, customers or suppliers, never believe what you have to say, even though you're telling the truth.

Solution: Most of us have been guilty of telling small lies to those around us in corporate life; it's embarrassing to get caught, as we do occasionally, but if it's nothing big then people don't think too much of it. Here we're talking about something else though: You are telling nothing less than the exact truth, but nobody believes you. You know how frustrating this can be, and the more you protest sometimes, the more the other party feels as if you really aren't being truthful.

It's important to realize that this impression on the other person's part is not something that could come from your present honesty: One rule of imprints is that *their content* must be consistent with *their result*; that is, you could never get a negative result (someone thinking you're lying to them) from a positive imprint (the imprint caused by being consciously truthful). Rather, their failure to believe in you comes from past acts of dishonesty, even relatively minor forms of dishonesty, and the imprints these have planted in your mind.

The solution then is to be strictly accurate in your words. Remember what *lying* really entails: giving someone else an impression of some object or event which does not strictly correspond to the impression that you yourself have of this same thing. So complete honesty in what you say is nothing less than assuring that the *impression* which your words leave on someone else matches the very impression you have in your mind. This is a lot more difficult than what we normally think of as honesty! But if you keep it up over a good period of time, you'll see your own credibility honored throughout your firm and the marketplace in which you move—it's a great feeling, and also quite profitable.

Business problem #26: Whenever you undertake any form of cooperative effort—be it a group project, a partnership for some business goal, or the merger of your company with another—it doesn't seem to work out.

Solution: Again, the fix for this kind of problem is a little different than you might expect. It doesn't have much to do, surprisingly, with getting everyone involved together in a room and trying to talk them into working with each other better. Rather, you have to be very careful, again, to be totally honest yourself. Always try to see to it that the way you describe things to other people *gives them an exact impression* of how you yourself see the thing—that is, the result of your words should be that the other party always gets the exact same understanding that you have about the particular object or event.

People say that "the truth stands on two legs, and a lie stands on one." This kind of total inner honesty, and especially your awareness that you are being totally honest, leads to a great peace of mind, and plants very firm imprints in your subconscious which later float up to the conscious mind as the perception of great unity, and success in whatever cooperative work you might undertake with others.

Business problem #27: You work in an industry where people cheat each other a lot.

Solution: This is a pretty common complaint that I'm sure you've heard from people in a large variety of businesses. "I'm sick of law—every lawyer I've met in this business, including the one I work for, is dishonest," or "Everybody in the music business is out to fleece you," or "Jewelry people are all shysters."

You can avoid this kind of world around you, again, if you are completely straightforward in all your business dealings yourself. Then, very gradually, you will meet fewer and fewer people who would ever want to cheat you or anyone else—because every person you ever come in contact with who would want to cheat someone is the result of an imprint you have planted in the past, by being less than totally honest yourself.

Business problem #28: Your boss often speaks to you in an insulting way.

Solution: This particular problem can be avoided by being very careful to manage anger whenever it comes up in your mind—say, when your boss speaks to you in an insulting way! If you really study the ancient books of Tibet, one thing strikes you most strongly: The natural reaction to a negative experience leaves the exact imprint which causes you to undergo this very same experience once more. In short, getting angry at your boss for insulting you plants the very imprint that would make you see him or her insulting you again in the future.

Withdrawal from this kind of war then has to be unilateral. We often see how small conflicts in the world escalate into major problems when individuals or groups or countries refuse to break the cycle of violence: *They hurt me, so I have to hurt them back.* The idea here is that you *back off* from the violence, even if the other side hasn't yet agreed to do so when you do. You refuse—once, twice, or even a hundred times ("Turn your face and show them your other cheek so they can hit that one too")—to respond to an insult with an insult, and in so doing you remove those imprints in your mind to have it go on. The cycle of violence is broken.

I often jokingly say to my friends that this is the real way to eliminate those people in your office who really irritate you—not by shooting them or anything like that, but by refusing to perpetuate violence with them. If you are kind enough long enough to anyone who is insulting you, if you refuse on a consistent basis to respond to negativity with negativity, then you will very gradually and very certainly see these kinds of people leave your life. They'll suddenly get transferred to another city; they'll retire early; another company will pick them up, whatever. I can honestly say that, after years of putting this particular principle into action at Andin International, I had a work situation where every single person in the division I was managing was a real pleasure to be with, all day long. It made going to work a true joy, and of course made our division very profitable: The minute that talented people are truly working in unison and personal harmony, half the problems that prevent a company from reaching its true potential disappear.

Business problem #29: You find that years in the business world are taking an undesirable toll on your personal appearance.

Solution: It may seem silly to list this as a business problem, but anyone who's been in the corporate world for any length of time can tell you that—whether it's fair or not—your physical appearance at work plays no small role in determining the kind of position and salary you pull down.

You also know, if you've been in any large company very long, that over time the whole corporate lifestyle seems to have a particularly negative impact on people's personal appearance. People show up out of business school looking relatively bright and attractive, and then after a few years of tough business in real life start to get gray hairs, potbellies, or big butts—that sort of thing. You tend to attribute it to the strain of the lifestyle: the late nights getting an order out, the constant corporate travel, the emotional ups and downs with the swings in your business fortunes from day to day. You imagine that, if things just calmed down a bit, you might go back to looking better—but you never really get a chance to find out.

The solution here is a bit unexpected, but it works. You have to be *extremely diligent* in watching your own mind for the slightest trace of anger toward another person. The ancient Tibetan books say that—if you're really going to be serious about this particular solution—you have to take one step back from the anger and be careful to avoid anger assiduously, even before the causes for an incident of anger have had a chance to convene. The particular causes for anger, by the way, are emotions in which you feel upset about something, just before you get angry about it.

So if you really want to become an expert at avoiding anger itself, you have to become an expert at not becoming upset about anything: avoid anger by avoiding its prelude, which is getting off balance or out of whack over any particular incident—be it a small disaster with an order for an important customer, or an unexpected traffic jam on the way to an important meeting. Consistently avoiding anger has the effect, over the long term, of planting very interesting imprints in your mind which will cause you to perceive, and see others perceive, your physical appearance as being quite attractive. The years in corporate life may go by, but you don't seem to age. It's a lot more easy and inexpensive than investing in exotic creams, exercise programs, or cosmetic surgery of different kinds.

Business problem #30: Regardless of how well you do in your work, the people around you are always criticizing you.

Solution: The solution for this problem is to be *very sensitive* about paying attention to how your actions and words affect those around you. That is, before you say or do anything, consider carefully how it might impact on others in the workplace. There is an ancient Buddhist book called *The Treasure House of Higher Knowledge*, written over sixteen centuries ago, which says that every good deed ever done has one of two different characteristics at the base of it: You are either being careful to act in a way which you can be proud of yourself, or you are being careful to act in a way which others would, justifiably, be proud to see you act. In other words, you are almost always planting very good imprints in your mind when you are trying to stay sensitive about whether what you're doing is something that will impact in a healthy, positive way on yourself and those around you.

We have to say a word here about the American image of a brash young business executive—sharp, tireless, witty, and continually scoffing at those around him who can't quite keep up with him. It's important to realize that people like this *are living off good energy from the past*: old energy from old imprints which, even as they live and breathe from day to day, are being worn out, used up. Their current arrogant, irreverent behavior, their willingness to ignore how their actions and words impact on those around them, can only plant seeds which will cause them to see themselves being criticized, by more and more people, as they grow up in their business careers.

Remember, it's not that being disrespectful of others' feelings leads itself directly to the criticism, although this may seem how the dynamic is working. Rather, the act of disrespect plants an imprint in the young executive's own mind which drops into the subconscious, stays there for a while gathering strength, and then returns to the conscious mind as the experience of being criticized by others. Conversely, if you have a particular problem of being criticized frequently by others, the most important thing you can do is to quite consciously, day by day, take a much greater interest in how what you do and say might affect those who work around you all day.

Business problem #31: Projects you hand out to subordinates never get done.

Solution: The imprint that causes this particular problem can be stopped by taking special care to facilitate the work of other people around you in the company. If someone needs MIS resources, you are their advocate with the ownership, to put in a plug for them so they get the help they need, even at your own department's expense. If another division needs a loan of several workers to get a project out that week, you give them up happily—and don't send the dead heads, by the way; give them your best. If someone's counting on you for some numbers to finish a report they're working on, make sure they get them, even if the extra time you take for their sake comes out of time you need to get your own work done.

The imprints from this kind of behavior are quite strong, and within a short time you'll see all the work you hand out coming back to you under budget, on time, and with quality exceeding your expectations.

Business problem #32: The business projects you undertake have smooth sailing at first, and then turn sour.

Solution: As with so many of the business problems we've described here, this one comes from an imprint that you might not guess, but which makes sense if you think about it for a minute. In the Tibetan tradition of ancient knowledge there is a special meditation that you can do called "gratitude meditation."

Sit down in a chair in one of the quiet corners of the firm somewhere (you know where they are, even though they're rare), somewhere where you know you won't be disturbed for five or ten minutes. Go through each of the good things in your life, and think about the people who helped make each of these things possible. Perhaps the particular skill you bring to your job is something that another person took great pains to train you in. And maybe that was years back; but don't you think that individual would appreciate hearing from you, a quick note of thanks for the gift given you that is serving you so well, so much later?

Are there people back home—spouse, parent, or someone who does some special job around the house for you—whose presence in your life *allows* you to do the work you do? When was the last time you thanked them? Is there not in fact a whole support network around you which helps you get to the office to do what you do? The dry cleaner? The dentist? The postman? The people at the grocery store, the people at your bank, the person who delivers your morning paper? You can say, "Oh, those people are paid to do those things—it's not as if they would get up in the morning and do this for me if they couldn't get anything out of it."

You're missing the point though. Paid they may be, but this doesn't change the fact that they are spending precious hours of their lives, valuable moments of their few healthy years, to help you accomplish what you want to. The failure to recognize how much others support you, the failure to appreciate how much of what we do is done only through the kindness of those around us, is very much a weakness of modern Western thinking.

There is also a direct relationship between the amount of gratitude we feel for others and how happy our lives are: Very happy people tend to be strongly aware of how much others have worked to help them be happy and comfortable (whether they were paid to do so or not; this is not something that a really happy mind is very much concerned about)—that is, really happy people tend to be very grateful for every small kindness which has contributed to their joy. Conversely, unhappy people tend to compound their unhappiness by avoiding any thought of how much others have given to them, how much others have sacrificed—whether they were paid for it or not—to help bring about their happiness.

So if you really want to assure that projects which have gotten off to a roaring start continue to roar, be very careful to plant the right imprints for seeing this become a reality: Take the time, and take the care, to show your sincere thanks, on a constant basis, to all those in the support network around you. Again the imprints don't necessarily have to be planted by some concrete action—although action is certainly eloquent. The main thing is that you maintain, on a constant basis, thoughts of gratitude—that you really appreciate, as you look down at your bowl of cereal in the morning, that hundreds or thousands of people have sacrificed those very precious moments of a brief human life to bring this food to your table. This kind of thinking is in very short supply in the modern world, and feels great once you start. Try it!

Business problem #33: In the course of your work, you are often exposed to an unpleasant environment—having to travel to and work in countries where the streets are filthy; commuting through areas with really polluted air; working in a plant where the particular product you manufacture requires noxious chemicals; or anything of the like.

Solution: A very typical solution for this particular problem is one that you could hardly guess, but all the ancient books agree on the necessary course of action. Go through your company or department and see if there is any kind of sexual harassment or lewdness going on at any level, and clean it out.

One of the most pleasant parts of working at Andin International was the nearly complete absence of all of the many forms of the harassment of women that you see in so many workplaces. From the owner on down, women were respected for the contribution they could make and were completely eligible for raises, promotions, and high positions, dependent entirely on performance. From the owner on down, no manager subjected a woman to the degrading behavior of unwanted touching or looks or whistles or lewd talk, or anything of the kind.

The entire lack of coarse behavior was noticeable and refreshing: no "good old boy" jokes about sex and women; no use of foul language; and no culture that encouraged married men and women to break their commitments to their spouses during the course of their work.

Again, it may seem quite simplistic to think that filth in your external environment could be created by a kind of filth in the way you talk or think. This idea is so foreign to our Western worldview that it almost seems like a child's tale. But think about it: All things have causes. There is a reason why certain parts of the country suffer from pollution, and others don't. In your mind you say now, "Of course there's a reason: Some places have more cars, more smokestacks, and less stringent laws to control pollution."

Ancient Tibetan thinking though, again, distinguishes strictly between the "how" and the "why." Saying that there is more pollution in a particular area because there are more sources of pollution addresses only *how* the pollution is produced. It *fails to address*, completely, *why* these sources of pollution happen to be present at all in the particular area at this particular time. We know that smokestacks create pollution. That's not the question. The real question, the one you always wanted to ask *but were told as a child to stop asking*, is **Why are the smokestacks there in the first place, and not somewhere else?**

Again the mind rebels, and says, "That's a silly question. That's just the way it is." But doesn't science say that everything has a cause; isn't it the foundation of our entire Western society to say that every event has a rational explanation? It's obvious that the *cause of the pollution* is the smokestack. But what about the *cause of the smokestack being there in the first place*? Shouldn't we be able to identify this cause as well? Because *isn't the fact that the smokestack is there in the first place* also an event in itself? And don't all events have causes which trigger them?

The fact is that the smokestacks are there because you are forced to see them—you are forced into perceiving them—by an imprint which has come up to your conscious mind from the subconscious one. *You* have created the pollution, and the sources which deliver it to you, by an action which was (1) *previous* to the result it triggered and (2) *similar in content* to the result as well. And the wisdom of thousands of years of extraordinary thinkers on the other side of the world says that the very particular cause of filthy or foul-smelling environments is sexual monkey business.

You don't have to believe it or not believe it—just try it. Root out these kinds of things in your company—things that probably hurt the morale of everyone in the company anyway—and see if the place gets physically nicer too. Seeing is believing.

Business problem #34: People around you are unreliable: You give them a job, and you're never quite sure if they're going to come through for you. You have to give three different people each single task to make sure it gets done, and you have to keep following up yourself on every little detail—an exhausting and inefficient way to work.

Solution: Again, one of the main actions you can take to assure yourself the perception (and therefore the reality) of reliability in the staff around you is for *you* to be constant and dependable in a very specific context: in your marriage or similar family commitments. It's not fashionable nowadays to talk much about this kind of reliability, but according to the law of the potential in things and the imprints of our actions, this is one of the most important steps we can take in assuring stability in our personal and business lives.

I grew up during the days of the Vietnam War, and the accompanying protest against what we considered foolish ideas of the generation before us, including the institutions of war and the possession of another person in marriage. My own mother was one of the first in our town to get a divorce, and I remember her paying for her decision in the looks and comments of others in the neighborhood, and in the struggle to make a living as a single mother.

But the combination of marrying on a whim and then divorcing each other easily, often after children have been produced who will suffer greatly in the process, is an action which plants very bad imprints on the mind, and greatly affects our perceptions of every part of the world around us. The great books of Tibetan wisdom state clearly that the lack of what you could call a social order in our Western culture—the simple fact that a person walking down the street in an American city throws a paper cup on the ground without the slightest thought for how this affects the next person who comes along—is a product of our newfound inability to keep our commitments to each other. If you want reliable employees, be someone that your spouse and children can count on.

Business problem #35: You have no financial independence; you can't be your own person—you can't make decisions about the things you have earned, especially, without consulting others.

Solution: The solution for this very specific problem is to respect the property and space of others very strictly. In a corporate environment, this would mean being careful not to drain resources say from other departments or managers without making sure first that they clearly agree; or else releasing the resources you have to others whenever there is a need, and you are in a position to be able to fill that need: in short, sharing with the other managers around you, in order to achieve common goals.

The concept here is that of "one body"; it is expressed eloquently in a Buddhist book called *A Guide to the Way of Life of a Warrior Saint*, written in Asia about thirteen centuries ago. Think of the idea of "my body" or "my self." We normally tend to equate it pretty strongly with the edge of our skin: If we are holding hands, then "me" stops at the end of *my* fingers, and "you" starts at the beginning of *your* fingers.

When a mother has a child though, it's pretty obvious that there's been a new definition of "me": the borderline of "me" has now been expanded to go around the child, and any injury done to the child is injury done to the mother, who reacts like a "momma lion." Your definition of "you" also expands just after you buy a new car that's going to mean new monthly payments which will eat up a major part of your salary. In New York this is expressed in real life when you see a bunch of teenage kids working down the block, checking the door handles of cars and looking through the windows into the backseats. Yesterday it was a nuisance and you might mention it to the guard when you get in the building; today, as they approach *your* new car, it's an outrage—and you might run out onto the street to stop them, or call the police in a flurry.

The "me" can shrink too: A surgeon tells you that one of your kidneys is cancerous and has to be removed, and after a bit of struggle with yourself you begin to *disassociate* with the kidney—you go through a process of beginning to divorce it from what you call "yourself," until on the day of the operation you are completely resigned to removing it from "me."

"Me" in the sense of "my interests" in a large company can shrink and expand as well. One certain sign of a healthy company is when the sense of "me" for each and every division manager stretches to include each of the other divisions—what's good for your division is good for mine, because it's all one company. It's important to realize that this is no fiction—it's no more artificial to make your "me" stretch to three divisions than it is to stretch it to your own division, just because somebody said on a certain day that you were the manager of this division—at which point you expanded "me" to extend to the *one* division.

What "me" is is a decision, at every moment in our lives, and restricting it to what appear to be "your" immediate concerns is—according to the ancient wisdom of Tibet—the source of all personal and corporate trouble. This is not some kind of noble sentiment—don't get me wrong. It's dead serious practical. All of us have the urge to be independent, both financially and organizationally. This is achieved by *being strict with yourself about* sharing all your resources with others around you in the organization. Get used to the idea. Nothing comes from nothing. Whatever degree of independence you ever achieve is a perception, and, therefore, a reality, driven by imprints planted in your mind by sharing your resources happily, and knowingly, with others in the firm.

Business problem #36: In your everyday business dealings, the people around you—customers, suppliers, and employees—tend to mislead you.

Solution: The solution to this problem is, again, one of those that you might not guess otherwise. We all know how frustrating it can be in business when we get into situations where we're not sure how much we can believe what the other party is telling us. A customer assures us that we will get a certain payment by a certain date; and then later we become aware that the payment is not coming anytime near that date, and that the customer knew this all along.

A supplier assures us that the raw material we need to complete a vital order to one of our most important customers will be in the house on time, and then we find out that the company doesn't even have the supplies—or worse, it had them and gave them to a competitor on the same date, because the competitor offered a bit more money for them. An employee goes away from a meeting in your office with a task to be performed which is an essential part of a larger effort; they've performed before, so you follow up only lightly from time to time, and each time you get assurances that their part is coming along well. Then the day comes to roll out the project, and you realize the whole thing will have to be delayed, because they haven't finished their contribution, and in fact hasn't made any progress on it for the whole time.

You can stop this pattern of people misleading you by acting on two fronts. First, be very sensitive to any feelings of pride that you may be a victim of. Corporate life is fast and cruel—stars rise fast and fall hard—and so you'd think that pride would be a rare affliction in companies. Businesspeople are among the most intelligent and talented in the Western world, but seem to have a blind spot on this point, an inability to control an emotion which is pretty uncalled for in a world where a single bad day can take you from divisional vice president to "older manager seeks entry-level administrative position."

Perhaps the most serious problem with pride is not how unpleasant it is for all of those around you, but rather how damaging it is for your own development. The Tibetan yak herders have a saying that "grass in the summer always grows from the lower meadows first, and only later works its way up to the base of the snow peaks." The point is that a person without pride—a humble person—is much better at listening to others, regardless of where these other people may be on the corporate totem pole, and uses what they learn for success—for more of the green.

There is always a potential for us to learn *something* from every person we meet in a working day, if only we would open our ears and *listen to what they have to say.* This doesn't mean that you have to accept every harebrained suggestion that you get from the people around you at the office; you have after all gotten this far presumably because you are able to make some good decisions. More often than not though you will learn something from your people that hasn't yet crystallized even in their own minds—directions they are going in or pieces of solutions that, collectively, should suggest a more comprehensive strategy in your own thinking—if you are very sensitive throughout the day, as you walk through your department or division, to pick up on the pieces you hear.

The second front you have to work on is to avoid the trap of living for the recognition of others. At some point in their corporate and personal lives, every person has to mature to the point where they do what's good and right not because someone else will thank or praise them for it, but simply because it's something that should be done, and they are in the best position to get it done. We can say in fact that—the better manager or administrator you are—the less you need any recognition from others. Mothers take care of young babies because they are exactly the right ones to do it at exactly that time, and learn to live without any hope of outright expressions of gratitude or recognition from the one they serve.

Really competent managers and leaders in a company are more on the lookout for ways that they can give recognition to others; at its best, this is not just another corporate strategy, but rather the managers' true perception of the situation around them: they are very sensitive and aware of the contributions of those surrounding them, and recognize and reward these contributions, *not* because this is a good way to motivate employees and so on, but sincerely because they *recognize* that those around them, not just they themselves, are each playing an important and integral part in the success of the company—even in their apparently more limited role as the operator of a machine or the guard of a door.

Get out of the habit of hoping for recognition or praise for yourself—get into the habit of looking hard for opportunities to give recognition and praise to those around you—and suddenly nobody in your world—customer, supplier, or employer—will ever be acting in a misleading way toward you. Again, this is the effect of the imprint of being sincerely aware of the contributions of those around you.

We should emphasize, finally, that you don't have to be insincere or make up excuses for giving praise or recognition where none is deserved. The point is that—if you work in a company of any size at all—it could hardly be operating on any level without the quiet and dedicated work of a certain core of people, people who have worked well at your side for so long, so consistently, that you probably don't even see how much they're doing for you anymore. One thing in corporate life, as in personal life, is that the closer and longer someone serves us the less we seem to recognize and reward this service. You know, kind of like the last time you took home roses and chocolates, and all that.

Business problem #37: No one in the company respects what you have to say; every suggestion you make is ignored or considered stupid.

Solution: Anyone who's done their time sitting around the table in the boardroom of a large company will appreciate this one. Sometimes it's so obvious that you really are afraid that you're going crazy. On Monday you have a six-hour board meeting (which goes on through lunch hour; the boss says "You can go out afterward and take some extra time at the restaurant down the street, it's on me"; but then there's a crisis in your department because you've been unreachable in the boardroom for the last six hours, and—oh you know the story, but that's not the point here).

The boss asks for suggestions about how to save money this quarter. (By the way, the exchanges you're about to read have really happened.) One person who happens to be in favor with the boss at the time says, "Let's try to reuse all the old computer reports in the company for scrap paper; encourage people not to pull good paper out of the copy machine and use it to take notes—instead keep a box of old used computer reports on the side of the machine, and let people use that."

The boss looks around the table; everybody seems okay with the suggestion, although most of us are thinking that it won't really save that much money if someone has to go around the company every day and distribute the used reports—but okay, the spirit is right.

"Good idea," he says. "Anyone else?"

I raise my hand. "How 'bout we put a special mat on the floor of the elevator, to catch the little diamonds that fall off people's shoes on the way out? I see a bunch of those in there every day on the way out, and they just get vacuumed up and thrown away by the cleaning guys who come in at night."

You see, the kinds of diamond parcels that we worked with on a regular basis had thousands of diamonds in them, and some of the diamonds were *really* small—like if you had a good sneeze, or the phone cord brushed across a pile as you sat back in your chair, or someone threw a pencil on your desk, then a good number of them might fly off onto the floor. As they strike the floor they also tend to mysteriously bounce or slide or scoot off across the room to the last place you could ever find them.

When this happens with a bunch of small stones you get up carefully (in case some of them have landed in your lap), and then tiptoe over to the corner for the small dust broom. The tiptoe is so the stones that landed point-up don't burrow into the soles of your shoes, and get carried out of the security doors into the bathroom or the elevator, where for some reason a lot of them seem to jump off—and this is why I was suggesting to put the mat in the elevator.

Then you get down on your hands and knees and crawl around on the floor, which nobody thinks is silly because everybody else does it too when they drop some stones. You sweep up carefully or maybe get down lower so your eye has an angle to pick up the flash off a lost baby, even if it's a few feet away. Diamonds—being the hardest substance known to man, and having the highest refractive index of any material and the greatest ability to throw light off their surface—have a very distinctive flash when a little piece of overhead light bounces off them, and every diamond man is sensitive to it.

You can be walking along a carpeted corridor in the executive offices, see this flash way off in a corner, and bend down and flick an incredibly small stone into your palm in a minute—it becomes just a reflex, an instinct. I remember there was a sidewalk in front of the International Paper Building on Forty-fifth Street and the Avenue of the Americas that was made some special way: a kind of sparkly powder was put into the cement before it hardened. It used to drive me crazy on the way home because my "stone-on-the-floor sparkle instinct" would go off, and I'd be bending down involuntarily to pick up the poor lost sheep.

Anyway, they don't always flash at you, since they're not always at the proper angle to the light overhead, so you have to sweep—very carefully and slowly—across the entire length of the room. Then you swoosh it all into a corner and hunker down to go through everybody's random hairs and dandruff (which looks a bit like really small stones); yesterday's french-fry bits; massive paper clips and staples (under which a stone could be hiding); and all the stones from about three weeks ago that you didn't find then. You *never* find all the ones you dropped. And some *always* get out to the elevator.

The boss swings around in his chair (he's the only one with a swinging chair of course, I never could figure that out) and growls, "That's the stupidest suggestion I ever heard of, Roach." There's this art form of making yourself invisible at the edge of the table during a boardroom meeting, and I proceed to do so.

"I have an idea," purrs the one person most in favor with the boss that entire month. "You know those chocolate bars we hand out to suppliers and customers for the holidays—the ones that say ANDIN on the top? They're really thick, you know. What if we unwrap them when they get here and *shave off* about a sixteenth of an inch of chocolate, and then make new chocolate bars from the chocolate that's left over?"

The boss leans back in his chair with an air of triumph, and gazes at her steadily. The rest of us aren't sure whether it was a joke or not (it wasn't), and so we're just trying to look neutral until the boss says "Stupid" (we nod our heads) or "Brilliant" (we nod our heads faster, with more gusto).

You know how the story ends up though. A week later the janitors are in the elevator laying down this black rubber mat with fine fibers across the top. You're on your way out to go home, your exhausted head down like a beaten dog, instinctively scanning the floor of the elevator for some lost stones.

"Hey, what are you guys doing?" you ask.

"Putting in these new mats in the elevator—it's a great idea. You know those small stones that get stuck on the bottom of people's shoes and get carried out to the elevators every day? These mats are gonna catch the stones, and then every night we'll tip them over with the gold scraps in the factory, and the stones will get recycled back to the diamond department, instead of getting vacuumed up by the cleaning guys every night and just thrown out."

"Wow," you say, "great idea. Whose was it?"

"Oh, the boss—he's really sharp you know."

This particular very frustrating perception is triggered by a specific kind of imprint—and that kind of imprint is planted by useless talk. It's interesting that the wisdom books of ancient India and Tibet, written thousands of years ago, describe useless talk as "willingly and happily engaging in wasted conversations about sex, crimes, war, and politics." People often ask me how I have time to manage all the projects we have going on all over the world—the answer is that I consciously try to avoid wasted talk. These are all the hours of conversation over newspapers and coffee where people review the state of the world of events and other people that they know little about, and which have no possible bearing on them at all, and on which they can have no possible influence.

You can throw in just about every news item from every television show, newspaper, or magazine; throw in nearly all of the rest of the "entertainment" part of television and radio; and just about everything you have ever said to someone else about someone else when all you wanted to do was hear yourself talk. A good check for whether a news item in the paper or a magazine is relevant to you is the three-day test. Three days after reading a major newspaper through in detail (because your flight got delayed and you finally had time to read the whole thing, or something like that), try to sit and write down all the bits of information you still remember from it.

You'll find that you don't remember more than one or two of the articles that you read, and very little detail about each of them. So what's the point of reading them in the first place? The power of the mind is magnificent, but not endless: You have, like a computer, limited space in your head for more information.

Buddhism puts a high value on silence, and for very practical reasons. We have a custom, which I'll describe more about later, of going on extended retreats lasting say a couple of days to a couple of weeks—where you very consciously avoid saying anything at all for the whole time. Most people in America and other Western countries have never tried anything of the kind; except for extraordinary situations (laryngitis, days at home sick by ourselves), there probably hasn't been a period of more than one or two days in your whole adult life when you haven't been talking to someone else. And most of this talk, as you will learn when you try a silent retreat yourself, is simply unnecessary and distracting.

Staying alone and silent for a while with yourself is an extraordinary method of gaining important insights into the state of your business—but more on this later. Suffice to say that the imprint which causes you to *see yourself ignored, even when you make a good suggestion*, is none other than engaging in meaningless talk. And if it's a problem that seems to come up a lot in your life, then be *very* strict, much more than other people, about not engaging in frivolous chatter.

Business problem #38: You find yourself afflicted by a lack of confidence; you used to feel very sure of yourself, and now you feel the opposite.

Solution: This problem again can be completely cured by avoiding all useless talk—not only the kinds we've just described, but another very important kind as well. This is the very typical sort of meaningless talk, so prevalent in business, where a businessperson makes grand plans and pronouncements and then never follows through to make sure the thing really happens. This phenomenon is particularly evident at corporate business conferences to plan the coming year: hour after hour of empty plans and resolutions that literally everyone in the room knows cannot, in reality, possibly be executed.

I'm not talking here by the way about the kind of excited over-commitment that a true entrepreneur makes; not the frenetic creativity that flows from one of those rare people who has vision and also knows how to do the grunt work to turn improbable dreams into reality. Rather we're talking about the repeated, half-baked plans and talk that dissipate resources and people's attention.

To assure then that you *will* be imbued with confidence in coming years, try to make sure that you talk only about things you really intend to pull off; that you don't waste the precious hours of your life talking of things that aren't really relevant. There is a delicate balance between dream and vision, between fantasy and hope—and the measure of the difference, in general, is whether you tend to actually bring a good number of your dreams into the amazing reality of a newborn.

Business problem #39: You find yourself unable to take your well-deserved rest; you have trouble relaxing, and never really enjoy a vacation—real leisure is beyond you.

Solution: The ability to relax, the skill of coming away from work and truly enjoying the leisure you have earned, is again something you can discover if you know how to plant the right imprints in your mind—it is not something automatic, it is not something that everyone is born with, and it is not a blessing bestowed only randomly among the population.

These particular imprints are planted, again, primarily by being watchful to speak only of those things which are meaningful, which have benefit—and to avoid talk which has no sense or point, whether it be gossip or silly ideas or plans that you never intend to act on anyway. The common thread here is a *sense of purpose*. The idea is to speak when there is a reason to speak, when there is purpose or action to be fulfilled; the result that comes back to you then is a sense of contentment or fulfillment, for you have fulfilled your life and words.

Remember again that—if you are the kind of person who already normally speaks only when it is meaningful to do so—this in no way means for sure that you have no *older* imprints from having indulged in useless talk in the past, or no *previously minor* imprints that have been in your subconscious for some time, picking up strength all the while, until they actually force you to see yourself as one of those sad people who is incapable of enjoying his or her rest.

It's important to realize that—if you *can't* enjoy your rest—then you *do* have these imprints. The power of the imprints can be blocked by being very careful not to engage in any similar type of action at all: not a single word of useless or meaningless talk. Other people may be able to "afford" it with *their* particular set of imprints, but you can't. If you are bothered by the specific problem that corresponds to a particular imprint, then you—*of everyone*—must avoid even the slightest brush with this kind of imprint again.

Business problem #40: You have a noticeable problem with *timing*. You get into a market big just before it drops; you get out of a market in the middle of a boom that keeps going long after you pulled your money out. Your new product always seems to come out head-to-head with a competitor's release of a slightly better product. Your commitment to an order from a major supplier reaches him several days after his prices went up.

Solution: Again, the problem here is that kind of useless talk where you divert resources and people and minds to plans that—if you think about for a minute—you never really intend to carry through on. Make very sure then that you do what you say you're going to do, and speak not of something you have no real intention of accomplishing.

Business problem #41: No one listens when you ask them to do something.

Solution: This is really just another take on #37, where no one respects what you have to say. The imprint which causes it is—as you might expect—consistently talking about things that have no real importance. So if you are afflicted by this particular problem, you have to address the imprints for it by always thinking carefully before you open your mouth to speak; by always coming out with something to say which is of benefit and real meaning to the people around you.

Business problem #42: People in your company seem to fight with each other a lot.

Solution: You know what a toll the little struggles among individuals in a firm take on the successful operation of the overall company. A division full of employees who support each other practically runs by itself; whereas a division full of division, where people bicker and strive against each other, is both an unprofitable and an exhausting environment. Hard work seems to give people strength, and a common bond; hard words have an immediate effect of draining the entire energy of a division and of each employee in the division. Almost every lunch hour of my time at Andin was taken up sitting with disgruntled employees and trying to get them to get along with one another, and it often occurred to me that I was being paid the ridiculous sum I was paid only to keep the peace. And if I did manage to keep the peace, then the production came through of its own accord.

As we mentioned above with business problem #6, fighting in a company—whether it's you fighting someone else or two other people fighting each other—comes from the imprints planted when you say things, in either a malicious or a gossipy way, which will draw other people farther apart from one another. The people involved can already be friends, or enemies, or even two employees who don't really know each other very well—but because of what you have told either one or both of them, they are a little more distant than when you started speaking. To counter this imprint, go out of your way to bring other people together, wherever and whenever you can, and even in very minor ways—all day long.

Along with this little hourly fence-mending, make a special point to avoid thinking malicious thoughts about anyone in the company. Every executive has a few other executives in the company who have given him or her some trouble, and there's a tendency to feel a twinge of pleasure when you hear that one of them is in a bit of trouble, even some trouble that's going to end up hurting the other people in the company, including yourself.

This is the one particular imprint that descends to the subconscious, swims around for a bit picking up strength, and then floats back up to the conscious mind as the perception of people around you fighting with each other. They fight with each other; they fight with you; you take a bit of pleasure from seeing them have a problem; that plants a new imprint for seeing the people around you fight; and—well—you get the picture.

Almost every bad imprint that you can ever plant in your mind is one that will make you see exactly the thing you were trying to avoid when you planted the first imprint. The wheel spins itself.

Business problem #43: You live in a business and social climate where integrity is simply not respected; where only fools are strictly ethical every hour of their business day—where "Nice guys finish last."

Solution: With this we have started to reach the most serious of all business problems: those that deal with the general purity of what we call "worldview" in your particular business sector or industry. It is true that we see whole markets or industries in commercial life which have a greater respect for integrity than others, and any seasoned businessperson can tell you that to work in an industry which does have a high regard for honesty and justice is, truly, a constantly uplifting feeling; whereas to labor in a little world where goodness is considered foolishness is in itself a degrading experience. It takes a very hard heart not to feel the difference.

If you find yourself in this kind of situation, it's important to realize that the corrupt feeling around you is not something you must seek primarily to avoid through external means; that is, you probably cannot escape being around people with no regard for ethics by changing your external circumstances, because these are not what's driving the very existence of these people. It is, rather, your own imprints. I have hired literally hundreds of people for a wide range of positions over the last few decades, and in the course have had a few quit on me suddenly—though very few.

The conversation usually goes like this:

"I've decided to leave the company."

"Why, what's wrong? Is there anything I can do to help?"

"It's no use; so-and-so (usually somebody sitting near the employee with slightly higher authority than him or her) is driving me crazy. I can't go on working with him; he's really incompetent, and I feel I could do much better in another firm under a more intelligent boss. In fact I've already been for the interview and accepted a position with that other company, so this is my two weeks' notice."

"All right then, I can see there's nothing I can do. But do keep in touch, and let me know how it's working out at the new place."

In the diamond business, by the way, you usually take the two weeks' notice thankfully, ask the disgruntled employee to stay seated where he or she is, and make three phone calls. One to the security office to have a guard come and stand next to the person while the individual cleans out his or her desk (in case there are any loose gems that floated into a drawer while the employee was working on getting disgruntled). One to the human resources department to get the individual's swipe card canceled so they can't get back into the vault area. And the last to the payroll department to cut an immediate check for the person's last two weeks' pay in advance: cheaper than having them walk out with even a few little brilliants.

At any rate, you get back in touch with the former employee in about three weeks to ask how things are going in the new position; doesn't hurt to hear a little about what your competitors are doing, after all. More often than not, the person seems to be relaxed and happy in their new situation. You ask the individual to get back in touch with you in six months to see how things are going. And then, almost invariably, you begin to hear the exact same complaints the erstwhile employee was making in your own firm.

The *imprints* for having bad people around you, you see, aren't changed by manipulating external circumstances. The Tibetans say that, when most of us go into a room with ten people in it, we find three people we like pretty much, three people that we pretty much don't like, and four people that we don't feel much about either way. Then if we go into another room of ten people it's just the same. Even if we take ten of the people we liked from three or four rooms like this and put them together in another room, we'd start to like three and dislike three others.

This is not a function of the external reality; in fact, there is no such thing. Rather it's a question of the imprints in our own minds. Don't look outside your industry to try to find another that's more honest; change your own imprints, train yourself strictly in integrity itself, in the forceful logic behind integrity, and then just sit back and enjoy the change in your own industry as it happens. The change will be wrought by your new imprints, not because you ran away from a bad situation, which in itself can never work.

Business problem #44: You find yourself losing your touch for business; nuts seem harder to crack now, you have trouble keeping up with the changes around you, you seem slower than you used to be when you grapple with complex business challenges.

Solution: So far we've been talking a lot about the kinds of imprints that create your environment and the kinds of people you will come in contact with throughout the day. But what about your own mind—what about the intellect itself? The ancient books of Tibetan wisdom say that this too, your very ability to think clearly, is a perception forced on you by the kinds of imprints you've planted in your own mind in the past. And they say that if you consistently fail to live by the rule that goodness leads to good things—that is, if you consistently fail even to recognize the existence of this deep truth—then your very intellect will suffer.

People who've had the honor to live in close contact with Tibetan Lamas have handfuls of stories to tell about the uncanny insight these masters display with the most common problems. A friend of mine was traveling in India by car with a newly arrived refugee Lama from Tibet; this was an elderly monk who had been living in a remote area of the Himalayas, and who had literally only recently ever ridden in a car. The car broke down, and the driver got out to raise the hood and examine the engine.

The Lama got out too, for—as the ancient books say—it's good to watch how people do things you don't know how to do yet, because you might learn something that will come in handy later to help someone, somewhere. He leaned over this thing he had never seen before, a car engine, and used the few words of English that he knew to ask how several of the parts worked. Then he pointed to the alternator and said, "This is what you have to fix."

And of course it was; I often imagine this Lama's mind as sort of a superfast computer that runs through all the possible functions of each part based on the functions of the few parts whose functions he understands—almost reinventing the combustion engine mentally, you see, as he gazes at this newfangled thing and visualizes its internal workings—and then coming to a conclusion, through iron-clad logic, about which part it must be which is broken.

This advanced ability to think, to reason out a problem infinitely faster and more clearly than most normal people can, is not a result of genetics or nutrition or even training; it is another perception, another perception triggered by a mental imprint, an imprint planted in the mind at a previous time. And the strongest way to plant these kinds of imprints is, quite simply, *understanding how imprints work* to create the world around us, and then acting on this understanding by following the path of personal integrity.

Business problem #45: The principles of justice don't seem to apply to your life: Whenever you are wronged, be it by a fellow employee or by a competitor, the authorities (meaning your boss or the courts) never seem to give you the help and protection that you were hoping for.

Solution: If you think about it, your failure to enjoy the help and protection that are due you by any authority represents a fundamental and disturbing breakdown in the very order of things—perhaps no situation in all of life is more frustrating than to be harmed, to seek rightful redress, and then be refused justice. This particular perception, this particular reality, has its own specific causes: an imprint planted in your mind *when you refused yourself to recognize the order of things*, the real way things work, by denying especially the very first rule of imprints. This first rule states that an imprint planted by a negative action, by an action in which you have consciously and purposely harmed another person, can lead only to a negative result: to a negative perception, a negative experience of the world around you or within you.

And you spit on this principle whenever you believe and act otherwise—in fact, whenever you knowingly undertake a harmful action hoping to gain something good in return. We're talking about small lies (negative imprint) to close a deal (desirable perception); cheating on taxes (negative imprint) to keep more money for yourself (desirable perception); or finding a way not to pay a fair import duty (negative imprint) to lower prices on your product and make it more competitive (desirable perception). **It is essential to understand that, in terms of *content*, a positive result (business and personal success) cannot come from a negative cause (such as hurting or cheating anyone else).**

To express this in a different way, it is completely impossible for a desirable perception to come from a negative imprint. Every time you even *think* this way, every time you deny the natural order of all things—implicitly or directly—you plant another imprint in your mind that will force you to see the external social order of your world turned upside down; meaning, the court or your boss will decide against you, even if "right" seems to be on your side.

The solution then is painfully simple: *Take the time and the trouble* to acquaint yourself with the new ideas presented here (well, new only in the West), with the entire concept that *your world is a creation of your integrity, or lack of it*. Overcome that very dangerous cultural sloth which refuses anymore to think about where the world and the bad things in it really come from. Why does one businessperson fail, while another succeeds, when each has essentially undertaken exactly the same actions? Negative events must come from negative actions; make sure you understand why, and how, and then sit back and enjoy the fireworks.

Business problem #46: You are slowly coming to the realization that, over the length of your career in the business world, the level of your own integrity has noticeably and disturbingly dropped.

Solution: The final solution to the final problem in this chapter, in a book about business integrity itself, is nothing you might ever expect—*for the loss of your integrity is a perception forced upon you by your lack of respect for integrity in the past*. To put it simply, you have for so long held the unspoken opinion that integrity has no relevance in business that you must now face the loss of your own integrity. And the real disaster here is that the very hidden potential which could have made you wildly successful will now work against you, for the imprint which causes you to misunderstand where things really come from is the most difficult imprint to overcome—and this is because *overcoming imprints is accomplished by understanding them*. The failure to understand how to be successful in your business and your life begets the continued failure to understand these things.

The solution of course is to work hard to overcome your natural resistance to the kind of thinking presented in this book. If you think about it, many of your opinions and beliefs about where success comes from were planted in you at a very early age: Many of your suppositions about life were imparted to you by first- and second-grade teachers whom, if you met and spoke with them now, would strike you as ridiculous in their thinking.

To be really successful you must learn to overcome ways of thinking and behaving that have proved themselves, over decades of your life, to be either counterproductive or—at best—almost random in producing the results you want. The truly great movers and shakers of every age, and of every part of the globe, have had to learn to reexamine each of the beliefs they grew up with.

Don't leave the success of your business, and your life, at the mercy of unexamined assumptions and prejudices of your own country and culture. Remember that what your culture says is good or bad or right or wrong or successful or unsuccessful has changed from year to year, even in your own lifetime. When I was a boy growing up in the southwestern United States, one of the most evil activities that a criminal could engage in was "running numbers."

I didn't know what "running" numbers meant, and asked my mother. She said that only bad people ran numbers, usually in the southern part of our town, across the railway tracks. They shot heroin into their arms and got drunk in bars and ran numbers. Running numbers was where people came to a dark room and gave money to a man who gave them a number, and then when lots of people had given lots of money and each gotten their own number, the man would close his eyes and pick one number and that person would win all the other people's money (after the man had taken out some of the money for his trouble).

Nowadays in the United States they call it a "lottery." The lottery is run by the government. People who ran numbers were put in jail. People who run lotteries are helping the public. They are doing exactly the same thing. Except now it's moral. In the 1920s in the United States it was a federal crime to own or to use alcohol. Now it's legal and sophisticated. The brilliant founding fathers of America kept black people as slaves, and had debates for decades about whether they were animals or people. In New York it's illegal to mistreat your pet, presumably because they have feelings. Millions of very similar animals are slaughtered in the United States every year for meat. Presumably they don't have feelings.

This is not a statement about gambling or racism or eating meat or not eating meat. It's just a statement about believing everything your culture tells you. You can't just blindly trust what you grew up with—whether it was taught to you by your elementary school teachers, or parents, or the people at your church or temple. You can't just blindly accept what is popular or legal or accepted at any given time in that little part of the world you call "home." You can't follow one way of doing business just because that's the way other people are doing it right now.

It never ceased to amaze me how the owner of Andin, Ofer, used to call us into the boardroom every few months and excitedly wave a book and say, "This is it! Look what I found in the airport bookstore on the way to Dallas! This is the answer to all our business problems!" And it would be a copy of the latest best-seller about how to do business.

"Ofer, do you realize who wrote this book?"

"Yeah, sure, it's this guy who gives motivational talks all over the country about how to succeed in business."

"And do you know how much money he makes a year?"

"I don't know. Look here, it looks like he makes about eighty or ninety thousand a year."

"And how much money do you make a year?"

"Well, I make a couple of million a year."

"So why are you reading this stupid book by a guy who makes only a fraction of what you do? Do you realize that he's saying you should do the complete opposite of what that guy in the other book last year was saying we should do?"

You spend so much time *doing business* that you should be willing to spend a little time figuring out *how business really works*; in the end, *it would save you years of your life* if you could figure out the basic reasons why business success does or doesn't happen in the first place. Success, personal or business, is a result—and all results have causes. When you repeat the same causes, you get the same result. If you're doing business in a way that doesn't always produce the same results, then you haven't found the causes. If you don't know what causes a result and you keep trying something that you know doesn't always cause the result you want, then you're just being lazy, and don't be surprised when you don't succeed.

One thing that the ancient books unanimously agree upon is the capacity of the human mind. Its potential is completely limitless. Read this book—not once, but over and over, especially the "correlations" or real solutions to specific business problems. It's not so important that you remember which solution applies to each problem—this you can always find out just from opening up the book and running down the list of problems—but that you start to gain a deeper understanding of *how reality itself, the very fact of business success or failure, is driven by imprints that we put in our own minds*, by the good or bad that we do to those around us, throughout the business day. Then you can pretty much design your own future, and it will come out just the way you want it.

chapter 8

The Act of Truth

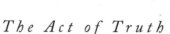

༄༅། །བསྐུ་མེད་རྒྱལ་བ་སྲས་བཅས་བྱིན་རླབས་དང་། །སྣང་སྟོང་འགལ་མེད་ཆོས་དབྱིངས་རྟེན་འབྲེལ་སློབས། །བདག་ཅག་ཅེ་གཙིག་མོས་པའི་བདེན་མཐུ་ཡིས། །ཇི་ལྟར་སྨོན་པའི་དོན་འདི་ལྷུན་འགྲུབ་ཤོག །

By the blessings of the fact that the Victorious Ones
And their sons and daughters can never fail;

By the power of the fact that the hidden potential
and what we see are completely compatible;

By the force of the deepest nature of things
And the truth that they all depend on perceptions;

And by the might of the truth of what
We wish for so deeply here in our hearts

May the thing that we pray for come to be,
Just as we hope it, all of itself.

These lines express what the Tibetans call an act of truth:

If what I have done is true,
Then may these things come to be.

Let's put it bluntly. We see people all the time in business who are good, people with integrity, who get chewed up and spit out with the best of them. And we see people who are selfish and greedy and immoral who rake in the dough. So how's this fit in with everything we've said so far?

"Why the wicked prosper," as the Bible would put it, and why those with integrity may not seem to prosper, has a very simple explanation in this system. There are a few basic principles here.

1. Causes come before their results.

This is so obvious that, as with most obvious things, we miss it completely. If someone is doing well financially, it must be coming—according to all we have said above—from imprints in their mind which they put there by being generous in the past. Present success, then, comes from having maintained a generous state of mind in the past.

This *does not necessarily mean* that the person enjoying the success *has a generous state of mind now,* any more than the presence of an apple pie on your kitchen table means that there is an apple tree starting to grow under the kitchen floor. The apple pie is a result of an apple tree that has already grown; and an apple tree starting to grow now is a cause of apples yet to come.

It is in every way plausible then that a successful businessperson can be enjoying the results of generous imprints planted in the past, and at the same time be planting new imprints for financial disaster in the future—by being greedy or stingy now.

2. Causes are smaller than their results.

Remember that imprints planted under especially powerful circumstances—a small good deed done with intense compassion, or a small gift to someone who needs it very badly—have immense power; and that all imprints build up force exponentially during their incubation in the subconscious. A person who is enjoying tremendous wealth now may have done some relatively minor kindness to another person under conditions like this; no problem.

3. Growing things takes time.

Imprints work the same as plants, don't doubt it. Nobody would plant some flower seeds in their garden on Monday, and then stand in the garden all day on Tuesday waiting for their flowers, angry and disappointed when they failed to appear by evening.

I've tried to present the information in this book in as modern a way as possible, while still sticking strictly to the meaning of the original ancient books. But there is one detail here that has to be admitted up front—a detail that won't be so popular in our McDonald's era of thinking. Planting and tending mental imprints take *time and patience.* I've taught this system to a great number of people, and a certain percentage always give up halfway through the exercise. Following the principles outlined in this book is something that must be done on a continual basis for months before you can expect to see concrete results.

People who fail to succeed with these principles invariably fail for one of two reasons: They don't follow them over a good amount of time, or they don't follow them very well (and usually believe that they *are* following them well, until they really stop and think about it). Mental imprints, remember, are being planted at the rate of sixty-five *per finger snap,* sixty-five per second. A few noble intentions during an entire day of mental irritation and whining at the events and the people around you will have practically no noticeable results, and you shouldn't expect them to.

The early Buddhists of Tibet were known as the Kadampas—they were simple people, herders and carpenters and small farmers, who took to the new ideas like fish to water, in their simple but exquisite way. They carried around a small bag of pebbles, half white and half black. Whenever they had a very good thought, or said something very positive to another person, or did someone else a kindness, they would take a white pebble out and put it say in their left pocket. Every time they had a negative thought about someone else, or said or did something unkind to another person, they would take a black pebble out of the bag and put it in their right pocket.

At the end of the day, just before going to bed, they would take all the pebbles out of their pockets and count up the black and the white. They immediately learned, as you will too, that the black pebbles far out-numbered the white pebbles. This isn't to say we're all evil and that we should always feel guilty or dirty—it just means that the basic condition of most minds in this corner of the universe (and there are many other corners) happens to work that way. A very, very important quality of our minds though—and you can see this is true—is that they are eminently *trainable*. With a little practice, your mind can learn almost anything; it's just a question of putting your mind to it.

4. It helps to have a tracking system.

The Diamond Division of Andin International used to be on the fourth floor of our building in Manhattan. Starting in the basement and coming up a few more floors was a large jewelry manufacturing facility, since moved largely overseas. Now making jewelry is not like making something like a car, with its thousands of moving parts. There are usually just two parts: the mounting, and the stone.

It's amazing though how many steps a diamond ring say has to go through to get to your department store. It starts in merchandising; somebody thinks up a new design and sketches it for the designer. Then the designer takes the sketch and works it up into a full-scale drawing, shows it around to the big cheeses, adjusts it a bit, and turns it over to the specs person.

The specs person looks at the piece from an engineering point of view: Is the shank strong enough to withstand normal abuse? (We once received a ring back from a customer completely flattened; the client said it was defective but when pressed she admitted she had smashed it under a falling toilet seat while cleaning the bowl; well, we replaced it anyway.) Is there enough metal around the stone to keep it from falling out? Can the piece be manufactured smoothly in mass quantities? Does enough light get into the stone from the sides and back so it can sparkle right? And so on.

Then the piece goes to a costing person who decides whether it's economically feasible. Does the customer get enough bang for his buck? Does the diamond look as big as it is, or even bigger? How does the piece compare in price with similar pieces on the market? Can we scrape some gold out somewhere without changing the look, or making the thing fall apart on someone's finger? What are the risks of making a bunch and keeping them in stock?

After this a piece or two is actually made and tested. The process of casting the gold for the ring literally hasn't changed since the days of the Egyptian goldsmiths thousands of years ago. This is called the lost-wax process; it begins with the model maker, who takes the drawings and carefully sculpts a master out of an especially fine and sturdy wax.

This wax master is then dunked into a little square of liquid rubber, which hardens around the wax. A mold cutter then enters the picture; he or she takes a very fine surgeon's scalpel and cuts the rubber square carefully sideways, like a hamburger roll, until they can carefully lift out the original wax. Then a channel is dug out from one side of the rubber square, from the surface down to the ring-shaped cavity left when the wax was pulled out. This now will be the mold for wax copies of the first master: these clones are simply called "waxes."

A wax injector technician takes the two parts of the new mold, binds them together with a strong rubber band, and then jams the channel into the nipple of a machine that spits out hot wax under pressure. The wax flows down the channel into the ring-shaped cavity, filling it up. When the wax cools the rubber band comes off, and then the wax is gently removed from the mold. If there are any scratches or other imperfections in the wax, a wax finisher takes a tiny brush and smooths them over; it's a lot easier to do with the wax than later, when the piece is gold.

Next a tree maker takes a handful of the waxes and attaches them to a wax rod; the waxes branch up off the rod like the limbs of a Christmas tree, connected to the rod by the twig of wax created when the wax was forced down the channel of the mold (this twig is called a "sprue"). The whole tree then is lowered into a small vat of plaster, upside down, with the base of the rod open to the surface.

After the plaster has hardened, it's put into a special oven, and the wax tree is melted out. This leaves the plaster alone, with a network of open channels leading to cavities shaped like the rings-to-be. A casting master then comes along and begins mixing his alloys to give just the right color and hardness to the ring: the alloys come in small cloth bags full of little lumps of pure gold or silver shot.

The challenge for the caster is in no way limited to getting just the right mix for the look and strength of the finished piece; even more crucial is *exactly* the right proportion of gold and other alloys to reach a true 14- or 18-karat mix; that is, 14/24 of gold or 18/24 of gold, and not a smidgen more or less. For herein lies one of the keys to the profit of a jewelry company. The cost of labor in the main markets around the world is essentially the same; the cost of gold is completely fixed; and everyone hopefully pays the same taxes and excise duties and so on.

So the only question is how closely you can control things like the percentage of gold in your ring: You have to come out with a legal 14/24 of gold—14 karat, if that's what you're selling—or you lose your reputation in the market. On the other hand you try *not* to give the slightest fraction over the 14/24, or else you've lost that much money. There are very sophisticated spectroscopic analyzers now used in the trade that can cost hundreds of thousands of dollars, but they can tell you exactly how you're doing, down to the hundredth of a percentage, on the finished ring.

We used one to determine whether a Thai supplier was giving us enough gold in our pieces, and he was a bit shocked when we showed him how much money he was losing by giving us *too much* gold. You see, you want your suppliers to be profitable too, or else they raise their prices to you, and their incompetence makes you less competitive in the market.

The alloys are mixed and melted into a liquid, then injected under pressure into the channels of the plaster. When the gold is cooled, the plaster is smashed, leaving a golden Christmas tree, with rings instead of Christmas ornaments at the ends of the branches. Now enters the "jeweler," a name which has nothing to do with a person who runs a jewelry store: in the manufacture of jewelry, this is a person who cuts or files gold after the casting is done.

The jeweler takes some heavy tin snips, or perhaps a pneumatic chopping tool that can leave your finger in two parts as well as it can a hunk of gold, and begins cutting the rings off the branch of the tree. The goal here is pretty simple: cut close enough to the finished ring not to leave a bump of gold that will be wasted, but not so close that Mrs. Smith's engagement ring has a gouge in it on one side or the other. Now the rings have become what we call "castings," and they're about to go for a dip overnight in the tumbler.

When the tree of gold cooled down back at the plaster stage, the outside part oxidized a bit and got a really ugly skin on it, like tree bark. So the castings at this point are not the lovely gleaming ringlets you normally associate with gold; they are dull burnt little things that need to have a few microns of skin peeled off. So you either give them a bath in some very nasty acids and arsenic, or throw them into a tumbling machine.

The tumbler is a little cylinder or wheel filled with special metal or plastic beads, mixed in a liquid slurry. You throw in a bunch of castings that were cut off the trees, turn on the tumbler, and leave it running until the next morning. Any process which can be done at night without supervision is highly desirable, since your lead time to get the rings to the customer can be measured in hours as the end of the order comes due.

The castings emerge with a dull shine and go to the setter. Setters are a strange breed, a clan apart to themselves. Often they are huge friendly guys sitting on small stools barely a foot or two off the ground. (This forces them to keep their backs straight as they work.) In front of them is a desk with a wooden tongue sticking out at them; above the table is a complicated network of drill holders with a variety of bits.

The setter gets a little package of diamonds from the stone department and dumps them out into a tiny cup. Then he takes a drill and opens up a nice little home for the stone in the casting; this may entail a whole new hole, or else just notches on some prongs that are already there, built in from the design stage. Next he takes a tiny cone of wax and coaxes the top of the diamond onto the tip; sort of like balancing an apple on the end of a cane. He flips the cone over deftly and inserts the stone into the hole, watching through a special visor as if he were a heart surgeon. Setters really have to have the steadiest hands in the business.

Then he takes a tool that looks like a little can opener and forces the gold over the stone. This requires just plain brute strength, and a lot of setters look like gorillas from the waist up. The strength though requires touch too, for this is where a stone can be chipped or broken, and the setter will have to pay a part of the cost of any stone he damages. Some setters get paid more, just because of the riskiness of trying to set certain kinds of stones. For example, more than a quarter of the emeralds used in a jewelry factory might get damaged at this stage, because they're one of the softest of all gems.

From the setter the ring goes to the polisher, who buffs the gold up to a nice sheen and takes out whatever unintentional gouges the setter has added to the piece. Then the piece goes into a boiling ultrasonic dip, which cleans off all the grit from the polisher's wheel and also bangs the stone around a few thousand times, simulating the use it might get from a hyperactive teenager in the first few months after purchase. If the stone doesn't fall out here, the ring is probably ready to wear.

Although there are more stages to making a diamond ring than you might have guessed, the fact is that there are still no more than two parts to put together. It's amazing then that in a normal factory maybe 30 percent of all the rings produced will have to go back at some stage for some kind of quality problem. The profit on a ring may only be a few dollars, and every time a piece has to go backward in the flow for rework it may well cost *more* than the entire profit, which is a polite way of saying that you will be providing the ring to the customer for free.

Imagine yourself sitting around the table in the boardroom with twelve vice presidents and the owners, the top of the table covered with hundreds of lovely, glittering rings, in a riot of colors: topaz, ruby, tourmaline, diamond, pearl, and amethyst. And every ring has some small scratch on it in that makes it worthless to send out to a customer. Each will have to be scrapped, which is a heartbreaking process of throwing a lovely creation, along with all the sweat and blood you've invested in producing it, into a boiling acid which dissolves the gold and leaves the gem (the gold is then filtered out of the acid and reused).

After a couple of hours of heated discussion (no one wants to admit that the scratches are being produced in a department that belongs to their division), you get to a pretty clear idea of where the scratches are coming from. Now that department happens to be populated by some pretty bullheaded employees who might figure out a way to put some new scratches on the rings if you reprimand them for their poor quality openly. So we at Andin worked out this system called, simply, "counting."

You get word down to the *cultural* heads of the department (the workers who influence most of the other workers, as opposed to the *political* heads—the middle managers who are often not so popular with the real workers) that you want a *count* of how many rings come out of their department with this particular kind of scratch on them. You just want the scratches tracked. No accusations, no blame, no punishment—just let us know every week on this piece of paper how many rings come out of the department with the scratch.

You know what happens then. Once the tracking starts, the scratches stop in a few days, and nobody feels bad. Results with no guilt, because guilt most often leads to new problems. Now what's this got to do with mental imprints?

You can understand the theory here perfectly well: Things have this hidden potential where they could become anything, and the imprints I put in my mind from the past play on this potential and decide how I see *everything*, even down to my own thoughts. But actually being able to follow up on this knowledge and turn it into success in your own business is a whole different thing. The best way of doing this is simply to install a tracking system—free of judgment or guilt—that you use just to *record* how you're doing, on a constant basis.

In Tibetan this tracking system is known as *tundruk*, or "six times a day"; we call it a six-time book. If you follow this system, you'll get results. If you don't, you won't. This is really one of the most important things in this book—so listen up, if you really want to succeed.

Go out and buy yourself a little daily planner that you can keep in your pocket. Then go back through the forty-six business problems in the last chapter and find three of them that apply to you especially. These are your three biggest problems, and these are what you're going to concentrate on. As a particular problem goes away or reaches a certain state of improvement, replace it with your fourth biggest problem from the list, and so on.

Divide a few pages of the daily planner into six boxes that give you room to write about five or six sentences each. Number the boxes, then write a few words to remind yourself of the solution to each problem, one solution in each of the first three boxes. Then repeat the process for the next three boxes. The first three boxes are to use before lunch; the second three boxes are for after lunch.

One time before you go off to work in the morning check the solution in the first box. Let's say for example that you're having trouble with business problem #36: People inside and outside the company seem to mislead you. The solution to this problem, you remember, is being careful to avoid pride and an unhealthy desire for recognition; stated positively, listening and learning from everyone around you, and finding ways to pass recognition on to those around you who deserve it.

Now in the left side of the box put a small "plus" sign, and write next to it that one thing you have thought, or said, or did in the last day or so which was closest to a success with this particular problem: Maybe you took the time to think of something good an employee is doing on a regular basis, and stopped to thank that person for it in a small way. Don't write a long story, or you'll get tired of tracking and give it up. Make it just a few seconds of honest self-reflection, and write something brief and quick.

No generalities here—they don't work. We don't want to see "I'm a pretty nice guy to people at work" as an entry. We want to see "At three-fifteen on Tuesday I went over to Susan's desk and thanked her in front of everybody else for keeping the inventories so well, so quietly, for the last six months." This kind of conscious tracking of your small successes creates a very strong good imprint in your mind, and you will find, soon, that the problem of people misleading you has started to vanish, so steadily and surely that you haven't even noticed what was happening.

Under the "plus" sign then write a "minus" sign, and search the last day or so for something you didn't do so well on this same problem. You might write, for example, "Refused to listen to Mark's suggestion about the purchasing policies yesterday, standing near his desk at two-thirty." Again, *be specific*—it's the only way the six-time book is going to work. Remember that imprints grow during their incubation time in the subconscious: Big results will come, even from minor imprints, but they have to be specific.

Finally put a little "to do" below the minus. This is a game plan for the day, something easy but very symbolic of the change that you want to make in yourself. It might be as simple as "Think of two good suggestions that Robert ever gave you," or "Thank at least one person in the colored gemstone department today." Make sure that the "to-do's" are modest; and in fact make sure that everything you put in your six-time book is short and sweet—you're a busy person, and if you make it a long story you'll end up petering out.

Above all, remember why you are keeping the book in the first place. It's not to feel guilty about things you are doing wrong—there's no word in Tibetan for "guilty." The closest thing is "intelligent regret that decides to do things differently." This is a very cold and calculating attempt to adjust your upcoming reality, to make it more profitable and meaningful— and there's nothing wrong with that, especially if it comes about by being kind and good to other people. You are now in the additional business of mental gardening: choosing the seeds or imprints you want to put in your mind by studying which imprints create the things you want to achieve— consciously planting those seeds, and then sitting back to enjoy the extraordinary success that will come to you.

Make an entry every two hours or so during the day then. Do it at your desk by yourself quietly (everyone will think you're a big executive checking your busy schedule), or if there are too many people around, or it's too crazy with the phone and the rest, then go off to some quiet corner near the coffee machine or something and do it there. I've even excused myself from board meetings on the pretense of going to the toilet, to write my next entry there.

It's important that the entries are spread out through the day—that's why it's called the "six-time book." The idea is one of continual maintenance, or catching yourself every few hours before anything very big can go wrong within your mind. If you make one entry at 8 A.M., then stop during your coffee break at 10:30 A.M. and do another. Then do one at lunch, one in the afternoon, and maybe one on the way home. In the late evening finish off with the sixth, and then—just before you go to bed— review the whole day and make a separate entry, with the best three things you did all day and the worst three things. Remember, you are not making a judgment about yourself or feeling guilty; you're just *tracking* what you have done, said, and thought during the day. By *tracking*, you will automatically *change*. By *changing*, your reality itself will change, into everything you ever dreamed of. If you keep this up over any decent period of time, you'll be amazed at the results.

5. Understanding what you're doing makes it infinitely stronger.

You can see then why people who live by integrity in their business life may not seem to get their reward on time! You have to be good *steadily*, on a constant basis, throughout the day, even if it's in a minor way. And you have to keep it up for a good while. Lastly, you have to leave time for the plants to grow—for this is the very nature of cause and effect, and of imprints acting in the potential.

There are a few more details here that will speed up the process markedly. If you *understand* the process while you are keeping the six-time book, the book works that much better. That is, stop every once in a while to reflect on what's really happening. You're having a problem in your business life—in exactly the same market or company or department where lots of other people *don't* have this problem—because you have imprints in *your* mind that make you see things differently than these other people. And you're on a quest to seek out these imprints and disable them, by planting the opposite imprint.

Knowing how it all works, keeping your mind on how it all works, makes it all work a lot faster and a lot more powerfully. This also explains why some people who appear to have a lot of integrity in business don't seem to be doing so well at any given time. It's not enough to live your business life even by a strict code of ethics if you're only doing so by instinct, or under duress imposed by the law, the custom in your industry, the behavior of your peers, or just strong advice from another person who can't explain to you how it all works. *Your ethical way of living and doing business must be driven by a clear and conscious awareness of what kind of imprints this behavior will plant in your subconscious, and how this will determine the very reality of the rest of your business career.*

6. Always end with the act of truth.

This brings us back to the act of truth. It's one thing to know that, in order to be successful in life or business, you *must* conduct yourself with integrity. It's another thing to act on this knowledge, from hour to hour, day to day. It's yet a higher level to know, clearly, the process by which these things *really work*. There's one more step though to get this power to work for you immediately, in a way that you can obviously attribute to your new way of looking at and behaving in the world.

And this is the act of truth. At the end of the day, maybe on your way home, pull out your six-time book. Look over all the positives that you've written down for the last twenty-four hours. Think about how each one has planted very powerful imprints in your mind, to see a whole new world in the future, to achieve success in your business and life frankly beyond what you can even now imagine. Enjoy even your smallest accomplishments in trying to follow the path of total personal integrity.

Imagine then what this kind of integrity implies. Imagine looking back on a day's work and being able to say, with total honesty, that you have been totally honest during every minute of the day—in the way you act toward others, in each one of the carefully considered words you said to others, in even your innermost thoughts. Good to each person around you, honest to them, living a life of complete personal honesty, and in a position now to look back and say, yes, it was a day of total integrity.

Whenever you have a day like this (and it will take some practice), or even something approaching a day like this, go on then to *the act of truth*. Calling on the power of an act of truth takes all the imprints for the day up to an entirely new level of strength. And it goes something like this:

> *If it is true that, during this entire day, I have been mindful of all which I said to others, and did to others, and even of my thoughts toward others, and acted thus throughout the day with complete honesty toward each person I came in contact with, then may a new power be born. And by force of this new power may I, and all those in my world, achieve through our work true happiness, and prosperity, together.*

When the Tibetans perform an act of truth like this they also imagine, coming out of their hearts, strong rays of golden light, as if the sun were in their chests. They picture the light going out to all those around them—first to those on the bus they're in, say, and then on to every person going home at that moment, and then to all the people waiting at home for each person going home.

Wish then for each of them the kind of success in their lives and work that you hope to reach yourself. If the principles that you've read about here—the concepts of hidden potential and of imprints in the mind—are at all true, then prosperity could come to each person who used them, to all of us, at the same time: There would be more than enough for everybody, and each person's cup would overflow.

goal two

Enjoying the Money,

or Managing

Body and Mind

chapter 9

Setting the Day
with Silent Time

Suppose now that you've understood the essence of *The Diamond Cutter:* You understand that nothing is the way it is from its own side, or else everything would seem exactly the same to everybody. You understand too that—since the way things seem can't come from nothing at all—then it must be coming from your own side. And you understand that the way things seem to you is caused by seeds or imprints that you put in your mind earlier, when you did or said or thought something good or bad about another person.

Finally you understand that, because of all this, you can essentially design your own future, just by keeping track of how you act and think during your day. The bottom line is that you have reached what every person throughout history, and throughout the history of business, has always hoped to reach: control of your own destiny. You know how to succeed.

I would like to say a few words here about some different methods of going even further, and getting the maximum enjoyment out of your success. Buddhist thinkers say that it's one thing to be successful—to attain material success for example—and an entirely different thing to enjoy the success. In this and the following chapters then we will talk about various ways of maintaining happiness on a constant daily basis while you go about the business of becoming successful. This begins with learning how to "set the day."

The Tibetan wise men call this process *penpa tang*: The expression means to set the tone for an entire day by spending a few quiet moments in the morning, and the phrase is close to another that means "shooting an arrow." This daily morning quiet time, sitting silently by yourself to prepare your thoughts for the day, is like the six-time book: absolutely essential for you to pull off the task of creating complete personal and business success for yourself in the years to come. The roots of this practice are found in ancient teachings of the Buddha such as the *Book of the Golden Light*, which was spoken over two thousand years ago; some details of the world may have changed since then, but not the basic principles of how to set the day, which have been passed on from master to disciple as a deep, personal, and lifetime practice in an unbroken tradition over all these centuries. Here's how you can do it too, every morning.

A very profound version of this practice states that you should actually begin the night before. After you have gotten in bed, first review the day just past, as we described it above. Check for the best three things you did or said or thought, and then the worst three. Concentrate especially on the good things, and as you go to sleep—as you enter the world of dreams, which the great Tibetan masters say is close in many ways to the twilight world between your death in this life and your awakening in the next— think ahead to the moment your alarm clock will go off the next morning. Think ahead to your first waking thoughts, to the first moments as you stretch and yawn and open your eyes. As you may have noticed in your life already, these few minutes—and in fact the following hour or so—are critical for getting the day off to a positive start. And the best way to get a good start is to set the day with a period of personal silence and reflection.

There are a few basic techniques for conducting this personal silent time that have been developed for centuries among the great teachers of Tibet, and before. If you know them and follow them, then this personal silent time—even though it's only a few minutes per day—will become perhaps one of the most important and cherished parts of your life. The techniques begin with finding a place in your house or apartment where you're going to spend the quiet time.

It's important that you have a separate place, physically, where you spend your morning silent time. We should say, first of all, that it's a bad idea to actually do it on your bed, a place where you have just spent a long time sleeping, and which is still covered with the feelings of drowsiness and darkness. Bed is a place where you have been conditioned, your whole life long, to get silent and then fall asleep; so if you do your silent time there it's very likely to get you sleepy. It's important to get out of bed and get moving.

In Tibet the monks go and splash water on their faces, and then blow their noses hard so they'll be able to breath very quietly during their silent time in the morning. At our monastery every morning this used to sound like a grand symphony of noses going off. Then you brush your teeth, so your mouth will taste good during the silent time; this is one more thing that keeps you from getting distracted. Next you go get something to hydrate your body with—say tea or juice or just a touch of coffee if you're used to it—and sip it while you clean up your quiet place.

This is a special corner of your house or apartment where you always go to spend your morning silent time. I guess the first thing to say about it is that it should be a place which is quiet, somewhere everybody else in the house has agreed to as a place where you can spend your morning silent time without getting interrupted. Some businesspeople I know clear out a nice little corner of the basement and fix it up; some in smaller places buy one of those neat Japanese blinds and set off a corner of the apartment; others make a deal with their family that they can have the living room alone from say seven to seven-thirty in the morning. Whatever you choose, make sure other people will respect your quiet space for the time, and be sure to remove all other sources of interruption.

This means disconnecting the phone to the room; making sure others are not going to be listening to loud radios or TV's nearby; and being careful to minimize outside noises by closing windows facing a busy road or street, for example. The time and space should be as quiet as you can manage, given your particular living circumstances. If the noise around the house or outside is too much at seven, then you might want to start earlier, although it is essential that you get a good night's sleep—as many hours as you personally normally need, in order for your silent time to be successful.

If your quiet place feels special, almost like a sacred space, things will go much better. It should be neat and tidy, and in fact the first thing we do when we enter it in the morning is to sweep up a bit, or dust, or straighten up. This we do even if the place is already pretty clean, because it gets the body bending and moving a bit. The Tibetan wise men say that as you putter around cleaning you should imagine that this represents cleaning up your business, and your life and your mind. If you become a "regular" (and you will have to, or none of this stuff works), you'll find that there's not much left to clean up in your quiet place: maybe just a few dust balls here and there, or a few loose pieces of paper. Then we just go to a finer level, and clean up any tiny thing that's still on the floor or whatever. This process represents the point at which you've gotten your business and your life together so well that there's only a little maintenance to do at times. But do the little maintenance, and never forget to think about what it represents as you work.

If your quiet place is really clean and tidy, it helps your mind get quieter. The next step is to find a comfortable seat, where you can go into your own personal silence. Getting into this silence is like going into a reverie or a daydream, or listening to your favorite music: You know, where you lean back and close your eyes, or just stare off into space, and let your thoughts go free while your body is relaxed and motionless. The point is to find a place where you can "park" your body like this while you go deep into the quiet of your own mind. The idea is to park the body in a position that will be comfortable until you and your mind decide to come back from your silent time.

In the ancient teachings of Tibet, it's best if this position can include a number of elements. The most important is to keep your back straight; there's something about the inner workings of the nervous system, say the Tibetans, that works better if you're sitting up straight, and helps you focus your mind during your silent time. It's good to sit on something soft but a little firm, and prop up the area under your tailbone (the back of your rear end, toward your backbone) a bit with a pillow: this helps you keep your back straight. You can cross your legs if this is comfortable, but it's fine too if you want to just sit in a normal position with your legs down, feet on the floor—the way you normally sit.

Lay your hands loosely on your lap with the palms up, and try to relax throughout your entire body. A good way to do this is to take a series of slow deep breaths. This practice has the funny name of *ook joong-ngoop* in Tibetan, and has been around since at least sixteen centuries ago, when it appeared in a text called the *Treasure House of Higher Knowledge*. The idea is to focus your mind within for your silent time by blocking out every other thought and experience; we do this by tying the mind to the breath, as it goes in and out.

Except we start with the out, and then go to the in! It works like this. You fix your mind on the inside of the two nostrils of your nose, up toward the holes. Imagine you're like a sentry who's been posted at these two little caves to watch and see if anyone is coming or going. As you breathe in and then out try to be aware of the touch of the air on the inside of your nose: the cooler, drier air coming in and the moist, warm air flowing out. Remember to stick to your post: Your mind is not allowed to stray from the inside of your nose and the touch of the air coming and going. If someone slams a door or talks loudly, you might be distracted for a second, but you are strict about bringing yourself back to your breathing as soon as you can.

The ancient custom is to repeat this for the length of ten breaths, with the caveat that—if you are distracted in a major way and lose count—then you have to start over again. The outgoing breath counts as the first half of a number, and the incoming breath as the second half. This way of counting a breath (which is the opposite of our own way, where taking, holding, and releasing a breath might be counted as a single breath, say, in swimming) is said to have an added power of bringing the mind inward, of focusing the thoughts within. If you find yourself losing count frequently before you reach ten, it's a sign that you're having trouble concentrating. This will affect everything about your business performance, and you should take special care to observe your silent time more regularly, every morning.

You can close your eyes or leave them open; it doesn't matter much, as long as you don't get distracted. If you close your eyes you might find yourself getting sleepy, again due to the conditioning of a lifetime of sleep. If you open your eyes you might find yourself looking around the room at things and losing your train of thought. The ancient Tibetan books say then that, if you leave your eyes open, you should try not to focus them on anything in particular: just let them stare out into the space in front of you, as if you were in a great daydream, and just looking off to nowhere. It's good though if you can turn your eyes downward a bit, with your eyelids down just a touch too.

Now that you're sitting correctly, how are you supposed to spend your silent time? And how long are you supposed to spend? Let's answer the second question first. It's good if you can spend fifteen to thirty minutes of silent time every day. And the "every day" part is important; these things don't work if you don't keep them up every single day, without a break. The best way to make sure you get your silent time every day is to do it *at the same time* every day. I used to commute into New York from central New Jersey at the same time every morning—the last half of the bus ride was a straight highway, with a little loop at the last minute going into the Lincoln Tunnel and then on to Manhattan. I would doze during part of the trip into New York, and wake up at exactly the same time every morning, right in front of the tunnel, to put on my tie and coat.

On the way home, it would be a nap during the first part of the ride to recover from the very hectic day and the lack of sleep from the night before; this would almost always start at the same time, say six-fifteen. This went on for over ten years, so that—even on my days off or during vacations—I would start to fall asleep wherever I was at exactly six-fifteen. The same thing started happening with lunch: We took our lunch break at one in the afternoon for so many years that, no matter where in the world I was or what I happened to be doing, I would start getting really hungry at 1 P.M. Eastern Standard Time. This same principle holds for your daily silent time.

Start carving out this time for yourself say at exactly 7 A.M. every day. At first, it's a little hard to get into the swing of things. You're not used to having the silent time, and you're not very good at it either. But if you just keep doing it at exactly the same time every day, it starts to become a reflex, like eating or sleeping. Then you get better and better at being silent until, after a while, it becomes your favorite part of the day.

Now how are we supposed to do this silent thing? When you look at a picture of His Holiness the Dalai Lama sitting and meditating in the morning, it may look like he's up to—absolutely nothing. But nothing could be further from the truth. From the beginning to the end of your silent time you go through a very specific series of mental exercises, much like a football player who has a regular routine at the gym. And by the time you get good at the silent time your mind, and your corresponding ability to run your business, is as sleek and swift and strong as any pro athlete.

When you first sit down, be sure to get absolutely comfortable. If you're not really comfortable when you first sit down, you can bet that you'll be squirming later. Adjust your position, making sure to get your back straight, and then just sit there for a minute or two, getting used to the silence. Try to be as quiet as physically possible. Try not to twitch at all. Bring your mind down slowly to your breathing, and start trying to count out ten slow, deep breaths—without holding your breath or forcing anything at all. Consciously try to shut down all the senses: Don't focus your eyes on anything, don't listen to anything, try not to smell breakfast waiting for you, and so on. When you succeed in reaching the tenth quiet breath, then you're ready to focus your mind on the issue you've selected for yourself today—it doesn't do you any good just to try to watch your breath the whole time, because this just calms you down for a while and collapses when you hit your first big problem of the working day.

The main silent time then should be dedicated to handling, in a very proactive and deliberate way, some problem that's keeping you from achieving success, either in your business or your personal life. Let's say you find yourself constantly grappling with business problem #18 from the first part of the book: Nobody in the firm, neither management nor rank-and-file, steps forward to help you when you need it in a crunch. Go down first into the silence of your mind, traveling along the road of counting your breaths, and stay there for a while, just enjoying the silence. Then consciously turn your quiet mind to your problem.

Think first of a specific instance in the last week or so (it won't be hard) when your problem came up again. Be careful not to generalize at this point: Actually think of a specific situation when someone failed to help you out when you needed it. Go into your mind and picture the exact day and place and time—see the room you were in, who you were sitting with, who else was standing nearby. Remember how you asked for the help you didn't get, and then carefully picture how it was refused. Remember the faces as the words were said, remember your feelings. Actually it takes a little self-control at this point not to get upset or angry over again, so be careful.

Next review the emptiness or potential that was present during the situation. Remember that this entails going over, in your mind, how different people were perceiving the event as it unfolded. The person who refused you help obviously didn't have a problem with the fact that you had a problem. In fact they probably didn't see it much as a problem at all. But you did; you saw it as a major problem.

This means that the problem wasn't, in fact, a problem from its own side—or else everybody present would have perceived it, equally, as exactly the same kind of problem. The fact though is that the problem was blank, or empty, or neutral: Some people saw it as a problem, and some didn't. This means that its *problemness* was coming from somewhere else—and as we have noticed before, there's not much choice except to say that it was coming from your own mind.

So were you just making up a problem where there wasn't any problem? Not at all. Just because your mind was making the problem a problem doesn't mean it wasn't a problem; in fact, this is exactly what makes anything a problem. And it doesn't mean either that, if you decided not to make it a problem, it wouldn't be a problem. It may be true that not getting the help you need is just a perception, but the perception and its ramifications are quite real: You won't be able to get done what you're supposed to get done, and management isn't going to take that lightly. You can wish all day that the problem wasn't a problem, and you could try to decide not to see the problem as a problem, but it is a problem, and it's going to hurt you.

Go next in the silence of the room and your mind to the source of the problem, which you now know is an imprint burned into your mind when, at some point in the past, you gave the same problem to someone else. After it was deposited in your brain the imprint swam around in the subconscious part of your mind, getting fatter all the time like a voracious fish, and then floated up to the conscious area when the moment was right. It colored, even created, your perceptions during the famous incident when you were refused the help. The villain was not the other manager or employee; it was yourself, and you're the one who's going to have to fix things too.

Now consciously take your mind ahead into the coming day and try to anticipate a similar situation that might come up. Try to imagine where you might be sitting, who you might be with, and what words might be spoken during the next incident where you're refused the help you need to do your job. Then do a little role-playing in your mind. Imagine how you used to react in a situation like this. Such and such a manager didn't help you out, and so you made a plan to make sure that they didn't get any help from your department in the coming weeks either.

But now you know that the "normal" reaction is the exact opposite of the right reaction. The minute you refuse someone else help in retaliation for not getting help, you burn a new imprint into your mind for seeing yourself refused the help you need in the future. So the last thing you want to do is shut down cooperation from your side when someone else has refused you their cooperation. In fact, you'd want to do the opposite: you'd want to plant an imprint for seeing yourself get the cooperation you need, next time. *And this can only be done by cooperating, unilaterally,* with the other person: giving them help even when they refuse to give it to you. Imagine what would happen if the whole world recognized that this was the best thing to do for everyone involved!

This kind of mental role-playing during your silent time is not just some noble sentiment. It's a very calculated exercise to bring you business and personal success. Some time during the next day or two, the situation you've imagined will actually happen. And you'll be ready for it when it comes. The behavior pattern set up by going over the logic of the situation, and planning how you're going to react to it this time, kicks in almost automatically. You begin to react the old way. The constant practice during your silent time makes you pause, and you remember to reach for the new way. The cycle of violence is broken at its heart: you refuse to perpetuate the failures of your life; you refuse to plant the imprints that will make you see them happen again.

You can see how this kind of quiet time can be very valuable for the workday you're about to start, and what a brilliant idea it was in ancient Tibet to practice dealing with problems before they even happen. The conducive atmosphere of your quiet time and place plants the seed very strongly in your mind to react the right way, and so the few minutes you spend in the morning during silence are an invaluable investment for the hours ahead.

There is a custom in Tibet to finish the silent time with a specific step. Take a few moments at the end to picture yourself exactly the way you one day hope to be. For example, imagine that you have already reaped the rewards of studying this book and the principles of potential and imprints.

Money is flowing in steadily; and the best thing is that you know exactly how it works, and exactly how to keep it coming. On top of this you know all the steps to take to make sure that, mentally, you also enjoy the money. And you are keeping your six-time book carefully, and observing your silent time in the morning, to deal with new problems immediately and make sure new ones don't crop up.

But don't stop here. Think to yourself: Is that really all you want to be? I don't think really that there's a human alive who wouldn't want to be more. Why don't we paint yourself not just rich, but also a successful philanthropist: You make a ton of money and you give away a lot too, and the world looks up to you as a man or woman who not only makes money but knows how to use it right too, how to help other people with it, and thereby get the ultimate satisfaction out of the money. And hey, why not picture yourself about as healthy as a twenty-year-old, because that's exactly how you'll get if you're careful to plant the imprints for this, by taking care of others' lives and health. Personally I'd throw in finally a bunch of really great personal qualities: loyal, sensitive, concerned, a person with total integrity, friend of anyone he or she meets, role model for all the children and other businesspeople in the country, good husband or wife, and father or mother; you know, the whole Boy Scout thing. Because this is what we'd all really like to be, deep down inside.

The Tibetan wise men say that this should be the last part of your silent time in the morning: picturing yourself as the most successful, and wise, and compassionate person you can imagine. Take a few minutes in the about-to-get-noisy silence just before you get up off the couch, and really work hard to see yourself as you could be. It plants a *very strong* imprint in your mind to get that way some time. You'll see. Now jump up and get off to work; you're probably late!

chapter 10

Staying Clear, and Healthier Each Year

༄༅། །དེ་ཚེའི་ཕྱིར་ཞེ་ན། རབ་འབྱོར། གང་གི་ཚེ་ཀ་ལྱིང་ཀའི་ རྒྱལ་པོས་ངའི་ཡན་ལག་དང་། ཉིང་ལག་རྣམ་པར་བཅད་པར་གྱུར་པ་ དེའི་ཚེ་ང་ལ་བདག་ཏུ་འདུ་ཤེས་སམ། སེམས་ཅན་དུ་འདུ་ཤེས་སམ། སྲོག་ཏུ་འདུ་ཤེས་སམ། གང་ཟག་ཏུ་འདུ་ཤེས་ཀྱང་བྱུང་ཞིང་། ང་ ལ་འདུ་ཤེས་ཅི་ཡང་མེད་ལ། འདུ་ཤེས་མེད་པར་གྱུར་པ་ཡང་མ་ཡིན་ པའི་ཕྱིར་རོ།

If you keep up your six-time book and your morning silent time, you'll soon find your workdays gradually changing. Slowly but surely, your refusal to perpetuate a cycle of negativity begins to clean up your world, bit by bit, corner by corner. First one problem goes, and then another; this irritating person becomes a friend; another is transferred; another moves to a different company, and in the end you begin to see yourself surrounded with people you enjoy, and work that is both stimulating and successful. The silent time in the morning, besides giving you ammunition for a whole lifetime of dealing with problems at work, also has the effect of making your mind much more contented and calm all the time.

In this and the next chapter then I'd like to go farther into how you can get the maximum enjoyment out of your success—and more specifically, how to make sure that your body is as healthy as your mind by the time you get good at all this. It's a sad fact of business life that by the time they've really "made" it in the corporate world many people have done so by sacrificing their health and their family life. Here we're going to talk a bit about how to have your cake and eat it too: how to be the most suc-cessful manager in the company, and at the same time the healthiest. Paradoxically, the best thing you can do to keep your body strong and young is to take care of your mind: to protect it from what the Tibetan masters call the "mental afflictions."

The definition of a "mental affliction" in ancient Buddhist philosophy is "any emotion which disturbs the peace of mind of the person who is feeling it." You might just call it a "bad thought." There are thousands of different kinds of mental afflictions, but in the end it boils down to six that are the worst: liking things in a wrong way; disliking things in a wrong way; pride; not understanding how things really work; lazy doubt about important truths; and wrong worldview.

Liking or disliking things in a "wrong" way has a specific meaning. Contrary to some mistaken presentations of the Buddha's thought, it's not at all wrong to like or dislike things. You're supposed to like your family, and your teachers, and goodness, for example; the Buddha likes to see us happy, and the Buddha dislikes the fact that we make ourselves so unhappy so much of the time. If you like something though in a way that makes you upset, or in a way that would impel you to hurt someone to get it for yourself, then this is a mental affliction: we call it "stupid" liking, because hurting someone else to get something for yourself is the best way *not* to get the thing for yourself.

The point here in this chapter though of learning about the mental afflictions is that they function to hurt your health from hour to hour, as you go through your day at the office. There are secret texts that were kept in the Himalayas which describe in more detail just how these negative thoughts affect your body; suffice to say that the very process of aging itself is tied intimately to these bad thoughts. That is, every time you feel upset at work, every time you are angry or irritated, every time you are jealous of another vice president or anything of the like, something inside your body is choked; a hair or two goes gray; a wrinkle deepens; your heart is strained a tiny bit more. In the end it all adds up, and causes you to get old and lose more of the strength you had as a youth. In the end, say these books, it is even responsible for your death.

The point of this chapter then is to give you some clues for dealing with these thoughts during the day. We'll start by returning to *The Dia-*

mond Cutter, at a point where the Buddha is describing an encounter he had gone through many lifetimes before. The story goes like this. The Buddha was a monk known by the name of "Teacher of Patience." He was out in the forest meditating with his back against a tree one day, in a place where the king of Kalingka and his entourage would go out on hunting parties. The queen and her own entourage had also gone out that day, to pick flowers and visit the woods while her husband and his hunters sought their quarry.

So the queen enters a clearing, and finds the meditating monk. She is deeply religious, and has been waiting for a chance to ask some important spiritual questions of a qualified master. So she interrupts the monk, who does his best to respond to each of her inquiries.

In the meantime, the king and his hunters are chasing a deer down—and it breaks into the very same clearing. The king looks down from his horse and sees his queen speaking earnestly with the monk; he assumes that there has been some monkey business going on, and orders his men to tie the holy man to stakes, spread-eagled on the ground. Then slowly he proceeds to cut off the monk's fingers, joint by joint, along with his toes and other parts of his body.

Here is how the Buddha describes the event in *The Diamond Cutter*; the wording is a little arcane, but don't get nervous—we'll go over it in detail and you'll get it perfectly by the time we're done with the chapter.

> **Why is it so? Because, O Subhuti, there was a time when the king of Kalingka was cutting off the larger limbs, and smaller appendages, of my body. At that moment there came into my mind no conception of a self, nor or of a sentient being, nor of a living being, nor of a person—I had no conception at all. But neither did I not have any conception.**

Here first we get Choney Lama's take on just what the Buddha is talking about; remember that words from *The Cutter* itself are in bold:

For what reason **is it so? Because** long ago **there was a time, O Subhuti, when the king of Kalingka** got the evil suspicion that I had engaged in relations with his woman. And so he **was cutting** off the larger limbs, and smaller appendages of my body. (The latter refers to the fingers and toes.)

At that moment I practiced patience, keeping my mind on an understanding of the lack of inherent existence within each of the three elements of the act of patience. As I focused on the "me" which exists nominally, **there came into my mind no conception** where I held any belief in some truly existing "me": and so I had no conception **of** anything from a truly existing **"self"** up to a truly existing **"person."**

At that moment **I had no conception at all** of any such conception that something was existing truly. At the same time though it was **neither** as if **I had no** other, nominal **conceptions** at all.

What Subhuti is saying here is the following. I did have the thought that I would have to keep my patience: I did have the thought to take the pain on willingly, and not to be upset about the harm being done to me. And I did have the kind of conception where I reconfirmed my knowledge of how I had perceived that no existing object has any true existence of its own.

The Buddha next begins to clarify himself:

⌒ **Why is it so? Suppose, O Subhuti, that at that moment any conception of a self had come into my mind. Then the thought to harm someone would have come into my mind as well.**

The conception of some sentient being, and the conception of some living being, and the conception of a person, would have come into my mind. And because of that, the thought to harm someone would have come into my mind as well. ⌒

Choney Lama clarifies:

Here is the reason **why it is so. Suppose that at that moment any conception of a self,** where I thought of "me" as existing in an ultimate way, **had come into my mind.** Or suppose any of the other conceptions mentioned had come into my mind. **Then the thought to harm someone would have come into my mind as well;** but the fact is that it did not.

It would seem then that the lines boil down to something like:

The king was cutting off my fingers and toes and other body parts, as punishment for something I hadn't done at all. If I had seen either one of us as persons, then I might have gotten angry, and the thought might have crossed my mind to try to hurt him. But I didn't have any such thought, and so I was able to keep myself from getting angry.

This is pretty heavy stuff. Just what's it got to do with not destroying your body at the office by indulging in negative emotions? We'll talk first about a couple of different ways that you could misunderstand these lines (and they have been misunderstood throughout the centuries), and then go on to explaining what they really mean.

There's one misperception going around that started with Buddhist books like this; with the ones that say there's no "self" or "person." People take it to mean that there's some kind of space you can go into when you're having a problem, a space which is just empty or where you see everything as unreal, and then the problem goes away, or you just don't attach yourself to the problem. People like this would say that if, for example, you were having a problem with someone who was angry at you, you could just sort of pretend the person wasn't there, or refuse to think about them, and then you wouldn't have any problem anymore. And they think this is what it means when we talk about "no self," which the Buddha goes on here to call "no sentient being, and no living being, and no person."

This isn't at all though what the Buddha has in mind, and it's not going to help you with your negative emotions at work either. It doesn't help for example to try to imagine that some negative experience simply isn't happening, or that somehow you aren't really experiencing it, or that you could somehow just detach yourself from it. When you're sitting there in a dentist's chair having a root canal drilled, and the dentist hits a nerve—or when you're staked out spread-eagle on the ground and someone is slowly cutting off your fingers and toes and the rest—it doesn't help to somehow imagine that he's not there and you're not here. Try it and see. It's not what the Buddha meant.

The part about "having no conceptions" is easy to misunderstand too. People have read lines like this and thought that the goal of a Buddhist trying to solve a difficult situation was to sit and try not to think about anything: to try to empty the mind of any thoughts at all, or maybe to see the thoughts going on but not listen to them or connect with them somehow. This wasn't at all what the Buddha had in mind either; you can try this too, next time you have a tooth drilled. It doesn't help. This is not the way to stop the pain. So what did the Buddha really mean?

Let's go to a real situation in the diamond business; your battlefield is going to be the boardroom or the factory floor, so we might as well take a real example from a real business. While I was working as a vice president at Andin, I used to go fairly often overseas to Asia to spend time at the Tibetan monastery where I did my studies. I worked out a deal with the owners, the Azrielants, where I would stay in touch by phone, and be ready to organize purchases of diamonds say from Bombay (not too far from the monastery) or Belgium.

"Staying in touch" at the time was no easy matter: the monastery was started in a few tents in the middle of a heavy forest in south India, after about a hundred surviving monks (our monastery originally had over eight thousand, most of whom were killed or forced to disrobe) escaped over the Himalayas during the invasion of Tibet. By the time I got there to start my studies there were a few hundred monks, and a modest assembly hall with simple cottages for the monks. The nearest phone that you could use to call the United States was in Madakeri, about a three-hour drive away. A short call to "stay in touch" then would take almost all day, if you could get through at all.

So I'm up in this little mud building at the top of a mountain in a forest in India, bending over an ancient phone, trying to hear what Ofer is yelling into the other end from his cushy glass offices overlooking the lights of the World Trade Center and the Hudson River:

"We need stones! Got a huge order! Gotta have ten thousand carats in

New York within ten days! Talk to Bombay! Talk to Antwerp! Get it going!"

Now ten thousand carats of these particular stones would mean maybe a million little diamonds; and for every one you actually buy on the market you might have to look at two or three. So you're talking checking a few million diamonds in ten days. Suppose it takes you ten seconds to pick up one stone and look at it with your magnifying glass. This means 6 stones a minute, and 360 stones an hour, per person. Suppose you can keep this up for five hours a day without frying your eyes out completely—you're talking maybe two thousand stones a day, max. So you're going to have to get at least a thousand man days out of your crew just to get close to finishing the order. So I ask again:

"Ten thousand carats, right, Ofer? You're sure—ten thousand?"

"Yes yes, right away; get on it tonight! Keep calling, wake everybody up around the world, it doesn't matter! Good luck!" Click.

I make a note in my diary about the quantity and the type of stone that's needed, and then proceed to spend several hours trying to reach all the international buyers around the world. By the time I leave the phone exchange on Madakeri it's almost dark; we walk out to a little garden overlooking a huge beautiful valley, enjoy the evening air and the smell of the wild Indian flowers, and watch the stars come out. I feel good, the good feeling of keeping a promise to do something even when it's a tremendous pain to do so. Then we pile into the rickety old monastery car and head back, for another week or so of intense studies with some of the greatest Lamas in the world.

About the time the diamonds pour into the New York headquarters from all over the world, I'm arriving too, dusty and sunburnt. Ofer calls me up to his office, and I saunter in with the self-confidence of an executive who's delivered the goods, despite the odds. I sit and wait for the congratulations to begin.

"What in the world is going on?" he starts.

"What do you mean?"

"What's with all the diamonds? Do you know what you're doing to the cash flow? What are you, crazy?"

You know the feeling. The sinking feeling. It's not just another miscommunication or business mistake—it's a whole statement on the condition of the world, our world. Why is it that things can't go right? I think you're getting an idea by now. But let's go on.

"Wait a minute, Ofer. You told me to buy them—you told me you needed ten thousand carats as soon as possible."

"Ten thousand carats! Are you kidding! I told you a thousand! What are you talking about? Why in the world would I order ten thousand carats!"

"But you *did* tell me to buy ten thousand. I remember, I asked you two or three times. I even made a note in my diary right there, while you were on the phone. Look, it's right here—it says ten thousand."

"How do I know when you wrote that? It could have been this morning! I never said ten thousand. Who would say ten thousand?"

In the study of negative emotions, when you're training in the art of avoiding the kinds of thoughts that will make you old before your time, this is the crucial moment. Business in general requires quick thinking and quick reflexes, but nothing compared to this. You probably have about three seconds to turn on your defenses before you get hit with some strong feelings of indignation, hurt, and anger. You will have to take action proactively, strong action, within these three seconds, or it will be too late. And the action is going to involve the "no-self" and the "no conceptions" that the Buddha just talked about. Except now we have to figure out what he really meant when he mentioned these things. Let's connect them to this real-life situation. We'll use the "three elements" that the Buddha mentioned with the monk who was getting his fingers chopped off by the king of Kalingka.

The "three elements" refer to three parts of the situation going on at this moment: the yelling boss (Ofer); the VP getting yelled at (me, unfortunately); and the fact that the whole event is taking place at all. Each one has its own emptiness, or what we've been calling "potential." In fact, there's a whole pile of emptinesses in this situation that are contributing to the mess, and which will contribute as well to the fix, which is why emptiness (the "potential") of things is so wonderful.

What's the potential in the boss? He seems pretty ugly at the moment, but remember that if his partner walked in—that is, his wife Aya—she'd say that he looks wonderful right now, saving the company from an irresponsible dumbhead who's gone wild buying diamonds we don't need and can't pay for. So he's not a monster *or* a genius from his own side, it just depends on who's looking; as we've said so many times before, he's just blank or empty on his part, and whether he seems good or bad at the moment depends purely on what kind of imprints I've put in my mind from the past.

Remember too the other thing we always mention at this point: That, although it's true that how he looks right now is something that's being conditioned and even created by my own mind, this doesn't at all imply that I can just wish him into a nice guy in the moment. And this is because I (unlike his wife) have imprints in my mind that are *forcing* me to see him as a very upset boss right now. The best I can do then is to be very careful not to plant any *new* imprints in my mind right now.

What kind of *new* imprints are we talking about? Well, how about an imprint to see a boss yelling at you for doing exactly what he told you to do? And how would a person get an imprint like this? Actually there's only one way to get this kind of imprint—and that would be to yell at someone like your boss, who's trying to address what he honestly believes is a serious and costly mistake. So what would be the *stupidest* thing to do at this moment, when you're getting yelled at? You've got it: yelling back.

If you let your mind go through this process, or even a significant chunk of this process, during the three seconds before frustration and anger sweep you downstream, a couple of things happen. First of all, you avoid a mental imprint that would give you a lot of trouble later. Imagine going to pick up a coffee on the edge of your desk and accidentally grabbing a cup of hydrochloric acid instead (something that could really happen in a jewelry factory if you were careless enough). You're having an animated conversation with someone so you don't notice; you raise the cup to your face; you start to tip it; and then at the last minute you catch a tiny whiff of the acid and set the cup down pronto, with a sigh of relief. The accomplishment of stopping your frustration and anger at the last minute—the victory of responding to your mind during the three-second window of opportunity and heading off your anger, and the time bomb imprint it's about to burn into your mind—is no less a relief.

Remember, a single moment of anger, a single moment of burning this kind of negative imprint into your mind, can lead to days or weeks or even longer periods in the future when you have to experience the result of this imprint in the world around you. When you are able to use this ancient wisdom to head off even a single instance of anger, then all the effort you've put into understanding the ideas in this book has more than paid off. You have just saved yourself from loads of trouble and pain; you have just taken a different road, and you will never have the accident you were going to have if you hadn't made that turn just now.

So what about the "no-self," and the "no conceptions"? Now that we've gone over an actual incident, these are easy. "No-self" means that your boss doesn't have any self-nature—no nature of his own, no nature coming from his own side, no nature that he was born with—of being a screaming unpleasant person, even at this moment. If he did have any nature like this, then even his wife would find him unpleasant right then—but she doesn't. So "no-self" means that whatever you see in him is coming from you, not from him. It doesn't mean he doesn't exist somehow, or that it would somehow be useful to pretend he's not quite there.

The "no conceptions" part means that you stop thinking about him the wrong way: Stop conceiving of him as being something that is bad from his own side, and start thinking of him as an empty screen, one that is filled with a hit movie for his wife, and one that's a horror movie for you right then. And the projector is, of course, your own mind, driven by the electricity called "imprints from what you've done to others in the past." Again, the point is not at all that it would be of any help not to think anything, not to judge anything as being good or bad, not to attach to any of your feelings or emotions. Remember: the entire event, and how you seem to yourself and others, and how your boss seems to you and others (these being the three elements), is certainly real. Real people will get hurt, real companies will suffer damage, real VP's will blow their next holiday bonus, but not for the reason you used to think caused them. It's all coming from things you did before.

So what's there to do now? It's one thing to understand clearly that—if you respond negatively at the end of the three seconds—you are going to plant some new negative imprints of the same flavor and have to eat them again later on. This we've covered already. But let's talk now about the immediate consequences of negativity: Let's face it, getting mad just doesn't help anything at all.

There's a famous verse from an ancient Indian Buddhist book that says,

> If a situation can be fixed,
> Why get upset about it?
>
> If a situation cannot be fixed,
> What's the use of getting upset?

We're talking here about the immediate benefit of refusing to give into anger. The main challenge has passed: You refuse to respond negatively, and thereby protect yourself from the same thing happening again in the future. Now go into your mind and refuse even an inkling of anger; in fact, go further, and wrestle your mind into a positive attitude. Instead of arguing about whose fault it was that the diamonds were bought, instead of fighting about who it was that messed up the cash flow, turn your mind immediately to the solution of the present moment. Here is perhaps the most important point of the whole exercise in this context: *You'll find that, because you fought the anger off even before it got fully into your mind, you're able immediately to turn all your energy to solving the problem.* Your mind is clear. Your face is calm. Your heart is beating normally, your breath is steady.

This is how you want to be when you deal with a serious problem, and this is absolutely the best thing for your body and your long-term health. Every time you refuse another few moments of anger or any other negative emotion, you are tacking onto your life and your business career several more hours of health and happiness, because it all adds up at the end. And for your immediate business it's just a lot more intelligent to attack your problems with a completely clear and calm state of mind.

A final note of advice. You've probably noticed by now that the whole approach presented in this book is very similar to gardening. Our premise is that problems are created by seeds or imprints you have planted in your mind in the past. Once these imprints have reached a certain level of power, once they are going off or about to go off and grow into a plant, it's essentially too late to do much about them. Conversely, it's naive to think that you can plant a seed in the morning and expect much of a result by the evening.

The point is that you should train yourself, in advance, to view the immediate results of your actions with a grain of salt. You may be able to calm your own mind immediately and be ready to deal with a problem with cool rationality, but this doesn't at all mean that everyone else in the room will calm down. *Nor does it mean* that the solution you come up with in your cooled-down state of mind is necessarily going to work: Don't forget that this depends upon seeds planted long ago. *It does mean* though that you are gardening for your future—*it does mean* that fewer and fewer tense situations will be happening in your world to come.

chapter 11

The Circle, or Working
for the Long Term

We've seen in the last chapter how watching your mind and avoiding negative emotions not only makes for a rosier future reality but also contributes in a major way to both your immediate physical well-being and your long-term health as you continue through the years of your corporate career; not to mention that it just makes every day at work much more enjoyable, if you can fight down and eventually beat completely every negative state of mind.

I'd like to describe in this chapter another trick that the great Tibetan wise men use to maintain their physical health, and a high degree of mental creativity, over the very long term. It's not at all unusual to find Tibetan monks in their sixties and seventies who display an ever-increasing intellectual appetite and curiosity, and who are physically able to maintain long hours and skip down stairs in a way that people in the West have lost by the time they're forty. The trick is called *tsam*.

Tsam in Tibetan means "border" or "dividing line," and the word is used to describe the art of getting away from your work every once in a while—going off somewhere else and, in a sense, drawing a circle around yourself where you can sit quietly and think for a bit.

During the more than fifteen years that I worked at Andin International, I followed the rule of the Circle. I had a strict policy, kept with the agreement of the owners, that I would always be off on Wednesdays, so I could get some distance between me and the office for thinking and seeking inspiration. In the beginning, I asked for and accepted a penalty in my salary for this time. Later on, when the benefits of the Circle became clear, my salary caught up with those who were not out once a week. We chose Wednesday because it would be least disruptive to the administrative needs of my job: I always had two days in a row, whether Monday/Tuesday or Thursday/Friday, to deal with a negotiation or a personnel problem that might stretch longer than a single day.

As a practical measure, I also developed a very strong second-in-command; this gave me freedom to go to the Circle and bring back the strength I found there as a contribution to the firm. It also gave our division a high degree of administrative power, which was useful especially in peak production times. People were accustomed to accepting direction on major issues from either me or my second, and so administratively it was less of a strain whenever we suddenly had to expand the labor pool by 20 or even 30 percent.

This by the way is a common phenomenon in the diamond and jewelry industry, since some 60 percent of all sales are connected with the Christmas season. We would be manufacturing up to eight or ten thousand rings per week in the autumn, and then have to shrink to one or two thousand after the New Year. All this means that you must be able to expand and contract your staff radically from month to month, and have the leadership power in place to deal with a division that might be twice as big as the one you had six months before.

It's important not to view the day spent in the Circle as just a rest day, a perk for a hardworking executive—although it did help me, with a two-hour commute both ways, to deal with the physical pressure of getting in and out of Manhattan every day. Circle days were, rather, strictly organized and executed, for maximum benefit. The whole idea is to break up the usual routine; to get some time to think about *why* rather than *how* with the work at work—time to plan, time to reflect, and perhaps most important *time to get new input*, new sources of inspiration.

During my time at Andin I interviewed and hired hundreds of people, most of whom were quite successful. I looked of course for the usual qualities: integrity, loyalty, team spirit, consideration for others, intelligence, and honesty. To tell you the truth I wasn't very often concerned about actual *skill*. My experience is that the human mind is so powerful that you can teach anyone how to do just about any job in the world fairly quickly, but it takes years to break bad personal habits and characteristics like lying or a lack of concern for others, and these ruin a worker long before any lack of technical skill.

One hiring trick though that I would like to share with you was the free-time test: I found out that the most important question you could ask a person was what they did with their free time. Andin is a hard place to work, and the hours—especially during the busy holiday season—can be brutal. The more hours you spend in a place, the less hours you spend someplace else. And there's a limit to how many new things you can learn around the same people in the same room, month after month.

If you never go anyplace else—if you never see anything new, if you never talk to anyone new—then your creativity is sure to suffer. And it's no exaggeration to say that a few minutes of true creativity creating new systems can be much more profitable to any company than weeks or even months of extra hours put in by managers stuck in the old system. So it's worth it to spend some time to find out what kind of creative input a potential employee is normally exposed to in their free time outside of work.

I found personally that almost everyone who answers "Mostly just watch some TV" to the question about their free time makes a very uninspired employee. Those who read a lot of books (except romance novels) often make thoughtful and creative employees. Those who write prose, and especially poetry, have great imaginations and can find original solutions to problems pretty easily. Young parents, by the way, have to be exempt from this question because they rightfully answer only that they spend all their free time taking care of their child—and by the way, children are one of the greatest sources of creative inspiration. It seems, finally, that people who devote any serious time to serving others in their free time—people who help out at a church, or who coach kids at Little League, or do a little volunteering at the local hospital on the weekends—are the most stable and creative employees of all.

Anyway, the point is that, much more than anyone imagines at all, it is essential for an executive to have a second life of some kind or another—a consuming second passion, whether it be writing or photography or sports or volunteering—in order to bring to the table new sources of creativity. I can remember, for example, coming back from a longer Circle session (which I'll describe later in this chapter) and sitting in front of a diamond stock box (something like a shoe box with a million dollars' worth of sparklies inside) and looking at the diamond papers as if they were something I'd never seen before.

These are little bits of folded paper that people have been using to keep diamonds in throughout the centuries; there's a trick to folding them the right way, as you might have assumed, so the stones don't fall out—but the basic shape hasn't changed I would guess for centuries. Neither has the way you write on the outside what's on the inside. Up at the top there's a general description of what's in the paper, say "quarter carat rounds." Somewhere around the middle maybe is some indication of the quality, like "white naats, J color." Down in the bottom right-hand corner is the weight of the packet of stones, down to the hundredth of a carat: for example, "10.27 carats." And of course somewhere under the inside flap is a tiny code with the price of the stones: something like ZLD4 might stand for "asking price $2,000; selling price $1,800; and don't take less than $1,600 under any circumstances."

Now in the old days of jewelry companies, there was a rule that a person who took a stone out of the parcel would make a mark on the inside flap, something like "CM took 3 stones to make ring samples, on 8/4." When the paper ran out of diamonds somebody might try to roughly add up all the stones and see if it made sense, but mostly nobody would pay much attention unless it was obvious that diamonds were missing. So I'm staring at a whole box of these papers from the new perspective I got from the Circle, from the weekly time off, and it gives me a new idea.

The idea went on for about thirty-six hours; I couldn't sleep much, and kept adding more details. The basic concept was that the paper would be preprinted before it was folded, with special lines that would force the diamond stock clerks to make some kind of entry, and write down the balance of remaining stones, automatically, whether they felt like it or not. When people ran out of lines, they were also forced to change the paper, and check the count and weight of the remaining diamonds at that point. I purposely made the lines thick so that the papers used most often (and thus in the hands of more people) would be checked more frequently.

Then we had the idea to color-code the papers, so that within a few weeks there was a whole rainbow of stone papers floating around the division. This way you didn't have to pick up the paper to see what quality or shape it was, and people could easily remember not to mix different colors together (a disaster when you're dealing with about a dozen slightly different shades of stones). A few hours later we came up with the idea of printing the papers in such a way that they were prepunched and could be flattened out and kept in binders after using; this way we had a permanent record of the actual signature of who had taken each stone from inventory, and an automatic backup to our computer inventories in case they went down or were corrupted.

Next we went on to play with the size of the papers; stripes on them for different cuts; and a lot of other innovations that made our inventory systems and loss control the most sophisticated in the stone business. And this, again, is one of the few places in the international diamond industry where you can definitely carve out more profit than the next guy, since the raw material is largely handled by a monopoly (no real deals are available) and the skilled cutting labor is pretty much fixed around the globe.

It was a very rewarding experience later to sit in little gemstone offices around the world and see that they had copied (and often improved upon) the system we had come up with. If over the years this inventory security method has saved even a single percent of the cost of the diamonds at Andin, we're talking millions of dollars of extra profit. And it all came from a day in the "Circle," a day away from work to get a fresh look at the work. It never ceased to amaze me how some other companies would try to squeeze every hour of free time out of their managers, and then be surprised when they were so exhausted that they never had any new ideas, or were never exposed to anything (other than the same old office) that could inspire these new ideas in the first place. So now you're sold on the *idea* of the Circle; let's see how you actually do it.

There are some basic rules for planning a day in the Circle. The most important is that the Circle should take place regularly, on the same day each week or every other week, and that this time should be *inviolable*. That is, if you choose Wednesdays for your Circle day, you should *never* break down and do normal work on a Wednesday. The reason for this is quite simple. Most capable people in the corporate world are addicted to work. They will work whether they really have to work or not, and this work will always be somewhat more than they could ever possibly finish.

This keeps the day interesting—keeps the adrenaline flowing and—as any executive knows—the adrenaline is completely addicting.

People would stay at Andin for years even after they could have easily gotten a higher salary elsewhere, just because the company was always growing and there were always challenging peaks to climb, every day of the year. You might think that the idea of the Circle sounds great, and you might even try it on two or three Wednesdays in a row, but you can be sure that you'll find an excuse to be back in the office for some "really big" emergency by the end of the month; and it's all downhill from there. Like so many of the other deep practices and concepts described in this book, the idea of the Circle *cannot work* unless you undertake it in a steady and persistent way. It's essential, at the beginning, that you buy into the concept that—*if you stop working for a day in the middle of your working week*—you will return to the office with great ideas that will pay for the time you took many hundreds of times over.

To hear these great ideas whispered into your mind while you're in the Circle, it's essential that you be *silent*. The first half of the Circle day, say the time up to 2 P.M. in the afternoon, *must* be spent by yourself, alone, in silence. No telephones, no TV, and none of the other kinds of noise that keep you from hearing the great ideas you have in your mind: no radio, music, newspapers, magazines, novels, kids, spouse, repairmen, or pets. Go to your quiet space, the place we talked about in the last chapter, and just sit there by yourself, silently.

It's really rather disconcerting for most busy executives to spend their time this way. The first natural reaction is this overwhelming sensation that you are wasting your time: The people at the office are slaving away, running here and there, maybe talking on two phones at once and putting out fires all over the company, while you sit here doing nothing. On top of that you have this big proposal due the next morning, and there's very little chance you'll get to it; it's also for one of the most important customers, and here you are blowing that last block of free time you have to deal with it.

Or else the spouse and friends and kids will start planning things for you to cover, knowing you're going to be at home all day. "If you're just going to be sitting around Wednesday morning, I don't see why you couldn't drop by the bank and be home for the parcel delivery—we're not talking anything more than half an hour." Tell them all to get lost. The Circle has to be a space of complete silence and concentration; it doesn't work if you get interrupted there, even if the interruption is only for a few minutes. You are reserving some of the rare, precious, irreplaceable moments of your life to go into the silence of your mind and find deeper answers to the challenges of both your business and your life. *Never* make the mistake of thinking that it's not worth it. You are not only unlocking the deeper creativity of your mind but you are proactively preventing a whole pile of health problems that you would have had otherwise, if you hadn't had the foresight to break the old pattern. And it doesn't take a genius to see where this old pattern leaves you. Go read the obituaries in any single issue of the *New York Times* and see how many smart and talented businesspeople worked themselves to death. Don't think you can't be the next.

After about an hour to an hour and a half of just silence sitting still in your quiet place, then do some kind of light exercise. The ancient Tibetan books say that, on a very subtle and profound level, the body and the mind are linked: the heavier and less erect your body becomes, the harder it is for the subtle energies of thought itself to flow. The traditional exercises for businesspeople around the United States have been things like golf or jogging or light weight-lifting, that sort of thing. These are fine; find the one that fits you the most and do it, because you'll be much more likely to continue with something if you enjoy it. Remember again that we *are not* talking about exercise for the sake of exercise, or just for some kind of vanity. If your body is healthy, your mind is clearer; if your mind is clearer, your business goes better; and (as we'll see later on) a *really* clear mind can transcend the limitations of the normal motivations for business: that is, you learn to go beyond the realm of mindless moneymaking and move into the realm of *meaningful* moneymaking.

Just a note: You might want to try some of the more exotic forms of exercise, ones that actually have a more powerful effect on your mind than for example just running around a track. I've met a number of businesspeople in recent years who have broken through the "embarrassment" barrier and attended classes in yoga, tai-chi, or even modern dance. I'm not talking here about the department-store version of these disciplines, where you dabble for a few weeks and never really get good at anything. Take the time, and spend the money, to get a real master of one of these arts to take you on as a personal student, and get some one-on-one training. Make and maintain a close relationship with a real expert over months and years. Learn to apply the discipline that you use in conducting your business to keeping your body running smoothly—again, not for looks, but for higher purposes.

Shake up your food schedule too on your Circle days; try, for example, only drinking liquids up till around 1 or 2 P.M. Your morning silent time will go much better, and so will the exercise, although you may want to take some juice before your exercise. Before you eat your first meal, sit quietly for a time and read some kind of thoughtful book about the higher meaning of your life—it could be a piece by someone like Gandhi or Schweitzer or the Pope or the Dalai Lama, the Bible, or anything of the like, but something that addresses the *purpose* of our existence, rather than just the *means* of existing, or making a living. Being around minds like this during your silent time is part of the whole idea of the Circle—escaping the very limited pool of understanding in your immediate office area at work, and exposing your mind to the very best thinkers of whole centuries. The quietness you have put yourself into enables you to hear what your mind is whispering to you, and some steady reading of the great minds and hearts of our world makes the whispers ever more meaningful.

After a light lunch, don't be embarrassed to take a nap if you feel the need. The appropriate amount of sleep for your own personal needs is listed in the great books of ancient India along with things like food and quiet concentration as one of the four types of physical sustenance; catching up on this need during your Circle day will not only refresh your mind but also invigorate your body, compensating for the wear and tear it gets from stress at work.

Later in the afternoon do some kind of practical study; this could be learning photography or computers or gardening, but the idea is that it shouldn't be directly "practical" for your regular job. In other words, you can't spend this time mastering a database that you want to use the next day in your work, but you could spend it putting together a home computer from a kit. Again it's best if you can get out of the house and do this study side by side with someone who's really good at it; the best kind of inspiration comes from live human beings who have mastered whatever they do, whether it's flowers or music or a craft. The point is to be exposed to creativity and excellence—the benefit comes more from learning to *think* like and have the *passion* of a master, than from being good at whatever he or she is teaching you.

In the evening make a conscious effort to get out and *help* somebody, at anything. It could be a children's sports team, it could be an elderly neighbor, it could be your spouse or family. There is a selfishness that comes with being the career breadwinner in the house, something that says that—if you are going out to a corporate job every day to support the family—you are then exempt from helping out with the more mundane tasks; whether they be with your family, or around the house, or especially with members of the community around you. People who make hundreds of dollars an hour at their corporate jobs feel as though driving old people to the grocery store in the evening—a job that anybody on minimum wage could do—is somehow a waste of their time and talents. They are more likely to serve on the board of a large local charity.

But this misses the point. Going into the Circle on our day off *is meant to get us out of the rut of a single corporate mind-set*, and getting out like this can go in a number of different directions. We are consciously trying to take our minds off the technical details of what we do and simply expose our minds to fresh resources of creativity: Silence, great thinking from the past, and then *perhaps most important* to take our minds out of the self-centered focus in which we spend so much of our corporate day. In other words, we are invigorating our souls and intellects not only by spending a day away from our repetitive patterns of business thinking *but also by spending a day away from concentrating on ourselves*.

For this, there is nothing like the everyday service of those around us who need us. This has been the greatest source of inner strength and creativity throughout recorded history for all the greatest beings to walk this planet; you should understand this fact, appreciate it, and then make a conscious effort to *take yourself outside of yourself* by providing free, personal, and not so glorious plain old help to those around you who need it, either because they are old, or poor, lonely, whatever. According to the wisdom of the East, there is *nothing* that will give you more power in your corporate work the following day.

At the end of the Circle day, as you get close to going to bed and the house and family quiet down, go back for some more silent time in your quiet place. This is the time to review the day and your thoughts and finish up your six-time book. Try not to think much about work and the things you will have to face the next morning; the trick here is to let the silence and the outside creative influences work on your mind all the way through the night and your sleeping hours, without thinking about the details of the next day. The inspiration you've set up will come to you the next day, when you need it; the seeds for it need the quietude of your sleep time as well, in order to grow to their fullest.

A last note here about your Circle days: it would seem that it's the time off, the hours of quiet and reflection, that gives you the creativity of the following day or two. But as we both know after all the wisdom of *The Diamond Cutter* we've been through already, the inspiration that "just happens" to you the next day has very specific causes, and these are the imprints you've put in your mind by the clear silence, and the closeness to great minds, and the willing service of others around you. It's not really anything different than what we've already talked about; in fact, nothing productive ever happens at all, unless an imprint from something good you did in the past forces you to see it happening. We are always in the business of gardening for the future.

So that's what we call a Weekly Circle. There's another kind of Circle that was really one of my greatest secret weapons throughout my entire career as a vice president at Andin. This is the Forest Circle, and you have to try it. There is no more powerful way to penetrate deeply into the future of your business career, no more powerful way to make the major leaps in your business that have to happen faster for you to reach your ultimate goals.

For the Forest Circle you first have to negotiate at least two weeks away from work. And we're not talking about normal vacation time here; this has to be *in addition* to vacation. Now how are we going to get this kind of time?

To get the time, first you have to believe in what you're going to do with it. We eat, for example, three times a day not because we need to, but because we really want to. Monks in the Buddhist tradition take a vow to spend the greater part of the day without eating; rather than being weak or thin, this custom makes the majority of the monks in a Tibetan monastery strong, light, and mentally very sharp. We find time to eat three times, we find the food and the place to eat three times, simply because we believe in it. If you *believe* in the Forest Circle, you will find a way to get the time off to do it: This again is the power of the human mind.

Let me tell you what you do in the Forest Circle, then we'll discuss strategies for getting the time off. It's important first to make sure that you have a clear cutoff date for your normal work—that you *stop* working on a certain day at a certain time. If you're any kind of executive by now, this is going to be extremely difficult the first time you do it. You got where you are because you know how to work and you like to work, and the projects you have lined up are all moving at a certain demanding velocity. It takes great wisdom to get them all detoured into other people's hands, delayed for the two weeks, or gracefully terminated all by the final hour you're in the office. But when the Friday afternoon comes for your Forest Circle, leave the work behind—physically and mentally. *Never* fall into the trap of "just another day" or even "just another hour" to finish that *very important* last step in a project. You *have to* think clearly up to the last minute at work, understand clearly just *why* you are going to do the Forest Circle. And it's because, if the Circle is successful, you'll come back to work with more than enough new ideas and creativity and energy to compensate even for a few projects that got hurt a bit when you took off and left them to go to the Circle.

To do the Forest Circle you have to find a place that's totally alone and quiet. Something like a cabin out in the woods, or at the shore in the off-season; outside of a city or town is best, a place where you can walk and not meet anyone, where no one will be knocking on the door for anything, and there are no traffic noises or anything of the kind. When you get to the place, clean out all the normal sources of stimulus: pack books or magazines or newspapers away into boxes; put the TV and any radios into a closet where you'll really have to work to get them out in a weak moment; and don't accept any mail or visitors at all.

This by the way is the key that makes the Forest Circle really work: you must have the ultimate kind of silence, the kind that comes in your mind when you're totally alone. Plan things so that you won't have to meet or talk to anyone: Make sure your family and friends understand this point clearly. Unplug the phone or better yet find a place that never had a phone anyway. Buy enough groceries to last the whole two weeks, and don't make any trips to town. The very best kind of place to do the Forest Circle is somewhere where you won't even see a sign of human life—no cars, no kids, not even any campers. Remember, this is not a vacation—it is a serious attempt to reach some of the higher things within you, and this journey is most powerfully done by yourself.

So now you're off by yourself—what are you supposed to do? Set up a good quiet place, as we did for the Weekly Circle—a special part of the house or room that's only for your silent time, and nothing else—better not to eat there, better not to have it close to where you'll be sleeping. The energy of the spot has to be dedicated to one purpose, and that's your silent time. It doesn't by the way have to be a formal meditation seat on the floor or anything of the like; a comfortable chair, with a back that forces you to sit up straight, is just fine.

A very basic schedule for the day would be to alternate between an hour or so of complete silence, just thinking about the larger issues of your life and your work; an hour in quiet study of those great minds and hearts we mentioned (including perhaps a study of the principles presented here, especially the part about business problems and their real solutions); an hour of quiet walks outside or some other exercise; and an hour of some light meal and some rest. It's important to eat very healthy and very light—lots of greens and protein-rich foods, while avoiding sugars and carbohydrates, which tend to dampen the creative energy you can get in the Forest Circle. If the quiet gets to be a little much and causes a bit of anxiety or light-headedness, make sure you're getting enough exercise, and eat some greasy or oily foods like macaroni and cheese, buttered popcorn, or lasagna.

After a day of this regimen you'll find yourself having the same doubts about the Forest Circle that you had about the weekly one—for a busy executive, it's hard to overcome the sensation that you're wasting your time *because you're not doing anything*. It is absolutely essential at these moments to recall what you're really up to. The silence and absolutely avoiding *any work at all* force all your creative energy within. You've literally never done this before in your adult life; never forced your mind within by purposely depriving it of any outer stimulation. What you will find happening is that your mind works in broad strokes of creativity and power on the broader problems of your work and family; answers are framed below the conscious mind in the silence, and will come to you in a flash of insight perhaps five days or a week hence. Relax and trust the process; it's worked for hundreds of thousands of wise men in the East over the past few thousand years, and it'll work for you. But you have to give it a try.

Remember to bring a little notebook with you to act as a diary or journal, and spend a lot of time with it. Talk to it. Write down all the little ideas you have at the beginning of the Forest Circle, and be ready for some major attacks of inspiration and insight after the first ten to twelve days. Also learn to expect some down days around a week into the Circle—this is a normal phenomenon, and is part of the process. The good side of your mind and the negative side of your mind are both enhanced and intensified during the Forest Circle, so you'll find yourself obsessing about the kindness of your family and about the lateness of your principal supplier, alternately. Learn to go with the first, and not get thrown off balance by the second.

The last three or four days of the Forest Circle are a special time to review your work and life in an overall way. Devote a certain part of each day to writing out all the great ideas you've had for your projects, and then begin designing your new daily schedule, with a short, do-able list of life resolutions. Under the influence of the silence, your mind will be working more clearly and strongly than ever before—and certain changes in your lifestyle, work, and home situation will suggest themselves almost automatically. It's important to realize that this may be one of the only times in your adult life that your mind is really working with full precision and clarity; you *must* recognize this fact, trust it, and trust "your life after the Circle" to the decisions and resolutions that come to you during the Circle.

Later, when you go back on the express train of your home and work life, some of the life and business decisions you made in the Circle will seem unrealistic, even naive. Don't believe it. This is how the vision born of silence looks to a mind that has gone back to the world of noise. The whole point of the Forest Circle is to return ready to create a new world, and new worlds are not built without a little risk and courage.

Just a final note about all the good ideas you're going to have in the

Forest Circle: Remember that they too, like the outside things around you, are coming from imprints you planted in your mind in the past by being good to others. These imprints swim up faster to the conscious mind in the very conducive atmosphere of silence and introspection; they're helped along by the peaceful thoughts you normally have out in nature by yourself. It doesn't hurt at all, in the week or two *before* you go out to the forest, to make a special effort to deal with your fellow workers and family members in an especially thoughtful and kindly way, and to resolve any personal issues you have open at the time. Then you have the right imprints in your head going into the Circle; and they are sure to ripen there.

By the way, we promised some suggestions here on how to get the time off. To put it bluntly, the only way you're going to get an extra two weeks is to offer to pay for it—that is, offer to have that much money (or a bit more) cut off your salary. This is a lot easier in a private company than a public one, but the general principle holds true that—if you are personally willing to make a sacrifice and are determined enough to go to the Forest Circle—you will find a way to do it. Keep your mind on the fact that it's not just your career at stake; it's your health, your peace of mind, your happiness, and your creativity. It's more than worth a couple of weeks of salary, and your boss or supervisor will appreciate your seriousness if you are willing to take a strong cut in exchange for the time.

Whenever I took time for the Forest Circle especially I would go and offer to take a cut for the time, an offer which was graciously accepted! Anyway it really sends management a message that you believe in what you're trying to achieve with the Circle. You're also going to have to get your family's permission for the time off, and in either case an important consideration is how well you can make arrangements for coverage of your regular responsibilities, so that there is no imposition on your fellow workers or spouse and children. It's important that everyone understands your goals, and that everyone supports the Circle experience wholeheartedly; the energy then is much better, and success more likely. This doesn't mean though that you shouldn't go ahead with the Circle if you get a little initial resistance—it's not just a luxury or a spare-time thing. We're talking inner work that will help determine whether your entire life and career are successful and beneficial to all those around you, even if at first they don't see it that way. So be strong and decisive. It's to help everyone.

There are some more details about the Forest Circle that are best learned live, as in sports where you learn most effectively from a living, breathing coach. If you're serious about using the Weekly Circle or the Forest Circle to put a rocket booster behind your life and your career, check out the "Resources for Going Deeper" section at the end of the book, to get in contact with DCI staff who can guide you through a session or two.

chapter 12

The Emptiness

of Problems

A discussion of how to keep your body and your mind healthy while you make your new money wouldn't be complete without the ancient Buddhist technique called "turning problems into opportunities." This can be done on two levels: the immediate and the ultimate.

Do you remember the story back in Chapter 10 where we bought the ten thousand carats of diamonds and almost bankrupted the company? The point back there was to deal successfully with intense criticism coming from your boss, to try to stop your own anger and frustration, even before they have time to form fully in your mind, during the first few seconds of getting yelled at. The immediate result there was that you left the boss's office with a clear state of mind, equipped and ready to deal with the problem at hand and fix it. The long-term result was that you stopped putting new imprints in your mind to see an angry boss: Your office life is going to get smoother and smoother from here on out.

So suppose we do walk out of the office cool—what to do about the extra ten thousand carats of diamonds though? In an immediate sense here you protect your mind, and in the long run prevent new wear and tear on your body, by putting your thoughts right away on the emptiness or hidden potential inherent in any problem. This emptiness means that the problem is a problem only so long as your imprints make you perceive it as a problem. And the mere fact of *knowing* about this emptiness allows you to turn any problem into an opportunity.

It's important at this point to realize that the ten thousand carats can be *validly and correctly* viewed either as a problem or the beginning of a new opportunity. Viewing them as a problem already makes you nervous; it puts you in a defensive position mentally and quashes your creativity. Decide that you must have had a killer idea last week and needed the ten thousand carats to pull it off; it's just that now you can't remember what your great idea was. So just figure it out.

A common strategy that we used to use at Andin was to back-design a product to fit the raw material we had overbought by accident. Not panicking in these types of situations means that you avoid tying up precious creative mental space (which would delay your having the idea that's going to solve the problem); it also prevents negative imprints that would, over the next few days and weeks, float up to the conscious mind and actually block your perception of the opportunity. So it's important to stay cool and concentrate on remembering, just what was it that I was going to do with those ten thousand carats? Suppose all the stones are these little dishwater brown mélange, or a mishmash of all kinds of shapes and cuts. These are the hardest thing to sell off on the market; little rocks that used to end up studding the tips of oil well drills—that is, until the resourceful Indian diamond dealers figured out a way to cut them cheap. And now they're going into the famous "one-carat heart."

This piece is a godsend to diamond dealers and jewelry firms that get stuck with large quantities of mishmash stones; and we at Andin took the concept to its highest expression. It goes like this. First you throw all the stones (and we're talking a *million* diamond chips here) into the diamond sieves, bash at the tiny iron cylinders all day long with little metal bars, and force the diamonds through a series of little holes that—in the end—direct all the microscopic brilliants of the same size into the same little pile. Then you do some very fine work with ultrasensitive diamond scales to figure out the average weight of each stone in each pile (remember you're talking something around one *millionth* of a pound per diamond).

You get about five piles laid out like this, with stones that are only microscopically different in size. Then you bring in a raw gold pendant with fifty tiny holes cast into it all over the place, in little cups; the whole thing comes out as a roughly heart-shaped collection of diamond chips set deep into yellow gold, which bleeds off some of the dishwater brown of the stones. You sit there with a calculator and figure out what combination of fifty stones from the five piles would come out perfectly with a weight of 99.5 percent of a carat, or whatever the legal minimum weight for a "carat" is at the time. The result at the end of the day is an exquisite, sparkling diamond creation that you can offer for a very good price because of the precision of control in the ingredients: in the gold and the diamonds. And the bottom line is that, when the piece hits big at the stores, you have just turned the ten-thousand-carat mistake into a ten-thousand-carat coup. You know how it goes after that. The boss tells you to go out and get another ten thousand carats of exactly the same stuff, and maybe you can't repeat.

But the point of the exercise is clear. Every existing object in the world is empty. This means that no object in the world is good or bad from its own side; one man's meat is another man's poison. An object *becomes* good or bad according to your perceptions, and these perceptions are dictated very precisely by the good or bad imprints you put in your mind in the past. Problems are not problems from their own side; rather, there is something in your mind making you see the problem as a problem. *Every problem* can be turned into an opportunity, because no problem is a problem in and of itself.

Try this exercise. The next time a business problem comes up, the next time a competitor gives you some kind of problem, pretend that the whole competing company is made of fairy godmothers who can see the future, who love *your* company, and who are trying to make you a big success. To do so, they see that they have to push you in a different direction than the one you've been going in. To get you to go in that direction, they have to block your progress in the old direction. Instead of feeling worried or upset that what you expected to happen isn't happening, open yourself completely to the new direction—try to see the new road where they want you to go, rather than looking back with longing at the old familiar path.

Is this way of looking at the situation realistic? Maybe yes, maybe no. It doesn't really matter. The end result is the same, in either case. Getting upset and concerned puts negative imprints in your mind; and the mental space it takes to get upset means that there is much less space for creative solutions. It can only make things worse. Concentrating on how to discover the hidden opportunity in the problem invigorates your mind and plants only positive imprints—imprints that will make you see a success in the future. So it makes perfect sense to go ahead and *see* things this way.

At the beginning of this chapter we talked about two levels of turning problems into opportunities: the immediate and the ultimate. The ultimate opportunity that you can derive from *every* problem is insight into the hidden potential of all things in the first place: their emptiness. How does this work?

Problems themselves are the highest opportunity we can ever have. If things go well all the time, says the wisdom of ancient Tibet, it's the worst thing that can happen. This is because we never question why things are really happening to us as long as things are good. You never see people tearing at their hair and crying, "Why did it happen to me?" about something good that has happened to them. It takes trouble for us to think about where things are really coming from.

Nothing is more sad, nothing is a greater problem waiting to happen, than a company or an executive who has become complacent, who has had success too long, too steadily. Things always change, and complacency is not a place from which people undertake the deep and difficult search for why things really happen. So it is not just a noble sentiment to say that the fact of problems is itself our greatest opportunity. Pain pushes us to find out what really drives the world around us, and if it leads us to discover the laws of the hidden potential and imprints, it is the best thing that ever could have happened to us.

goal three

Looking Back,

and Knowing

It Was Worth It

Shirley

ཨོཾ། །སྐར་མ་རབ་རིབ་མར་མེ་དང་། །སྒྱུ་མ་ཟིལ་བ་ཆུ་བུར་དང་། །རྨི་ལམ་གློག་དང་སྤྲིན་ལྟ་བུ། །འདུས་བྱས་དེ་ལྟར་བལྟ་བར་བྱ།

Our journey through the wisdom of *The Diamond Cutter* has taken us through two great lands so far. One is the world of the hidden potential and imprints in the mind—the fabric of the very reality around us, made of a blank screen on which our perceptions project pictures of business and personal success or failure, dependent entirely upon how we have behaved toward others in the past. In short, we have learned where money really comes from, and we have been given a truly foolproof method for getting it.

Money by itself is completely meaningless if we cannot enjoy its use; and we have learned too how to maintain a clear and healthy body and mind both in the office and out of it—how to keep our careers going year upon year with youthful vigor and creativity. Here at the end though we must speak about the inevitable; which is to say, regardless of how well you succeed in making money and then maintaining the clear heart to enjoy it properly, you must one day come to the end of your business, and even your life. In the Buddhist tradition, a businessperson is not really successful because he or she has made a lot of money, nor even because the person has made a lot of money and knows how to enjoy it fully. The end is as important as the beginning and the middle; you must be able to come to the end, the inevitable end, and look back on your life in business and say honestly that it was all worth it—that all your intense hours and years of effort have had some real meaning.

The decision to make sure that your business has some real meaning and benefit in the world cannot even come to you unless you are able to look at your life and your career from the perspective of its inevitable end. You cannot resolve to see that your life has meaning unless you are able to see yourself in the final hours of your life, unless you are able to put yourself in those future shoes, and practice looking back upon what you have done with your life. And so this chapter is about Shirley.

To get to Shirley we have to go back to *The Diamond Cutter*. Perhaps the most famous lines of the ancient book are those found at the very end; together these are called the "Verse on Impermanence," which is considered so important in the Buddhist world that Tibetan monks are required to chant it on the full moon and the new moon, without fail. It goes like this:

> **Learn to see that everything**
> **Brought about by causes**
> **Is like a star,**
> **A problem in your eye,**
> **A lamp, an illusion,**
> **The dew, or a bubble;**
> **A dream, or lightning,**
> **Or else a cloud.**

Choney Lama explains the verse as follows; again, the words of the original book are in bold print. You can see that he finds in the verse not only an instruction on impermanence but also a strong connection to the concept of the hidden potential in things, or emptiness.

Next comes a concluding summary, which shows how all **things brought about by causes** are empty of any nature of their own, and are also impermanent. All this is contained in the verse about the "star, a problem in your eye, a lamp," and the rest.

We could take for example the five parts of a person—the

physical body and so on—or any other such objects. All these can be described in the following metaphors.

Stars appear at night, and then by day they no longer appear. The parts to a person and other things brought about by causes are just the same. If a person's mind is full of the darkness of ignorance, then stars or these parts appear to exist in an ultimate sense. Suppose though that the sun rises—the sun of the wisdom which perceives that nothing exists in and of itself. Then these objects no longer appear to exist in an ultimate or inherent sense. As such we should see these things **as** being **like a star**.

Suppose your **eyes** are blocked by some **problem** in them—by particles of dust or something of the like. The thing that you're trying to look at then doesn't look the way it really is; rather, you see it some other way. It's just the same with the eye of the mind when it's blocked by the problem of ignorance. Things brought about by causes then appear to this mind as something other than what they are.

The flame of a butter **lamp**, supported by a thin plant wick, flares and then quickly dies out. Caused things, each supported by its various causes and conditions, also go through a continuous process of rising and quickly dying out.

An illusion is something that looks different than what is actually there. Things brought about by causes also appear to exist in and of themselves, to a mistaken state of mind.

Dew vanishes quickly; things with causes are the same—they die away speedily, without lasting even into the second instant of their existence.

Bubbles pop up at random, because some water is stirred up or something of the like, and then they burst and disappear just as suddenly. Caused things work the same way: when the various conditions all come together, they pop up suddenly, and then they die out just as suddenly.

Dreams are an example of a misperception that is caused by sleep. Things brought about by causes as well are misapprehended—they seem to exist truly, to the mind which is affected by ignorance [of the hidden potential].

Lightning flashes and dies out quickly. Caused things too rise and die out quickly, depending on the conditions that assemble to bring them about.

Clouds are something that gather and fade in the sky, depending on the wishes of the serpent-beings and such. Things brought about by causes are the same; depending on the influence of imprints, which are either the same for various members of a group or not, they rise and die out.

Each of the metaphors above is also meant to represent how no object brought about by causes has any existence in and of itself.

The explanation given here applies to things brought about by causes as an entire group. A more restricted application is quoted from sutra by Master Nagarjuna:

> *Your physical body is a bubble that forms,*
> *And feelings resemble the froth of a wave;*
> *Discrimination is just a mirage,*
> *And the other factors like empty cane;*
> *Awareness is similar to an illusion—*
> *Thus did the Cousin of the Sun speak.*

[These are the five parts to a person mentioned above; the "Cousin of the Sun" is another name for the Buddha.]

Master Kamalashila relates the final three metaphors to the three times [the past, present, and future]; this is a little different from the explanation here, but the two are in no way contradictory.

To put it briefly, Lord Buddha is telling us that we should "See that each and every thing brought about by causes is impermanent, and is empty of any nature of its own, all just like the nine examples given above." We should also consider these lines as indicating both the lack of an inherent nature to people and the lack of such a nature to things.

The verse just covered refers primarily to the impermanence of a person—to the fact that, as individuals, we must come to the end of our careers, and to the end of our lives. To go to a much deeper level (not that it's our goal right here), this too can be explained in terms of imprints and the hidden potential. That is, there are imprints in our mind which create our perceptions of the very world around us, and even of our own bodies and minds. These imprints are like any other form of energy—like anything else that is ever set in motion through circumstances or conditions.

Flatly put, *the fact that things are put in motion*, the fact that some things like imprints drive the appearance of other things like the world around us or even our own bodies and minds, *necessarily means that those things must at some point come to a stop*, **due to the very fact that they have begun.** It doesn't take anything more, according to Buddhism, for a thing to stop than for it to begin. The minute you hit a baseball with a bat you are assuring that the ball will, somewhere, somehow, roll to a stop. Your business career will end because you got your first job. Your life will end because you were born, and no further reason is needed. Trying to make sure that your personal life and your business life end up having some meaning depends on being absolutely convinced that they will, one day, end.

The day I walked into Andin for my first real job I ran into Shirley; it wasn't hard, because she was the only other employee at the time. I was just coming out of eight years of intense, single-pointed concentration on studies and meditation in a small monastery with my Lama; the noise and stench of New York City would literally make me nauseous coming in on the bus for nearly two hours every morning, but then to watch Shirley go through the day would counterbalance everything. She was a strong, proud Jamaican woman with flowing black hair and a smile the size of the room; growing up in Arizona, I had never met someone from the Islands and was entranced when I saw this living sunlight walk up and down the corridors, singing some beautiful song in a lovely British lilt. Shirley and her husband Ted quickly became like family; we suffered along with the owners, Ofer and Aya, as Andin took off, doubling and tripling in sales almost by the year, until reaching its current volume of more than $100 million per year. In time, both Shirley and I were running large divisions of the company: she the distribution, and I the diamonds.

Shirley's unshakable good humor and the love she poured out to all those around her were lengendary; we could work until one or two in the morning and she would be as cheerful at the end as she had been at the beginning of the day. A song was never far from her lips, even under the pressure of directing nearly a hundred employees and packing and shipping ten thousand pieces of fine jewelry per day, against impossible deadlines. She would be the first in and the last out, and would die for her people; this and other traits earned her the fierce loyalty and love of anyone who worked for her. The inner strength that shone from her eyes, and the deep convictions of her living Christianity, made her a rock of strength for all of us.

I remember when the first problem came; something was wrong with Shirley, people said, and did we want to go visit her at the hospital. This was one of those profound shocks you get when someone you thought was invincible proves to be more than fragile: the feeling I had when my mother got a large lump on her breast, or the time my father blacked out hunting and started falling down a mountain, with me the teenage boy trying to stop his huge body from rolling off a cliff. It turned out that Shirley had a fairly serious case of diabetes, but all would be well if she would take it easy a bit, eat well and regularly, swallow a few pills at the right time of day.

You have to realize that the company was burning up the market; we were invincible, running circles around a whole world that didn't seem to know how to do anything right. Shirley and I reached a point where we were playing with hundreds of thousands, or even millions, of dollars on an hourly basis. Our salaries grew nearly as wildly as our work and our staff—we became little gods in office kingdoms, discussing the future of a person or a whole room full of people over lunch, as if they were dolls or toy soldiers that we owned, and moved here and there at our whim. Andin was an all-consuming passion and mistress; the company made impossible demands of us and drove us to performances way over our abilities, only to reward us with money we had never had any dream of seeing. And Shirley began to stay later and later into the night, entranced in a way, as we all were to some extent.

Nothing was as important as work. She would miss a meal here, and then there, and then frequently. Maybe she would remember to take her medicine, and maybe not, but the monster shipment to J. C. Penney would go out without a minute to spare. The hours and the abuse of her body began to take their inevitable toll, but she refused to slow down. I think one of the most important corporate lessons I ever learned came to me around this time: Really good employees will continue to drive themselves until they hurt themselves, and it takes great wisdom and self-control on the part of managers to know when to force people to slow down, even when the operation will suffer as a result.

There came a time when Shirley wasn't well enough to run a large group of people, but out of pure affection the owners created a job—a customer service department—that she could continue with at a slower pace. And then she left and moved up to New Hampshire, to rest and begin expensive kidney dialysis treatments. Andin continued to roll and it was hard to keep in touch; my day was moving at a thousand miles per hour, sometimes three or four phone calls going on at once, gemstones flying through the division not in little envelopes but in garbage bags and bins— not in hundreds but in thousands and tens of thousands. Shirley's day though was slowing down.

The last time I spoke to her I accidentally called at the very moment she had returned from the hospital after both her legs were amputated. She was, as always, incredibly cheerful and caring, talking more about me than about herself; and then for the first time wondering out loud what she would become. Within a short time she was dead.

With the news of her death, with the knowledge that the woman we had stood next to over the years, and shared every conceivable sorrow and joy with during most of our waking hours, was no more, and could not be with us again, we looked for the first time back on our lives at the company, with the eyes of a person who had reached a permanent turning point. It was inevitable that, for the first time, we would begin to ask ourselves if it was all worth it. It was fun; it was more than fun, it was consuming; but the illusion of grandeur and importance faded instantly against the fact of death, forced upon us by her permanent departure. The lusty war for money would never be the same again. Now it was something serious. Now it was something for keeps. We were spending real life here, and at the end we would run out of life. No one could continue to ignore the fact that—regardless of our company's growing power in the market, and regardless of the authority and money we ourselves accumulated in our positions as Andin grew—it would be no more than an ill-remembered dream only a few days after we retired. We were forced to question why we were there at all.

The Buddhist approach to business says that we should walk into the office this way every morning, with the question: "If I were going to die tonight, is this the way I would spend my last day?" This is not just a way to depress yourself, or some kind of morbid thinking. It's very practical; it frees you; and it makes for great business, business you can really be proud of when you come to the inevitable end of your business career and look back. Here's how it works.

There's a practice called "Death Meditation" in Tibetan monasteries. The idea you get in your mind when you hear this phrase is probably lying down on a cold piece of sidewalk somewhere and trying to imagine a lot of tubes up your nose, relatives crying at your side, and heart monitors going off with a beeping sound. But this is not the point at all. To put it simply, you just wake up in the morning and stay there in bed, lying down, without opening your eyes. And you say to yourself: "I'm going to die tonight. What would be the best thing to do with the rest of my time?"

A couple of things will go through your mind right away. It would be like having a surprise day off, and since you're going to die tonight well, then, maybe try something you always wanted to do that was a little off-the-wall or maybe even a bit dangerous but—what does it matter, if you're going to die tonight? So I suppose you might get the urge to try skydiving that day, or maybe go sing in a karaoke bar, or get the most expensive tickets to a Broadway play (assuming there's a matinee).

The Death Meditation practice has to be done on a regular basis, over an extended period of time—and that's when it has its strongest effect. One result you'll find comes pretty quickly is that you streamline your life: You cut out the things that you own or do that slow you down. This is the beginning of a new kind of freedom, both physically and mentally. How many pairs of shoes do you have? And where are the pictures of your old vacations, the ones that you don't look at anymore? In your mind when you hear these questions you start picturing all the different shoes that you have: Your mind goes into your closet and looks at least at the ones you use most often. And then your mind goes to a cabinet or dresser somewhere and sees a few stacks of photo envelopes; goes inside one or two; sees roughly what a couple of the photos are of.

All this proves that, somewhere, on some level, you are keeping a mental inventory of all the things you own. Which also means that some part of your mind space is taken up with these details; remember that the mind is like the hard drive of a computer—it only has so much space. You know how computers start acting when their hard drives get near to full: programs stop working, everything gets slower, systems crash. And you know how fun it is to use a new computer with a lot of hard drive space— everything is flying. The idea of Death Meditation is to go from one to the other. A quick, dirty way to achieve this is to start throwing out things in your house that you don't need or use. This can be up to about 75 percent of the things there—a good rule of thumb is, have I really used this thing in the last six months or so? If not, throw it out.

As you practice this meditation longer, you'll start to do with your schedule what you've done with your things. If you were really going to die tonight, would you sit and read through the whole Sunday paper, or most of the magazines you subscribe to? Would you really surf around the TV looking desperately for anything of even minor interest? Would you still go out and spend an hour or two at lunch or dinner, gossiping about the other managers? Decide then: *If not on the day I die, then not now either.* Because, frankly, it may really be today.

At some point in this process you will begin examining your career itself. Is this really the job you'd want to be doing if you were going to die tonight? Is there something else you would rather be doing, but were afraid to try, because you weren't sure you could make enough money at it, or because you're afraid to try something that's completely new, or just because you're a little lazy to fully move on? Life really is very short, and your working years are very limited—your years of maximum energy and health and mental sharpness. Maybe it would be worth it to make a little less money, if you could live each day doing what you really felt was important.

At the final evolution of the Death Meditation, this kind of thinking flowers into an instinctive attraction to those things in a human life which really are of the greatest beauty and meaning. You have, through a process of internal thought and meditation, pushed your thinking ahead to what it will very likely be toward the end of your career and your life. You have already probably made a pretty good amount of money. You have met your own basic needs, even comfortably, and provided for those of your family. Occupationally you are at a place where, even though your physical energy and to some extent your mental powers may be a little less than they were at your peak, you have a wealth of experience that makes you capable of pulling off almost any kind of task successfully.

This is the point, mentally, when successful business people in their later years begin to be attracted to philanthropy. This is not happening because they have nothing else to do; rather, these people have picked up a kind of wisdom over the entire course of their life that has pinpointed the single most meaningful thing you can do with the money and power and experience you've accumulated. People like this are at the point we were talking about before: They are looking back on their career from the viewpoint of the end of career, and have begun the inevitable process of asking themselves, "Was it worth it?"

The idea here is to anticipate where you're going to be in a few years, and make some decisions now that will allow you to look back with total joy and satisfaction. The knowledge that you'll be able to do so makes not just the goal, but the entire trip—your entire career—infinitely more fun and interesting. So try the Death Meditation now; my guess is that you'll end up in the state of mind we describe in the next chapter—what we call "exchanging self and others."

You have to go through this process of mentally going on ahead in your life so you can look back at your life and know with satisfaction that you've done the most important and meaningful things, not only with your career but with the entire business itself. Companies are no different than people: They are born, they live their life, and then they slow down and die, by the very nature of things. You have to come to evaluate your business from the same viewpoint you've used to evaluate your life—you have to go to its death and look back.

And businesses do die—a businessperson who really recognizes this fact, even in the midst of the wildest success, is in a much more powerful business position, all the time. This attitude keeps your head clear and your life priorities straight. The Buddha himself looked clearly into the end of his own business—the end of Buddhism itself—and often spoke about this end, to keep his clarity, and the clarity of his followers. *The Diamond Cutter* includes a good chunk of one of these talks; the exchange begins with a question to the Buddha by Subhuti, the god of wisdom disguised as a common monk:

> ⌒ O Conqueror, what will happen in the future, in the days of the last five hundred, when the holy teaching of the Buddha is approaching its final destruction? How could anyone of those times ever see accurately the meaning of the explanations given in ancient books such as this one?

And the Conqueror replied,

> O Subhuti, you should never ask the question you have just asked: "What will happen in the future, in the days of the last five hundred, when the holy teaching of the Buddha is approaching its final destruction? How could anyone of those times ever see accurately the meaning of the explanations given in ancient books such as this one?" ⌒

The issue is whether or not there will be **anyone** at all **in the future** who believes in, or has any great interest in, **ancient books such as this one**—ancient books which **explain** the nature of the reality body, and the physical body, of a Buddha. In order to raise this issue, Subhuti asks the question that begins with **"O Conqueror, what will happen in the future, in the days of the last five hundred, when the holy teaching of the Buddha is approaching its final destruction?"**

In reply, the Conqueror says: **"O Subhuti, you should never ask the question you have just asked."** What he means here is that Subhuti should never entertain the uncertainty of wondering whether or not there will be anyone of this type in the future; and if he never had this doubt, Subhuti would never ask the question.

And again the Buddha spoke:

⌒ O Subhuti, in the future, in the days of the last five hundred, when the holy teaching of the Buddha is approaching its final destruction, there will come warrior saints who are great beings, who possess morality, who possess the fine quality, and who possess wisdom.

And these warrior saints who are great beings, O Subhuti, will not be ones who have rendered honor to a single Buddha, or who have collected stores of virtue with a single Buddha. Instead, O Subhuti, they will be ones who have rendered honor to many hundreds of thousands of Buddhas, and who have collected stores of virtue with many hundreds of thousands of Buddhas. Such are the warrior saints, the great beings, who then will come. ⌒

O Subhuti, says the text, in the future, even when the holy Dharma is approaching its final destruction, there will come warrior saints who are great beings. They will possess the extraordinary form of the training of morality; they will possess that fine quality which consists of the extraordinary form of the training of concentration; and they will possess the extraordinary form of the training of wisdom.

And these warrior saints who are great beings will not be ones who have rendered honor to or collected stores of virtue with only a single Buddha, but instead they will be ones who have rendered honor to and collected stores of virtue with many hundreds of thousands of Buddhas. This fact, says the Conqueror, is something I can perceive right now.

Master Kamalashila explains the expression "days of the last five hundred" as follows:

> "Five hundred" here refers to a group of five hundreds; it
> refers to the well-known saying that "The teachings of
> the Conqueror will remain for five times five hundred."

As such, "five times five hundred" refers to the length of time
that the teachings will remain in the world: 2,500 years.

On the question of just how long the teachings will survive in
this world, we see a number of different explanations in the various
ancient books and the commentaries upon them. These state
that the teachings of the Able One [the Buddha] will last for a
thousand years, or two thousand, or two and a half thousand, or
five thousand years. When we consider their intent though, these
various statements are in no contradiction with each other.

The reason for the lack of contradiction is that some of these
works are meant to refer to the length of time that people will still
be achieving goals, or still be practicing. And others refer to the
length of time that the physical records of these teachings remain
in our world. Some, finally, appear to be referring to the teachings
in the Land of the Realized [India].

There are many examples of the kinds of warrior saints mentioned
in the text. In the Land of the Realized, there have been
the "Six Jewels of the World of Dzambu," and others like them.
In Tibet there have been high beings like the Sakya Pandita, or
Buton Rinpoche, or the Three Lords—the father, Je Tsongkapa,
and his two spiritual sons.

It's striking for those of us in the West to read an exchange where
the founder of a major religion, during the very hours of the founding of
that religion, predicts the disappearance of his religion from the world
over two thousand years later. The constant tendency throughout all our
institutions—business, politics, families, and individuals—is to believe, at
the very depths of our hearts, that anything which is going well at any
given time will continue to do so. Buddhism though says that all things are
driven by our imprints, by the perceptions forced upon us by these

imprints. And imprints are like trees—their seeds are planted, the sprout comes up, the tree grows and flowers and inevitably dies as the energy of the seed is exhausted. Since the world around us, and we ourselves, are perceptions driven by the power of mental seeds which act exactly the same as physical seeds, then we as individuals, and our world too, must inevitably come to an end.

Even as we ride on the peak of our career, even as our company rips up the market, we must maintain this knowledge. To go through our lives, and to conduct our business, from the clearest perspective of all, we must travel ahead mentally to the day of our retirement, and the day of our death, and the day of the death of our company itself, and look back at what we have done. Was it worth it? Was it meaningful? Was it the best way to spend a short, precious human life?

In the next chapter we will look into ways of making sure that it *was* meaningful. And don't worry; the point is that you can have your cake and eat it too—the goal is to (1) make a lot of money; (2) stay very healthy in your body and your mind so you can really enjoy the money; and then (3) use the money in a way that you can look back and be proud of. The best way to use the money also happens to be the best way to run a large company, and your family, and your life.

chapter 14

The Ultimate

Management Tool

།རབ་འབྱོར། འདི་ལ་བྱང་ཆུབ་སེམས་དཔའི་ཐེག་པ་ལ་ཡང་དག་པར་
ཞུགས་པས་འདི་སྙམ་དུ། བདག་གིས་ཇི་ཙམ་སེམས་ཅན་དུ་བསྡུ་བས་
བསྡུས་པ་སྲོག་ཆགས་སྐྱེས་པ་རྣམས། མངལ་ནས་སྐྱེས་པ་རྣམས། རྡོ་
གཤེར་ལས་སྐྱེས་པ་རྣམས། བརྒྱ་ཏེ་སྐྱེས་པ་རྣམས། གཟུགས་ཅན་རྣམ།
གཟུགས་མེད་པ་རྣམ། འདུ་ཤེས་ཅན་རྣམ། འདུ་ཤེས་མེད་པ་རྣམ།
འདུ་ཤེས་མེད་འདུ་ཤེས་མེད་མིན་རྣམ། སེམས་ཅན་གྱི་ཁམས་ཇི་ཙམ་
སེམས་ཅན་དུ་གདགས་པས་བདགས་པ་དེ་དག་ཐམས་ཅད་ཕུང་པོ་ལྷག་
མ་མེད་པའི་མྱ་ངན་ལས་འདས་པའི་དབྱིངས་སུ་ཡོངས་སུ་མྱ་ངན་ལས་
བཟློ། །དེ་ལྟར་སེམས་ཅན་ཚད་མེད་པ་ཡོངས་སུ་མྱ་ངན་ལས་
བཟློས་ཀྱང་སེམས་ཅན་གང་ཡང་ཡོངས་སུ་མྱ་ངན་ལས་བཟློས་པར་
གྱུར་པ་མེད་དོ། །སྐྱས་དུ་སེམས་བསྐྱེད་པར་བྱའོ།

I don't think there's a single business executive in America who doesn't have a very clear gut feeling for the difference between what's meaningful and what's not meaningful. We may get sidetracked from time to time by possessions or relationships that are purely self-serving, but their very nature is that we quickly become tired of them—their meaninglessness is unavoidable to any thinking person. The ancient Buddhist books say that every person is driven, deep down inside, to discover what is truly meaningful, and we are incapable of being happy until we find it. And *The Diamond Cutter* is quite clear on what is, in an ultimate way, meaningful.

We'll start with the root text itself:

⌁ Subhuti, this is how those who have entered well into the way of the warrior saint must think to themselves as they feel the Wish to achieve enlightenment:

> I will bring to nirvana the total amount of living beings, every single one numbered among the ranks of living kind: those who were born from eggs, those who were born from a womb, those who were born through warmth and moisture, those who were born miraculously, those who have a physical form, those with none, those with conceptions, those with none, and those with neither conceptions nor no conceptions.
>
> However many living beings there are, in whatever realms there may be—anyone at all labeled with the name of "living being"—all these will I bring to total nirvana, to the sphere beyond all grief, where none of the parts of the person are left at all.
>
> Yet even if I do manage to bring this limitless number of living beings to total nirvana, there will be no living being at all who was brought to total nirvana. ⌁

The feeling behind this selection is clear; many of the expressions used are not. Let's go to Choney Lama's explanation for help, and then see how all this applies to corporate management:

> What the root text is saying is: "**Subhuti, this is how those who have entered the way of the warrior saint must think to themselves** first **as they feel the Wish to achieve enlightenment:**
>
>> **Whatever realms there may be, and however many living beings there are,** they reach to infinity, they are countless. If one were to classify **those numbered among the ranks of living kind** by type of birth, there would be four: **those who were born from eggs,** and then **those who were born from a womb, those who were born**

through warmth and moisture, and those who were born miraculously.

Then again there are the sentient beings living in the desire realm and the form realm: those who have a physical form. There are also the beings in the formless realm: those with no physical form.

There are "those with conceptions," meaning the beings who live in all the levels except the ones known as the "great result" and the "peak of existence." There are "those with no conceptions," which refers to a portion of the beings who reside at the level of the great result. In addition are the beings who have been born at the level of the peak of existence: those with no coarse kinds of conceptions but who on the other hand are not such that they have no subtle conceptions.

The point, in short, is that I speak of all living beings: of anyone at all labeled with the name of "living being." All these will I bring to total nirvana, to the sphere beyond all grief, where one no longer remains in either of the extremes—and where none of the two kinds of obstacles, and none of the suffering heaps of parts to the person, are left at all.

To summarize, these warrior saints develop the Wish for the sake of bringing all these different living beings to the state of that nirvana where one no longer remains in either of the extremes; to bring them to the dharma body, the essence body, of the Buddha.

The reference here is either to someone who is feeling the Wish for the first time, or to someone who has already been able to develop it. The first of these two has been practicing the emotion of great compassion, where one wishes to protect all living beings from any of the three different kinds of suffering they may be experiencing. This has made the person ready for his first experience of the state of mind where he intends to lead all sentient kind to the ultimate nirvana. The latter of the two, the one who has already developed the Wish, is refocusing his mind on his mission, and thus increasing the intensity of his Wish.

Don't worry about the part about the different kinds of beings here; according to the ancient books of Buddhism, there are realms and creatures spread throughout the universe that we have almost no idea of. The main point is that the Buddha is describing a person who wishes to bring every living creature, wherever it is in the universe, to ultimate happiness: to highest nirvana. This particular Wish is recognized in Buddhism as the source of all happiness itself—but what's it got to do with business management? And what about that last part; the part where the Buddha says, "Even if I did manage to bring every living being to complete happiness, nobody would get there at all"?

Remember we've been talking about giving your life meaning—both your business life and your personal life. In the last chapter we covered death, or the end: the end of your career, the end of your company, and ultimately even the end of your life. Death is a fact of life, and we will judge our lives in retrospect, from the vantage point of their end. You have to be able to look back and say not only that you made money, and not only that you enjoyed making and spending it, but also that you made a difference in the world, while you made the money and afterward.

And this is perhaps the greatest secret of the ancient books of Buddhism: a simple, daily method to give your life and career meaning, so that they are more than just the gradual crumbling of power and wealth and vitality into old age and death. It just also happens to be the greatest management tool of all time. In the Diamond Division at Andin we typically had over ten different nationalities working together on the same floor: ruby and sapphire experts from Thailand; topaz people from Sri Lanka; emerald sorters from India; pearl sizers from China; gemstone matchers from Puerto Rico and the Dominican Republic; diamond buyers from Israel; stone setters from Vietnam and Cambodia; quality control and colored stone buyers from Barbados; buying coordinators from Guyana; and more. You can imagine what it sounded like to have ten different languages going in a stone sorting room at once; ten different exotic food smells emanating from the microwaves at lunch; ten different sets of cultural etiquette to be satisfied simultaneously: Don't point your feet at the

Thais; don't offer a Gujarati anything to eat that grew underground; don't forget something gold for the bride at a Cantonese wedding.

But the division ran as one person, and one thing I can honestly say is that it was a true pleasure to work with every person there; despite our hugely different backgrounds (the most frustrating thing was that *no* normal American joke would seem funny to *everyone*, and since nobody had grown up in the United States you couldn't make references to old TV shows or songs or anything else), despite the obvious and also the unspoken gaps between us, we ended up with a deep feeling of mutual love and respect, which in turn made the division work like a well-oiled machine. A big part of this was simply *the absence of personal problems that could have happened but never did.*

I think we achieved this in a large part because of the initial philosophy of the division from the day it began—and the core of this philosophy was the ancient Buddhist practice of "exchanging yourself and others." If you really want your business or your department to be a success, I suggest that you try this practice; it's simple, extremely powerful, and costs you nothing. It's just an attitude that you start from the top—it begins with you, and then leaks down to the entire staff. No memos needed, no announcements, no meetings.

That thing that the Buddha was talking about just now—the Wish for enlightenment—has the exchange of yourself and others at its core. It involves three essential steps, and the third of these steps includes the answer to the question about why the Buddha said "nobody gets there when you get everybody there." This profound practice is over 2,500 years old; we'll present it here in the classical way, but with modern, real-life examples.

I like to call the first step the Jampa Method. Jampa is a shy, young Tibetan monk who lives in the little Mongolian monastery where I did a lot of my training, in New Jersey. He's the cook, mows the lawn, takes care of the older Lamas, and does a million other selfless tasks, constantly and quietly. He turns the Jampa Method on whenever a visitor shows up in the little kitchen next to the abbot's quarters. He does it to you and you never know. He opens the door with a big smile that covers your face with his sunshine, but he's already doing it. What's "it"?

Jampa was trained at our home monastery of Sera Mey, now relocated in India after the invasion of Tibet, and he was trained by some of the best—by two high Lamas named Geshe Lothar and Geshe Thupten Tenzin. The minute you step in he has you down on a chair at the kitchen table, and he's puttering around the stove and the refrigerator to prepare you something to drink or snack on as you describe why you're visiting the monastery. While he walks around the room he watches your eyes and your body language. As your eyes scan the room, do they stop and rest on the kettle on the stove, or do they hesitate at the refrigerator when he reaches for the handle; that is, would you like something hot to drink, or something cold? There's a bowl of candy on the kitchen table, and a plate of cookies farther down, and the perpetual pot of soup on the stove— which one do your eyes come back to most often?

Within a few minutes, Jampa has figured you out completely: he knows whether you like tea or coffee, hot or cold, with milk or sugar or not, cookies or crackers or noodles, and a dozen other details about your likes and dislikes. The next time you show up, you'll find your favorite beverage on the table before you say anything, because he remembers—he makes it a point to remember. And he makes it a point because he *really wants to give you what you want.*

The Jampa Method is, in short, learning to be very observant of what others need and like. This is so you can give them what they want the most. This may sound a little naive, but the simple exercise of taking the time to *educate yourself about what others like and want* has a profound effect on your entire business world. The nature of business, and the nature of corporate life, is that executives tend to concentrate on the immediate issues at hand for themselves—they are expected to perform as individuals, and they are rewarded as individuals. When was the last time you and *another* vice president were given a holiday bonus to split between you for doing a good job together? This individual focus causes us then to concentrate on ourselves, at the expense of paying attention to others.

The Jampa Method, the first part of the exchange of self and others, takes us out of this exclusive focus on ourselves and starts us off on the process of being sensitive to others. This has all sorts of immediate benefits on the work flow, and on your finances. It also plants some of the most powerful and profitable imprints possible in your mind. Here's how we apply it in a corporate setting.

As you walk around your department, watch the people who work for you. Most of us make it a point to be an expert in the finances of running our operation; in the important occupational regulations affecting our business; and in the state of the suppliers who provide the services and materials we absolutely need to get our product out. The idea here is that you now consciously train yourself to be an expert in one more thing—and that's the likes and dislikes of the people around you. We're talking here about *everything*, every detail about what makes them happy: how they fix their coffee; what kind of cushion they like on their chair; what kind of pen they prefer; how many children they have, what the children's names are, and how they're doing; when was their last vacation, and where did they go, and how did they enjoy it.

Then go and sit down in your office and *memorize* these details for each of the people close to you. If you have to take some notes, then do so. I find a laptop computer very useful for this; you can pull the file up again on the way home from work and review what you learned. This exercise inevitably leads to some kind of improvement in your behavior toward the person, even if it's just handing them sweetener rather than sugar the next time you're standing next to them at the coffeepot. Deep down, people really notice this kind of thing; in a way, we're all like your dog at home—he knows it when a person who loves dogs walks in the room, and he knows it when a person who hates dogs walks in the room, and he acts accordingly, even before anything is said or done.

People have an instinct that informs them when you don't care that much about what they like or need, and they have an instinct for the opposite just as well. It may seem a little artificial at first to track their likes and needs so blatantly, but that's part of the process—it is, exactly, artificial at the beginning. Later it becomes second nature, but only because you've done everything artificially at first.

It is true that what most of your employees would really like is if you gave them a six-week vacation, or doubled their salary. But these are not the kinds of likes and dislikes we're talking about. We're not suggesting that you make any major financial or personnel move here. Just that you watch and observe quietly, and within your immediate capacity supply those around you with what they seem to like the most. Inevitably the tables will start to turn, and they will get in the spirit of doing the same for you. Imagine the feeling of a whole division of people acting this way.

There was a point in my career at Andin when I realized, clearly, that the primary reason I was being paid such a ridiculously high salary was because I could get people to work together. I realized that the most important role I filled was simply that of an arbitrator between any two or three of the people who worked for me; that the most important hour for me in the entire day was lunchtime, when I would almost always be taking out two supervisors who couldn't get along with each other very well. This kind of friction bleeds a company silently but surely: Supervisor A has a little beef with Supervisor B, and avoids talking to that person unless it's absolutely necessary. A little issue comes up on an important order that can be handled easily in its early stages on Monday, but which will form into a disaster by Friday.

Supervisor A knows about the issue on Monday but doesn't say anything to Supervisor B, who could have fixed it easily. It's not the kind of issue that should have or would have been brought up on Monday at the staff meeting, but it is something that Supervisors A and B would have mentioned to each other if they were in the habit of hanging out at the water cooler together to shoot the breeze once in a while. What I'm trying to say is that a little good will among your staff members is worth much more money than you ever dreamed of. And the Jampa Method is the first step.

Again, no announcements or policy statements—you just start doing it, and others follow. I remember when His Holiness the Dalai Lama visited my home state of Arizona to give a series of talks, and one of my old high school friends had a chance to ask him a question: What's the best way to teach young children how to lead an ethical way of life? "At that age," said His Holiness, "it doesn't matter what you tell them to do. They will watch and imitate you; they will do what you do, and so you are faced with the hardest task of all—to be ethical yourself." You have to start spying on the people who work for you, a kind of very beautiful spying, to see what they like, what they find important in their own lives; and then go about helping them get it.

The second step in the practice of exchanging yourself and others is to pretend to put your mind in their body, and then open your eyes and look at you, and see what it is that you (they) would like from you (you). If you think this sounds confusing, try to imagine how hard it is to translate an ancient book on this subject from Sanskrit or Tibetan!

This step, called Switching Bodies, is a little deeper and harder than just watching the people around you to see what they like and don't like. I can remember trying it with a young man from Guyana who had just joined the division; he came recommended by a friend of his mother's, who already worked for us (people who work with stones always come on recommendation; there's not really any way to stop them from walking out with a few hundred at any given hour of the day, so they have to have a traceable history). We sat him down the first day in front of a huge pile of diamond chips and set him to counting out hundreds or thousands for specific ring orders.

By the end of the day I had learned a bit more about him; he was pleasant with the people around him, a fast learner, quiet, humble, and quick as hell. On the way out I learned one more thing: I looked into his face and saw a mix of enjoyment for the place and a twinge of despair at the thought of having to sit in a chair and count little rocks for the next few years of his life. And then I did the Switching Bodies thing, I put myself in his body, and looked at my face, and asked myself what I would like me (me) to say to me (him). So I said, "Come into my office in the morning and we'll see if we can't find you something a little more challenging." And I felt my eyes drop a little shyly, and a smile stretch across my (his) face.

From that moment on it was a steadily putting my mind in his body; we got him (me) something that I (him) had always dreamed of—a chance to learn to work with computers. We put him under one of the best programming cowboys we had, and after he had proved his determination we helped him get through a series of college courses. In the diamond business, this kind of night school is traditionally a no-no: During the busy season, everyone's working very late hours, and even off season you don't want tired people messing up sensitive inventory systems or piles of diamonds. But every time I saw him I knew it was what I (he) wanted when I looked at my (his) face, and I knew the sense of fulfillment and accomplishment it gave, and we found ways to work around his (my) absence on school days. In the end he became the best programmer we had, and even more important an employee who knew we had done what we knew would be best for him, even when it hurt the company a bit. And in this way we had created a person who would really give when the crunch came, and who throughout the day would be looking for ways to help the company and those around him.

You can't put a price on these kinds of people, sprinkled around your department, constantly on the lookout for ways to smooth out problems with orders or systems or people before you ever hear about them. And when the day is over, when you reach the end of your own career and look back, it won't be the sales you made or the projects you completed or the P&L that you remember at all. It will be looking into the young man's face looking up at your own, and knowing you have given him something precious for his entire life. And if you keep up this kind of thinking, this kind of putting yourself into your employees' bodies and looking to yourself for help, you will find a profound kind of satisfaction growing within you, the kind of deep contentment that you have at very rare and special moments, except that—the more you keep this up—the more frequently the feeling comes to you. This in fact is a sign that your work *is taking on true meaning*. And it's important to point out again, I think, that this kind of thinking is not only *right*, but also *the most profitable*, as your department and your company begin to run themselves, begin to be run by people who really care, because you care for them as you would for yourself. Money and happiness. You can have your cake and eat it too.

Are you ready for the ultimate step? This takes some practice, and it's important to appreciate the fact that you have to work up through the first two stages before you try it. But don't think it's not worth the effort. It is the final evolution of the practice of exchanging yourself and others, and in fact it is—according to the ancient books of Buddhism—the final evolution of the human heart and mind. It's hard to do, it's hard to even want to do. But nothing in the world will make you a more successful executive, and a more successful person.

We call this third step the Rope Trick. You can do it on any one of your employees; just walk up and stand next to an individual some day at her desk. Pretend that you have this huge Roy Rogers lasso in your hand,

and that you drop it on the floor around the both of you—it surrounds you both. Now imagine that the two of you are, literally, one person.

You see, in the first two steps we did some pretty radical things about learning to watch and think about what those around us really like—we even got to where we could switch bodies with someone and look at ourselves and see what we (they) wanted most from us (us). *But there was still the distinction between "you" and "me."* It was a question of "me" watching "you," or "me" trying to get into "your" body. With step three we take the practice of exchanging yourself and others to a completely more radical level: You *are* your employee, and he or she is you: you are one person.

In this third step, your mind has broken completely out of the self-centered mode of so many business executives, the really very selfish mode which is so encouraged by our normal corporate reward system. It's not a question now of my getting a bonus, and not even a question of that person getting a bonus—the question becomes, how can *we* get *our* bonus? By this point you are so much into the minds of those who work for you that you are actually treating your and their welfare as one and the same thing. It's as if you had just become a Siamese twin with someone. Now you have two mouths on your head to feed; now you have two sets of legs, and four pairs of shoes to buy when you go to the store (maybe one pair of wing tips and one pair of high heels); now it's four ears that have to hear the Big Boss yell if either one of your two pieces forgets to order those half-carat princess-cut diamonds.

If you're any kind of normal American businessperson, this line of thinking has gone a little too far for you. The implications are enormous; and two problems come up in your mind immediately. The first is that the process of exchanging yourself and others has, by this point, become something totally artificial—I mean, how could you *actually be* another person; or more precisely, how could the two of you become a single person? But it is totally possible that this could happen; and the key for making it happen is hidden within that thing the Buddha said at the beginning of the chapter; the statement that "on the day I bring all beings to total happiness, there won't be anyone at all who gets to total happiness."

To get this let's go back to our discussion about making money; let's go back to the reasons why everything that ever happens to you happens to you. We've said many times now that the things around you are sort of neutral, like blank screens: This is the hidden potential in things. A yelling boss at work seemed unpleasant to you but perhaps pleasant to the person sitting next to you, and therein lies his "emptiness" or his potential— meaning that he is basically neutral, and whether I experience him as pleasant or unpleasant, whether I interpret the sounds and shapes coming at me as something good or bad, is not something coming from "out there," from him. Rather, it's a function of the imprints in my own mind, imprints that I placed in my own subconscious in the past by acting in a positive or negative way toward others. And these imprints now are floating up to my conscious mind and coloring—nay, actually *creating*— the way in which I see my world (the yelling boss being just a little piece of that world).

Forget the yelling boss for a moment—let's come back to the poor person getting yelled at; let's come back to me. If all this stuff about the hidden potential in things, and about the imprints I've planted in my mind to see what I see, is true, then *I'm the same as the yelling boss*. That is, *the way I see myself* is driven by exactly the same kinds of causes that drive how I see the yelling boss. *I see myself* the way I am for the same sorts of reasons I see *him* the way he is. I see myself as I see myself because of imprints in my mind, coming up to my conscious mind, flowering, and determining what I see. And the important point here is to understand that they not only determine *how* you see yourself, but the very *fact* that you see yourself. That is, you define yourself as you do, you draw the boundaries between yourself and other things and people, only due to past habits and imprints in your mind. You are used to thinking of yourself as the one who stops at the edge of your skin, and so you plant imprints that later make you see yourself the same way. "You" ends where it ends not because it is a natural place to end, but only because it's where you're used to you ending.

We talked about this a bit before. Anyone can see, with only a bit of thought, that the place where "I" end and "them" begins is a very slippery matter. When mothers give birth to children, their sense of "me" suddenly gets stretched to cover another, tiny, body: Do harm to *this* particular child, and you can expect *this* particular woman to react with all the passion that she would show if you attacked her own body. People with really bad cases of diabetes act the opposite: their feet form sores, and the sores become gangrenous, and the doctors tell them they either have to amputate the leg or die.

The minute you decide that losing your leg would be better than losing your life, you have in effect *shrunk* your definition or border of "me" to a smaller space than before. This proves that you have the power to expand or contract "me" to greater or smaller areas, so don't tell me it's impossible to do the Rope Trick and throw the rope around another person until you become one person. It's only the imprints from your past, your *habit and choice* of thinking of the edge of yourself as the edge of your skin or the edge of *your* stomach, that keeps you from making someone else you too. Imagine, just for a moment, what would happen if the entire world thought and acted as if everyone else were they themselves. We could bring everyone to total happiness, and "no one" would reach total happiness—because "everyone" would only be one of us: us.

Which brings us to your second objection, the second hesitation you must have in your mind about this whole proposal. Suppose I do do the Rope Trick; suppose I do take the border of "me" and stretch it around one or even more other people. Where do I draw the line? What's the limit? Life is hard enough as it is; it seems almost impossible to provide successfully for all the physical and emotional needs of a person who has even just a single body and mind—that is, my current me. If taking care of myself, if trying to keep my own body from falling apart, and keeping my own mind from breaking down every day or two, is such a struggle, then what hope would I ever have of taking care of one or more other people *as if they were truly "me"*? Where would I ever find the resources?

The irony here is that *the resources would come from the very act of expanding yourself to include others*; that is, the very ability to handle, physically and emotionally, the job of taking care of lots of people as if they were all "me" comes from *the true decision to do so*. If the whole idea of the hidden potential and imprints creating our very reality is true, then there can be no greater way *of creating wealth* than *sharing it indiscriminately*. Put simply, if the only way I can ever *see* a dollar is to have planted an imprint from *giving* a penny, then the very act of making sure that all those around me have money *as if we were, all together, a single person* would bring me almost limitless resources. Imagine, in short, a world where everyone considered everyone else his or her responsibility, as if everyone else were all "me." And there's no reason why they can't be.

Any intelligent person reading these lines right now can sense, can smell, that we're barking up the right tree. To overcome the tendency *not* to think of others, to spread your idea of yourself to include all your employees and everyone else around you, to work *not for the sake of others*, but as if *there were no "other"*—this would be real happiness, this would be true contentment. You know in your heart that it would be right, you know in your heart it would be right to start it now, and you know that, if you spent your whole career and your whole life this way, purposely trying to work for the good of those around you as hard as you work for yourself, that you could look back with pride, for this is the real meaning of a human life. This is the ultimate wealth.

chapter 15

The Real Source

of Wealth, or

the Economics of

Limitlessness

|དེ་ཅིའི་ཕྱིར་ཞེ་ན། རབ་འབྱོར། བྱང་ཆུབ་སེམས་དཔའ་གང་མི་
གནས་པར་སྦྱིན་པ་སྦྱིན་པ་དེའི་བསོད་ནམས་ཀྱི་ཕུང་པོ་ནི། རབ་
འབྱོར། ཚད་གཟུང་བར་སླ་བ་མ་ཡིན་པའི་ཕྱིར་རོ།

If you think about the whole concept of economics, of every economic
system from capitalism to socialism to communism, it all boils down to
how we share our resources, our wealth. How much for me, and how
much for you, and the rules for dividing what we have. And if you think
about it a little more deeply, all our systems have exactly these same two
premises in common—that there *is* a separate "me" and "you" to "share"
things; and that we *have* to figure out a system to share things, because
things are *limited*. Well, as we have already demonstrated, you can just
throw both of those premises out now. To see how, let's go back to *The
Diamond Cutter* for some final brain-busting words from the Buddha:

> ⌒ **Why is that? Think, O Subhuti, of the mountains of merit
collected by any warrior saint who performs the act of giving
without staying. This merit, O Subhuti, is not something that
you could easily ever measure.** ⌒

Let's go, as usual, to Choney Lama's explanation of these words for some help. One would have to admit that a person who is still locked in the chains of grasping the idea that things have some inherent quality of their own could still collect a great amount of merit through acts of giving and the like.

But suppose a person frees himself from these chains and then goes on to practice these same acts of giving and such. Their merit is certain to be ever so much greater than before. And it is to emphasize this point that the Buddha says, **Why is that? Think, O Subhuti, of the mountains of merit collected by any warrior saint who performs the act of giving without staying. This merit is not something** whose limit **you could easily ever measure;** in fact, it would be quite difficult to measure.

And the Buddha continues:

> ⌒ **O Subhuti, what do you think? Would it be easy to measure all the space in the universe to the east of us?**

And Subhuti replied,

> O Conqueror, it would not.

The Conqueror spoke again:

> **And just so, would it be easy to measure all the space in the universe to the south of us, or to the north of us, or above us, or below us, or in any of the directions in between? Would it be easy to measure all the space in the universe, in any of the ten directions from where we now stand?**

And Subhuti replied,

> O Conqueror, it would not.

Finally then did the Conqueror say,

And just so, O Subhuti, it would be no easy thing to measure the mountains of merit collected by any warrior saint who performs the act of giving without staying.

Some of the ideas here are pretty obvious, and at least one is not so obvious. The Buddha is trying to describe to us, first of all, the idea that "merit" or goodness or the power of certain imprints in the mind could be limitless. Secondly, he is saying that, in order for this power to *be* limitless, we "warrior businesspeople" have to "perform the act of giving without staying." What the heck does it mean to "give without staying," and just what is a "warrior saint," anyway? The answer to both these questions is the entire basis of what we call the Economics of Limitlessness.

We'll start with "giving without staying." This is really just a wrap-up of all the ideas we've talked about already. Any businessperson worth his salt would admit the truth of the apparent randomness of business strategies: Sometimes a conservative financial move fails, and sometimes it's the only thing that works; sometimes a risky financial move succeeds, and sometimes it leads to disaster. It's the same for smart businesspeople and not-so-smart businesspeople: Some smart ones succeed, some smart ones fail; some not-so-smart ones fail, but some not-so-smart ones succeed. None of the usual criteria, if we are really honest with ourselves, seems to work in a foolproof or predictable way at all. To a Buddhist state of mind this is, first of all, a definite indication that *we have not found the real cause* for wealth: We don't really know what creates it.

If you think very carefully, you can see a profound truth in the very distribution of wealth among the people of our own world. Wealth comes and goes as individual people come to power and then die; it comes and goes as whole countries and empires rise and fall; it seems to spread throughout the world itself in times of great prosperity, and then shrink throughout the world in times of depression or war. Individual inventions—such as penicillin or the gun or the personal computer—can effectively, in only a few years, cause an increase or decrease in the well-being, the "absolute" wealth, of the entire population of the world. What I'm trying to say is:

The *amount* of wealth around is not a fixed thing, and never has been. It fluctuates. This throws suspicion on the entire concept that there is only so much wealth, only so many resources, in the world; and that we just have to work out a good system of sharing what limited amount we have available. Maybe there's another possibility. Maybe if we figured out *the real cause of wealth* then we could *increase the entire amount of wealth in the world*; that is to say, maybe everyone could have enough, or more than enough.

We proved pretty well I think that a yelling boss is something created by your own perceptions. Let's go through the logic here briefly once again. Technically speaking, strictly speaking in a scientific way, a yelling boss is really only a collection of colors (mostly red!), shapes (mostly waving at you), decibels (mostly loud), and vowels and consonants (a+b+c coming at you in a pretty steady stream). Your mind, under the influence of imprints you've planted there long before, is moved to interpret these shapes and sounds as an unpleasant, yelling boss.

And remember the person sitting next to you (who maybe doesn't like you so much), or perhaps the boss's wife: they see this same set of shapes and sounds as being something pleasant, something right. The "unpleasantness" and the "pleasantness" then can't be something that *belongs* to the boss; it must be something that is coming from somewhere else, because otherwise we would all find the boss either pleasant or unpleasant. The only other choice really is that *the qualities of unpleasantness and of pleasantness are being imposed on the picture* by our own minds. And it's obvious too that this is not something we would do *voluntarily*. The yelling boss may only be a perception orchestrated by our minds, but we don't seem to have any power to turn the perception on and off. Something within our minds is forcing us to have the perception, and that's the imprints coming up to the conscious part of our minds from the unconscious part.

It's painfully obvious, finally, that whether a yelling boss really exists out there completely on his own or whether he is a result of my own particular set of perceptions doesn't at all affect the reality of his existence; I mean, in either case, he's still going to cut my holiday bonus if he's mad, whether his being mad is a quality that adheres to him or whether it's something I'm supplying from my own mind. Where the knowledge that he's my perception really helps, then, is not in changing what's going on at the moment, because that's already happening. Rather, it helps *a lot* in determining how I'm going to react to this yelling boss; that is, do I really want to see him like this again? Because the one thing that would force me to do so is if I responded to him with the same kind of stuff he's dishing out to me now. The only thing that can create the perception of a yelling boss is an imprint for a yelling boss, and the only thing that can plant an imprint like this in my mind is—you guessed it, *yelling back at the boss.* So what's this got to do with economics?

If all this theory is correct (and it happens to be), then in theory I could *stop any future yelling bosses* if I just understand what's going on and refuse to yell back at him. Then at some point in the future he'll come in the room and we—*both me and the person sitting next to me* (remember, the guy that didn't like me so much and enjoyed seeing the boss yell at me)— will *both* find him pleasant. If you think about it carefully you get the whole point here: The *wealth* in the room, the amount of happiness or well-being in the room, *has just doubled,* and *at no expense to anyone.* It's not as if I was happy at my office mate's expense. Now there's just twice as much happiness as before. And money works exactly the same way.

When you *give* something away to another person, when you help any single other living being with your hands or your time or your funds, then a certain imprint is planted in your mind; the act is *always* recorded by the consciousness of the act, and consciousness is turned on and recording all the time. This imprint stays in the subconscious gathering strength, growing in power like any physical plant or tree. At some point it makes its way to the head of the line of your awareness, into your conscious mind, and colors—even creates—your impression of the world around you, and even of yourself.

Business transactions, and business decisions, are like an empty screen: *whether you see them work or not,* whether they are successful or not, is determined not by any outer factors like the business climate or your intelligence or the amount of risk you choose to take, but rather solely by the perceptions of the transaction or the decision forced upon you by the imprints in your mind. The fact that the outer factors don't determine the success of your transactions or decisions is painfully obvious from several pieces of evidence; from the fact, for example, that the same strategies don't always work—or from (if you think about it deeply) the sheer fact that some new products are a hit, or that some old products begin to fail. Why do people suddenly decide that a scene from a comic book by Andy Warhol is valuable, or that a drawing by Picasso which any child could have done is priceless? Why do some idiotic songs or TV shows become hits, while more thoughtful or even more idiotic ones fail miserably? Something's going on here. Success is, ultimately, not a thing that is decided by anything we thought it was.

Now if all these theories are right, then the reason that any particular venture (brilliant *or* idiotic) is a success and makes money is due only to the good imprints in the mind of its creator: Those who succeed get to see themselves making money *only* because, at some point in the past, they planted in their own minds an imprint to see themselves making money. And this particular imprint can be planted *only* by watching yourself *giving all you can to others.* As we've seen, this giving begins and should begin in a limited way: Small kindnesses done to people in your own department, or your own family, based on watching them closely to see what they want and need.

Then the giving graduates to a broader level, say to every department in your company, with the gift taking on more substantial proportions—financial yes, but also in terms of giving your own time, and your emotional and professional support, and helping people with *ideas.* By this point too your giving is driven by the deeper practice of moving into other people's bodies to see what they hope for from you. At its peak then the generosity reaches a place where you are seriously investing all your personal financial, emotional, and professional resources and abilities, and those of your company, in a well-thought-out plan to bring happiness to your entire family, company, community, and even world—because you have consciously readjusted the borders of "me" to include all of "them," and you are, basically, just taking care of a (much) bigger "me" now.

Remember that this last step cannot be done successfully—and in fact, you cannot really be assured the ultimate financial and personal success described in this book—unless you really take the time to understand the principle of the hidden potential and the imprints that play upon it. Only then will you truly appreciate how limitless wealth can be created by giving, and only then can you truly recognize how "me" must rightfully become something that extends past your current very limited self.

Suppose one person already understands all this and has used it to be a financial success. Then suppose that individual goes and teaches it to someone else, who uses this information to become a financial success himself. They're like the two guys sitting and watching the wonderful boss who used to be a yelling boss. Now there are *two* rich people where there used to be only one. And *because the wealth* is the result of an imprint, because a business transaction or decision which is in itself only neutral or blank or potential has suddenly become successful, then *we can say that the new wealth occurs at no expense to the preexisting wealth*: that is, there is twice as much wealth, *in absolute terms,* as there was before. Now suppose the second guy goes and teaches a third guy, and—well—you get the picture.

In deep terms, we can say that *the fact that some people are wealthy now, and others are not*, is evidence that—if we understood how this situation in itself has come to be—*everyone could be wealthy*. Put differently, wealth can be limitless in the world because wealth is limited now. You can just throw out the idea of sharing limited resources, and by the way you can throw out the idea of poverty itself. Wealth is a perception (and *therefore* a reality) forced on anyone who has been truly generous in the past. It is therefore available to all people.

The mind—a mind crippled by the assumptions and, frankly, fairy tales of the entire history of our civilization, passed down by well-meaning parents over its entire length—balks at the possibility that *every living person could have more than enough wealth*. It's not something that has ever happened before in our recorded history, says this state of mind, and so it could not happen now. We've heard this argument before; it wasn't true then, and it's not true now. Watch out, Columbus, you'll fall over the edge, because the world is flat. Iron could never fly in the sky, or float for that matter. It's not possible that practically every person in the world could have the same access to the world's information, running through wires made of glass or beamed down from a place beyond where the highest bird can fly. Where did all these things come from? Did they not alter the *absolute amount of wealth* in the world? Where does new wealth really come from? Now you know.

Just a couple of notes here on the mechanics of the Economics of Limitlessness, and then we'll stop so you can drop the book and go out and give it a try. The process of *creating new wealth* works infinitely better if you understand how it works; that is, you should read this book over and then over again until you really get a clear picture of hidden potential and imprints—how they work together. Giving with this knowledge is what the Buddha means when he says "give without staying" in the ignorance of how things really work. The ancient books of wisdom say that, to really throw yourself into this stuff with the amount of effort it takes to pull it off, you *must* start from a firm belief that it works. They say that you can only get this firm belief if you have figured out, to your own satisfaction, that logically it really *should* work. And there's one more detail you're going to need.

Remember the "warrior saint" thing? It may not surprise you that a "warrior saint" is, very simply, just anyone who has gone through the three steps of the practice of exchanging themselves and others that we outlined in the last chapter. It makes sense, doesn't it? The only person who could really give away enough to others to plant the imprints in their mind to see a great deal of wealth coming their way later would be someone who didn't really see much distinction between themselves and others. The person who has the best chance of truly being generous to others is a person who has figured out the biggest secret of life—the biggest source of all happiness; a person who has figured out that just working for a single "me," a single mouth and a single stomach, is profoundly boring, uninspiring, and false to our whole human purpose.

It's a lot of *fun*, it's an unexplored and endless joy, to expand yourself to include other bodies, and then take care of them. And if all this stuff about hidden potential and imprints is really true, then the best way to take care of others would be to turn them on to how to become wealthy themselves, and how to enjoy the wealth, and how to make the wealth meaningful. If you really think about it, the very act of sharing wealth in this way—the unlimited proliferation of the knowledge of how to create wealth—is the most profound way to plant the seeds in your own mind for wealth you've never imagined.

This gets into the subject of whole forms of wealth beyond what we can even imagine, sort of like walking into a garden to find a single flower and leaving laden with treasures we could not even imagine when we entered. But that's a subject for later.

Cutting Diamonds

In the 20 years since *The Diamond Cutter* was first published, I have been invited to speak, along with our staff of the Diamond Cutter Institute for management training, to over 200,000 people in more than 75 cities all over the world. As you might expect, standing in front of large audiences hundreds of times every year has helped us to develop very effective tools for helping people to achieve personal and business success even more quickly.

What you will find here in the first new section of the book are three of the best tools we've developed. If you learn to use them, you will reach your goals faster, and with greater success. I call these three tools The Pen; The 4 Steps; and Two Husbands in the Kitchen.

The Pen

"The Pen" is a clear & simple demonstration of the idea of the hidden potential in things, which is at the core of this book and of the original Diamond Cutter Sutra, which was written over 2,000 years ago. There's an ancient tradition of teaching this all-important concept by holding up any simple, common object and asking a few questions.

And so if I hold up a pen and ask you what it is, you reply, naturally, "It's a pen!"

Next I ask: "Well now, suppose a dog comes in the room, and I wave this thing in front of his nose. What will he do with it?"

"He'll bite it," you answer.

"So does the dog see this as a pen?"

"No—he sees this thing as a chewtoy!"

"Well then who's right?" I ask. "The human or the dog? Is this thing really a pen, or is it really a chewtoy?"

You think for a second and reply, "Well, they're both right. After all, the human can use this thing as a pen; and the dog can use it as a chewtoy; and they're both perfectly happy with it!"

"Exactly. Now suppose I put this object down on the table here. And then I ask all the humans and all the dogs to leave the room: they go out the door, and we close it behind them. Now the room is empty. At that moment, is the object on the table a pen, or is it a chewtoy?"

You think for another moment and answer, "Well, at that moment, when the room is empty and there isn't a single human or a single dog around, I'd say that this object is just sort of—nothing, nothing yet."

"Good. Now suppose one of the humans opens the door and comes back in the room, and approaches the table with this thing on top of it. They reach the table and then they look down. At that moment, what does this object *become?*"

"Well," you reply, "at that moment this object becomes a pen!"

"Right. And if the dog walks in first, before the human? What does this same object become *then?*"

"Well, if the dog walks in first, then this same object becomes a chewtoy."

"Right again. So now think carefully for a moment and give me a good answer: If this object becomes a pen when the human walks in; and it becomes a chewtoy when the dog walks in; then *is the pen coming from the human's mind, or is the pen coming from the pen itself?*"

"Well, since it becomes different things when different types of beings walk back in the room, then it *can't* be coming from its own side. So the pen *must* be coming from the mind of the human!"

"Right once more. But let's look at that idea. Is the whole world then just a product of positive thinking? If we have just proved that the whole world is coming from us, then can we simply close our eyes, and think *positively*, and make things become whatever we want them to be?"

"Well no. I mean, it is true that the pen is somehow coming from my mind. But it's also obvious that this doesn't mean that I can make things whatever I want them to be, just by wishing. If that were the case, then everybody in the world would have everything they want, all the time— and obviously we don't!"

That's all completely correct. Things may be coming from my mind, but it's obviously not the case that I can *choose* how they come from my mind. There must be some force or power in my mind that makes me see a pen as a pen, and there must be some *other* force or power in the dog's mind that makes them see the same object as a chewtoy. That power is a mental seed, which we'll discuss next.

So by itself, this object is neither a pen nor a chewtoy. By itself, it's just *waiting* to be something. The object by itself is a lot like a white movie screen, before the theater employees turn on the movie projector to show the movie on the screen.

This object waiting to be something—this blank white movie screen—is exactly the meaning of the hidden potential in things, as it is presented in the Diamond Cutter Sutra, and here in the Diamond Cutter business book!

The 4 Steps

The second great concept presented in the Diamond Cutter Sutra is something we can call the Seed System: the idea of seeds in the mind, and how they are planted.

This is best understood with the explanation of Master Vasubandhu, who 17 centuries ago was perhaps the earliest commentator on the Diamond Cutter Sutra. In the fourth chapter of his famous *Treasure House of Higher Knowledge (Abhidharma Kosha)*, he explains how these seeds create the world around us, and how we can actually "design" our world to be a perfect world, if we know the precise method for planting the necessary seeds.

Let's go back to the human approaching the table with the object lying on top of it. As the human looks down at the thing, seeds in their mind split open. As a seed opens, a tiny image of a pen emerges from the seed—and the mind pushes this tiny picture out and lays it over the object on the table.

As the overlay settles down on the colors and shapes that were waiting on the table, the mind begins to see this object as a pen. A different picture or overlay emerges from the seeds in the dog's mind: for them, it's a picture of a chewtoy coming out of the seed; settling on top of the colors and shapes out there; and making them appear as a chewtoy.

As we all intuitively felt, the chewtoy is just as valid as the pen. In fact, subsequent seeds will open and cause us to see the pen producing letters on a piece of paper; or just as well, tickling the taste buds on a dog's tongue.

And so we can rightly say that—even though the people and things around us are empty, and even though they are products of pictures coming out of our own mind—they still *work*, quite normally. A pen that's coming from seeds in my mind can still make a mess in my pocket, if it breaks open there.

The process by which the world comes out of the seeds in my own mind is called, in the ancient wisdom tradition, by various names: "cause-and-effect"; or "dependence"; or—less friendlily—"dependent origination." Whatever we call it, the point is clear: the world by itself is a blank white movie screen, empty, waiting to be something. And then the seeds in my mind-projector break open and make the people and things around me what they are.

Now if we could learn to control this process—if we could learn the precise method for *planting* these mental seeds—then we could, in theory, make a perfect world: no more hunger, no more war; no want, no death. Here's where we need Vasubandhu's 4 Steps for planting mental seeds. They are simple, and anyone can use them, regardless of what country or race or religion they may belong to—

Step 1
Decide what you want.
Define the goal you would like to reach. Classical goals for most people around the world are five: right now in my life I would like to reach—

(1) financial independence,
(2) beautiful professional and personal relationships,
(3) great health & youthful energy,
(4) a highly creative and peaceful mind,
(5) a world where each and every one of us
   shares all these blessings equally.

Choose some easily-defined aspect of one of these goals which you would like to reach within the next 6 weeks or so. For example: I would like to see my income increase by 10%, so that I could help more people. Perhaps, for example, you would like to be in the position of the politician Prince Jeta, or the businessman Anatha Pindada, who at the beginning of the Diamond Cutter Sutra purchase and provide a garden where the sutra can be taught for the first time, two thousand years ago!

Step 2
Choose a seed-planting partner.

Mental seeds can normally only be planted by interacting with another living being. This means you are going to need a seed-planting partner. This has to be someone who seeks the same general goal that you do. In our example here, this means that you're going to have to find another person who wants to increase their income, because they want to do some kind of good in the world.

Step 3
Help them once a week.

Mental seeds are planted when we see or hear ourselves do something— even if it is just hearing ourselves thinking a thought. In practical terms, to reach our goal, we're going to have to undertake some concrete action to help this other person reach their own, similar goal.

You will need to spend at least one hour a week helping, for free, your seed-planting partner with one small part of their goal. It might be calling customers for them, for example; or helping them find the perfect employee. The sound of each word you say, and the image of each gesture you make, makes an impression upon your own mind—and within a few hours, this impression becomes a mental seed.

Step 4
Put water on the mental seed.

So those first three steps plant the mental seed. But a big problem with mental seeds is that they can sit around in the mind for a hundred years before they crack open and produce our goal. There is an ancient method for "watering" the mental seeds to speed up this process.

After all, if it takes three years for the seed to produce my extra income after I help another person, then it will be very difficult for me to connect that extra income to the actions I took to help this other person. And then I won't much believe that the system works, and I won't use it very often. So watering mental seeds is important!

The traditional method for "watering" the seed so it grows stronger and faster—and quickly enough for us to gain faith in this system—is a simple meditation that at DCI we call "Coffee Meditation" (from something my own teacher said to me when he taught this trick many years ago). As you lay down on your bed and put your head on the pillow to sleep, you pause for a few minutes to think about the kindness you paid to your seed-planting partner this week.

This is not an act of pride. (Pride would say, for example, "No one in this whole city can help people as well as I do!") Rather, you just play back the mental movie of every little thing you did this week to help your seed-planting partner. And—very importantly—you celebrate mentally that you have a new and infallible system for increasing your income!

These two trains of thought have a direct and immediate effect on the seed, and it opens much quicker and stronger, to create the income and the world we want.

Two Husbands in the Kitchen

Perhaps the most important point in the Diamond Cutter Sutra— repeated over and over—concerns the intersection between The Pen (hidden potential) and The 4 Steps (cause-and-effect).

That is, how does the blank white screen (The Pen) provide a "space" for the movie coming out of the projector (mental seeds planted by the 4 Steps)?

This is illustrated perfectly in the DCI teaching tool called "Two Husbands in the Kitchen"—and if you understand the Two Husbands, then you truly understand the Diamond Cutter.

The Two Husbands allegory begins with a working mother who has two young children, and a husband who enjoys watching football all day on television. One day her boss at work asks the mom to come in an hour early the next morning, to participate in a phone conference with overseas staff.

Accordingly, she comes to her children's bedroom that night and says: "Kids, Mommy has to go to work an hour early tomorrow. So can you both be up, and dressed, with homework all finished and ready to go, at 7am?"

The two kids give their solemn promise to be ready!

Next morning, at 7 sharp, Mom opens the door to the children's bedroom. They are both still in their pajamas, and jumping on the bed and screaming for fun. Mom gets upset:

"You two are the stupidest kids in this whole city!"

The children's feelings are hurt; but they quickly get ready and the day begins. (It's important to note here that these hurtful words were heard, not just by the kids, but of course by Mom herself. So that means the words planted some mental seeds.)

A week later, Mom is dragging herself home after an especially hard day at work; and picking up the kids; and buying the groceries for dinner. She's totally exhausted, but as she reaches out to open the front door to the house, she reminds herself that the best thing she gets from her husband is those amazing hugs, whenever she comes home.

She opens the door to the kitchen; sets down the groceries; and throws open her arms.

Her husband (who as it turns out, expected dinner an hour earlier) sticks his finger in her face and abruptly yells, "You're so *stupid!*"

Mom's reaction, of course, is to think: "I didn't do anything! I just open the door and he starts yelling *Stupid* at me!"

But, having gone through The Pen & The 4 Steps, we know *it's not true that Mom didn't do anything*. When she yelled at the kids the week before, Mom heard what she herself said; this created an impression upon her mind; and that impression soon became a group of mental seeds, planted in the soil of the subconscious mind.

A week later, in the instant that she opens the door, these seeds crack open—and out comes that tiny image of a yelling husband. Just as with The Pen, this image flies out and overlays the external shapes and colors, and creates the very *real* reality of a yelling husband.

There are some very important points here, which in fact help us grasp the original Diamond Cutter Sutra more fully, and see how we can use it for our own personal and business success:

1) How to prove we're stupid

Of course, normally we indulge in our normal human reaction, and yell back at our husband immediately: *"I'm* not stupid, *you're* stupid." This reaction *proves* that *we're* the stupid one, because by hearing ourselves yell back we plant new negative mental seeds in our mind. Next week, these seeds open in the kids' bedroom and we see them misbehaving again.

2) Sansara: the downward cycle

When the kids do misbehave, we of course yell at them again; and that plants more seeds to see our husband yell; and then we yell at *him* again, and so on and so on: another downward cycle.

These types of mini-cycles throughout our week add up to a big negative cycle which is called, in the ancient Asian literature, *sansara*—or the "cycle of pain." As we see in its opening pages, the goal of the entire Diamond Cutter Sutra is to break these cycles, and reverse them into a constant upward cycle.

3) Two husbands in the kitchen

If you think about it, there are always *two* husbands in the kitchen anytime one of them yells at us and we *haven't* learned about the Seed System. There's one husband in the kitchen that we feel, instinctively, is *not my fault:* "I just walked into the kitchen, and *before I had a chance to do anything,* he yelled at me." So we can say that Husband #1 is the one who is *not* coming from me: who is *not* like The Pen.

And then of course there's a second husband in the kitchen. This is the one that—if we just think about it for a few seconds—is popping out of the bad mental seeds I planted when I heard myself yell at my kids last week. Husband #2 *is* my fault.

4) The cause-and-effect husband

Husband #2 is the cause-and-effect husband: he has emerged from the seeds that I planted when I yelled at the kids. In the lingo of the ancient Asian sources, this is equivalent to the "dependent-origination" husband—which now you know means simply "the husband I planted myself, when I yelled at the kids." We need to appreciate that the cause-and-effect husband really *does* exist.

5) The hidden-potential husband

Husband #1 can also be called the "hidden-potential husband." In the ancient books, he might be called the "emptiness husband." That's because he is *not* coming from me: he's *not* my fault, because *I didn't do anything, and he starts yelling at me.*

We call him the "emptiness husband" simply because *he doesn't exist.* The old books often put it this way: "He doesn't exist *now;* he *never* existed before; and he *will never exist* afterwards."

Because he's simply impossible. If The Pen proves anything, it's that *nothing exists which is **not** coming from our own seeds:* from exactly how we've treated other people!

6) Only an emptiness husband can make you upset

Now when you get upset at your husband after he calls you "stupid," which husband are you getting upset at? Is it Husband #1 (who is *not my fault, because I didn't do anything and he's yelling at me)*, or is it Husband #2 (who is coming out of the seeds I planted by yelling at the kids)?

Well it has to be Husband #1 that we're upset at. This is because with Husband #2 we realize whose fault he is: *MY OWN*. It's not possible to get upset at a person if you know that they are coming 100% from what I myself did last week to the kids!

7) When you do get upset,
you are literally getting upset at nothing

If all this is true, then every time we get upset at someone (or even some-*thing*, like the weather or the traffic), *we are actually getting upset at something which is not even there, and could never be there.* This means that every negative emotion we've ever had in our life *was aimed at a thing or at a person which didn't even exist.*

When we understand this, we can forever stop being upset, at anything. (Unless you want to be upset at yourself, for planting the seed in the first place!)

According to the Diamond Cutter Sutra, this is the **only** *way that a human being can permanently stop the emotions of getting upset, or getting angry.*

And there you are. These three tools actually give you everything you need to know to make your whole life—in business and at home—a success.

Success:
5 goals, 5 continents

⌢

In the 10th anniversary edition of *The Diamond Cutter*, we included 39 success stories from around the world, to help demonstrate that the method taught in the book really worked!

Looking back, I notice three things. First of all, a significant number of the success stories in the 10th anniversary edition went on to become even more successful; and very often became mentors for the next generation of successful people. And so what you read here are some stories about that third DCI success generation (counting myself as the first generation!).

Secondly, we have decided in these success stories to focus on a fewer number of people than we did before. This is because we want to go deeper into how the success happened, and what it looked like, in each case. We have also adopted an interview format, to let each person speak to you directly. To tell these longer stories without taking up too much space in the book—but still give you the feeling of how global the success has spread—we include one story from each major area of the world.

Thirdly, to be honest I think we tried too hard to portray the successful friends in the 10th anniversary edition as being completely perfect, with completely perfect success. Of course it's true that—if we are able to follow the Seed System perfectly—we will have a perfectly successful home and business life.

But remember that mental seeds are planted at the astounding rate of 65 *per second.* And that they *double in power every 24 hours.* This means that we can ruin half a day of success with just a few minutes of being upset with our business partner; or a customer; or our kids—and who among us can avoid those few minutes, once in a while?

And so, in real practice, we tend to see that people who try very sincerely to plant success with the 4 Steps also unintentionally plant some lousy seeds mixed in with this success. They are still wildly successful compared to other people, but they also come across as *real* people who still have *real* problems and challenges in their life, even with the success. And so we have tried to paint their pictures that way—in a more real way—in the following success stories.

As we mentioned in the previous section of this new 20th anniversary part of the book, people all over the world would like to reach five different goals in life; this is what success means to a great number of the people living on our planet:

(1) financial independence: enough money to do whatever I would like to do with my life, including helping as many people as I can

(2) beautiful professional and personal relationships: there are few things more sad than a wealthy person with no friends or family

(3) great health & youthful energy: a person with serious chronic back pain, for example, can hardly enjoy financial success and good relationships

(4) a happy and peaceful state of mind: success has to stretch inside of us, not just outside

(5) a world where each and every one of us shares all these blessings equally: and there is not one of us who wouldn't like to be someone who helps make this happen in the world; we love movies about superheroes because each one of us would like to be one!

And so another reason we have selected the particular success stories you're about to hear is that, all together, they cover these five goals—and we hear how each of the goals has actually been achieved.

There's nothing to stop us, then, from using the Diamond Cutter to reach these goals ourselves. Let's get started.

A new home
& the perfect partner

John Brady & Connie O'Brien
North America—Sedona, Arizona

Geshe Michael Roach:
Can you tell us what kind of work you both do?

John Brady:
Right now I'm the executive director of the Asian Legacy Library (ALL), which is a free online library of ancient Asian literature. We started at Princeton University 33 years ago, with the help of the Hewlett Packard Corporation.

My colleagues and I travel the globe looking for rare, ancient books; and then we train and pay people living in poverty, in different parts of the world, to digitalize them.

We have scanned 4.7 million pages of these manuscripts, and cataloged over 300,000 volumes in libraries around the world. Our staff worldwide has typed 16,000 rare woodblocks into searchable format. In fact, the original manuscript used as the basis of *The Diamond Cutter* business book was one of our biggest discoveries; we found it in a giant warehouse of old books in St Petersburg, Russia.

Connie O'Brien:

When the 20th anniversary book was first being prepared, I was helping start up a project called "Green Stretch Pen." This is an effort initiated by the Government of Mexico to help 23 million children in the country avoid obesity, by eating more *greens* and other healthy foods, as well as by exercising and *stretching* on a regular daily basis. The program also seeks to protect children from bullying, and in the long term keep them from joining drug gangs, by giving them an understanding of how seeds are planted in their minds from how they treat others, and how these seeds help create the people and things (such as *pens*) around us.

During the last few years I have been focusing on a second project known as the Yoga Studies Institute (YSI). Again, this is an effort to help both business people and families to maintain a healthy level of exercise and good diet, so they can have maximum energy and health to do the things they want to do. An important part of this project is to translate ancient yoga books that my husband's organization finds, and use this precious wisdom in our yoga and healthy eating programs.

GMR:

As you know, this part of the 20th anniversary edition of the Diamond Cutter *book is about success stories from the five continents—talking about how people have achieved the five most common goals of life: financial independence, great relationships, good energy & health, a peaceful mind, and doing something to help the world at large. Can you give us an example of how the two of you have used the Seed System principles of the book to achieve your own financial independence?*

John:

I'll tell you an amazing story. A big part of financial independence is having a good place to live—your own place to live. This is especially important because more and more of us in the world are working much of the time from home.

I think all of us would like to have enough room to live comfortably; we'd rather have our own place, so that we don't need to keep paying higher and higher rent; and we'd also like it if the house or apartment were spacious, safe, and sunny! It's getting harder and harder for people around the world to find living space like this.

Connie and I were spending a lot on rent, and we didn't have much hope of buying our own house, since homes in the small city where we live are quite expensive. Although we do make modest salaries from our main work—and as lecturers and professors for DCI and for SCIM, the DCI teacher-training college—we also devote a large part of our time traveling to different countries around the world, sharing without charge the deeper teachings and meditations that provide the foundation for the DCI success trainings. We often have to cover all of these expenses ourselves.

And then suddenly, out of the blue, one of the students in these courses offered to pay for a beautiful, spacious house for us. We were very encouraged to see this proof that the Seed System really works!

Connie:

What John's not mentioning, because he's so humble, is that our house had a very specific seed! Since the project to save the ancient books doesn't charge anything for people to use the manuscripts it digitalizes and puts up online, the work depends entirely on donations.

There was a period when the American economy wasn't doing very well, and the project was desperate for new ways to fundraise. At the time, John was also working as the vice-president of one of the largest catalog sales companies in the United States. He had a large income and had purchased a penthouse apartment on Central Park in New York City—one of the most expensive pieces of real estate in America.

When the ancient book project was almost ready to collapse, John actually sold his apartment and donated a large part of the income to the project. I myself, and most of us who know and love John, believe that this provided the main seed for our much larger and elegant house—in fact it was originally built by a well-known American architect for her own family to live in.

GMR:

That's a wonderful testimonial to the Seed System! So just to make sure our readers who want the same result get a specific plan, could you guys spell out the 4 Steps they should follow to plant a nice place of their own?

John:

Sure, with pleasure. Here is the classic, specific 4-step plan that Connie and I would suggest:

Step #1
Say what you want:
> "We'd like a beautiful place of our own."

Step #2
Choose a seed-planting partner:
> Someone you know who wants a place like that.

Step #3
Help your seed-planting partner:
> Once a week, for an hour, for free, help them look for their own place.

Step #4
Do your Coffee Meditation:
> When you put your head down on your pillow at night to sleep, think in detail about what you did to help your seed-planting partner, and how you will help them again, this week.

GMR:

Now, you two keep mentioning "our" house—and our readers may not realize that you are married. Did the Seed System play any role in your meeting each other, and deciding to tie the knot?

John:

That's a wonderful question. For many years before we got married, both Connie and I had a deep interest in meditation. Separately, we ended up taking the entire series of 36 courses of the Asian Classics Institute (ACI), which prepared us to do a number of short-term, solitary retreats.

As *The Diamond Cutter* book itself describes, these "Circle Retreats" are a powerful tool that we both used in our business career: myself as an executive of a large Manhattan corporation, and Connie as the founder and owner of one of Vancouver's most successful restaurants.

We worked our way up from weekend silent "creativity retreats" to deep retreats of a month or more—which have an even greater impact on business and personal creativity. Finally, after these many years of preparation, we went for the Olympic Gold Medal of all meditation retreats: the traditional "Great Retreat" of 3 years, 3 months, and 3 days in silent contemplation.

We entered the Great Retreat at Bear Springs Retreat & Conference Center in southern Arizona, along with about 35 other people. On one hand, it was perhaps the greatest experience of our lives. On the other hand, it was also one of the most challenging, when a young man who had just left the retreat passed away.

Connie:

Actually, John and I didn't know each other that well at the time, but we were sort of thrown together into the role of counseling the other retreatants. We did this for months, and gradually came to realize that we had fallen in love.

We were married not long after the retreat, and looking back we take that counseling work as having planted the mental seed for our relationship: by taking care of the emotional needs of others, we had actually gone through a traditional 4-Step Plan to plant a beautiful relationship.

Just to review, for someone else who might be hoping to plant their partner this way, here are the 4 Steps you would use:

Step #1

Say what you want:

"I would like to plant my perfect partner."

Step #2

Choose a seed-planting partner:

Find a person who is lonely, and offer them companionship. A nursing home is the perfect place to find a lonely person like this—choose the one who is most lonely, with no family members left to help or visit them.

Step #3
Help your seed-planting partner:

For example, once a week, for an hour, take this elderly person out for a coffee, or tea, or movie.

Step #4
Do your Coffee Meditation:

When you put your head down on your pillow at night to sleep, think in detail about what you did to help this lonely older person, and what you will do to help them again, during the upcoming week.

GMR:

This Coffee Meditation seems to be at the very core of mental-seed-planting. But in my experience, a lot of us have trouble acknowledging, even to ourselves, our small daily attempts to plant good seeds. Do you two have a suggestion for those of us who find it difficult to do this particular one of the Four Steps?

John:

I have a special problem of my own with my Coffee Meditation, which is that I tend to fall asleep almost immediately when my head hits the pillow. So I've learned to just focus on one very small, specific detail of something I've done during the day to plant a good seed by helping someone else.

I don't try to do some grand meditation on a major project: I just choose one small, specific thing that I can celebrate—whether it's something I did myself, or I saw someone else do today.

Connie:

I go along with what John said, since I have the same problem (or blessing) that I fall asleep almost immediately at night. One very important thing I would add comes from those ancient books that John is saving with his project. They say that it's possible for us to "target" our

Coffee Meditation. For example, if I'm having a challenge with someone at my job who talks too much, then I can think about a moment today when I was a good listener and allowed someone else to say their piece.

I can "send" (target) that good energy to my friend who talks too much at work, even though it will only change them in my own perception. By the way, it's also important to know that Coffee Meditation is an excellent way to spend the time when we're already in bed but have trouble falling to sleep, or wake up for a period during the night.

How to

be the next

great entrepreneur

Stanley Chen & Zhou Xiaoping
Asia—Shenzhen, China

GMR:

Well, to start with, can you tell us a little about yourselves?

Zhou Xiaoping:
(whose name is pronounced *Jo Shao-ping*):
I grew up in the Xiamen, which is a pleasant oceanside city in the southeast of China. The population of the city and surrounding area is about 5 million.

Like most Chinese families, we are all close, and growing up I was always particularly close to my grandparents. I did well in college, and ended up majoring in English linguistics & literature, as well as English translation.

I had read the Chinese version of this *Diamond Cutter* book, and was already interested in it, and then one day I got a volunteer opportunity to translate onstage for Geshe Michael. Since then I have become a close part of the global DCI family, and a big fan of using the Seed System in my own life.

Stanley Chen:

I grew up in Shaoguan, China, which is an inland city of about 3 million people not that far from where Xiaoping grew up. Our city is famous though, because the Nanhua Temple is located here.

This temple is one of the major centers of Chinese Zen Buddhism, and was the home of Master Huineng (638-713CE). He is the famed Sixth Patriarch, and is considered perhaps the greatest Zen master in Chinese history. For example, he wrote the famous *Platform Sutra*, one of the most influential spiritual works in our country.

Master Huineng is also said to have attained awakening when he accidentally heard someone reciting the Diamond Cutter Sutra. So I guess it's not completely coincidental that I was also studying human resources management and English translation in college; got interested in this same **Diamond Cutter** book; and had a chance to translate for Geshe Michael on stage at a **Diamond Cutter** Institute event. And with that, I also became a fan of the Seed System.

GMR:

The two of you are business partners, and together you are some of the most successful entrepreneurs in the entire global DCI network. First off, can you tell us a little about your main business?

Stanley:

Like a lot of entrepreneurs who use a big toolbox of business techniques they learned from DCI, Xiaoping and I have started a number of different companies; but our main business is called "Future Diamond Institute."

One of the primary programs of the Institute is called Classics Soft Power Global Executive Training (CSP). And we have another commercial translation company called Pure Gold Translation Services.

GMR:

We've also heard some news that you guys are starting up an exciting new project, with the creation of a new international university that will offer US-accredited degrees. Can you say a word about that?

Xiaoping:

Actually yes, in the next month we are opening Diamond Silk Entrepreneur University (DSEU), which will have campuses both in Kyoto, Japan, and also Sedona, Arizona, in the USA. The university will offer accredited BA, MBA, and EMBA degree programs, in an option of either English or Chinese language. The unusual name we chose for DSEU is meant to reflect our goal of offering a standard, high-quality business university program, which at the same time includes great entrepreneurial wisdom from centuries-old Asian traditions; in an attempt to "re-connect" the old Silk Road between the Western and Eastern parts of our planet.

GMR:

What are some typical services that your first two companies offer? How did they get started?

Xiaoping:

Classics Soft Power provides an in-depth, 18-month management program to help established business executives expand and improve their companies, especially for doing more business overseas.

Stanley:

We had this idea to emulate a special concept which is found in a number of very famous Chinese sources. One of these is the well-known *Yi-Jing* (sometimes spelled *I-Ching*), or *Book of Changes,* said to have been written by the Duke of Zhou (Zhou Gong) about three thousand years ago. Another is the *Analects* composed by the great master Confucius, who lived 2,500 years ago. And a third source is the renowned *Dao De Jing* (also spelled *Tao Te Ching*)—the *Way of Virtue*—written around the same era by Laozi.

All three of these ancient authors talk about the concept of a *junzi,* which can refer in modern times to *a successful businessman or businesswoman who at the same time is very knowledgeable about the best of their country's ancient culture, and uses this culture to become even more successful.*

And so the Classics Soft Power program, which is itself also very successful financially, trains top executives to be more effective and successful, by using great ideas from the ancient books.

GMR:

What are some of the great books of Chinese history that you use in your Classics Soft Power program?

Xiaoping:

Well, readers of *The Diamond Cutter* business book here will already be familiar with one very good example, which is the ancient Diamond Cutter Sutra itself. The Chinese edition of the sutra is the oldest printed book in the world with a date inside; so we thought it would be a great place to start from, to share with the world the best of the ancient wisdom of China, which can be like a "secret weapon" for anyone to use for success in their business and their family life.

Many of the greatest of these ancient sources though are either not generally available internationally, or have not yet been translated into modern Mandarin and other present-day languages. This is where our second company comes in: Pure Gold Translation Services.

Aside from doing thousands of pages of technical translation for commercial companies every year—for example, the major business training manuals used by DCI itself—we also have a division which locates and translates famous books by ancient Chinese authors that contain great ideas which will help corporations become even more successful.

For example, right now we're working on a projected 8-volume translation into modern Mandarin and English of an important text written by Master Yuance, a great thinker from the Tang Dynasty and a direct student of the famous Master Xuanzang, who made a great 17-year journey along the ancient Silk Road. This epic was later described in the famous *Journey to the West*; and Xuanzang is also known for translating many ancient manuscripts himself.

We feel that the Tang Dynasty era (618-907CE) represents one of the main periods in history when the best features of China's cultural richness extended to the whole world, along the Silk Road—and we seek to continue this tradition.

GMR:

We can say, I think, that the two of you have been very successful in three different ways. First, you are good examples of the model of the hip young entrepreneur who tries something new and makes a great business out of it— you yourselves are modern examples of the ancient model of the junzi. *Secondly, I have seen myself how, at the same time, you are respected and loved by all the senior business people in your program—which is unusual in Asia, where younger people are generally expected only to follow the lead of the elders. And thirdly, the two of you seem to be enjoying a fun and successful business relationship together. Can you share with our readers how you think these three happened?*

Xiaoping:

It's true, the two of us are only around 30 years old, and we've already had these three kinds of success: becoming successful entrepreneurs with new ideas; respected to and listened to by the people around us, which is something everyone enjoys when it happens in their life; and sharing this enjoyable and creative business partnership between us.

I think the reason we've reached this triple success is that we learned the Seed System of *The Diamond Cutter* at a young age, and we worked hard to put it into practice. We learned the 4 Steps and we really tried to use them on a daily basis; and this is the result we got. And so we really encourage others to check the Seed System out, and try it themselves!

GMR:

Let's get practical here. What specific steps would you advise another young person to take, if they wanted to have the same success that you've had?

Stanley:

Well, our friends John Brady and Connie O'Brien have already given our readers 4-Step Plans for achieving a new home; and a great relationship. What we'd like to share here are the 4 steps for becoming a successful entrepreneur.

In our early years getting to know the Seed System, we both translated for Geshe Michael on stages in different cities around the world. Gradually we began to recognize the 4 Steps that he himself used in Manhattan, as a young entrepreneur helping to build the largest diamond jewelry company in the world. These are the same steps that we used ourselves, and that we recommend to our readers:

Step #1

Say what you want:

I would like to be the next great entrepreneur in the world!

Step #2

Choose a seed-planting partner:

Now, you could obviously choose, as your seed-planting partner, another person who would also like to be the next great entrepreneur, and that would be a good choice. But what we noticed with Geshe Michael, is that with his diamond company *he chose the great ideas themselves to be his seed-planting partner.*

That is, he planted his seeds by sharing the wisdom of the seeds itself, and by preserving ancient great ideas about the seeds. To do this, he worked with John Brady for many years to locate and share the old manuscripts with these ancient ideas; and that sharing of the understanding of how to plant a great entrepreneur became itself the greatest seed to become one.

Step #3

Help your seed-planting partner:

And so Xiaoping and myself work very hard at preserving these ancient Chinese cultural ideas and making them available around the world.

Not long ago, we even had a chance to share the ideas of the Diamond Cutter Sutra with the members of the Congress of Mexico, and in my photo in this section you can see me there, giving my speech about Classics Soft Power and the 4 Steps.

So *just sharing The Pen; and the 4 Steps; and the Two Husbands* with other people—once a week, at home or at work, maybe just as you sit around with others on your coffee break—is a powerful Step #3.

Step #4

Do your Coffee Meditation:

Of course, the real key to success as an entrepreneur is to do your daily Coffee Meditation, just before you sleep, thinking about all the help you have given by sharing these ideas with other people.

GMR:

Here in the new success stories for the 20ᵗʰ edition of The Diamond Cutter, *we are asking each contributor if they have any special tricks that they use for this Coffee Meditation. Can you guys share with us one trick that you two use?*

Xiaoping:

We sure can! We all know that, during Coffee Meditation, we are supposed to think about how we helped someone else this week, for an hour a week, and about how we plan to help them more in the coming week.

What many people don't realize, though, is that we can do Coffee Meditation on the good deeds that we have seen others do today. In fact, the ancient books say that we can even get for ourselves 10% of the energy of the other people's good seeds, just by being happy like this about what *they've* been able to do.

And so Stanley and I like to do Coffee Meditation *on each other,* not just before we go to bed, but also as we work with our clients and staff during the day. We take every opportunity we can to share with other people what great things the other one is doing; for example, I might get up on the stage at one of our executive training events and talk for a few minutes about how hard Stanley has been working all week to get ready for the event.

This kind of Mutual Coffee Meditation has been an important key to the great success we've had as young entrepreneurs, and we strongly recommend it to others who seek the same goal!

Succeeding in a major corporation and fighting depression in our family

Victor Gonzalez & Zazi Abarca
Latin America—Mexico City, Mexico

GMR:

So far, our success stories have focused on 4-Step Plans for the goals of building our own business; creating a relationship; and planting a beautiful place to live. The two of you though have a different success story to share with our readers; that is, how to use the 4 Steps to succeed in a major corporation, and how to use them to make our family life a success, especially for fighting depression. So Victor, can we start with the large corporation?

Victor Gonzalez:

Sure. Earlier on in my life, I was an executive with two very large corporations in my home country of Mexico. The first was Coca-Cola FEMSA, which is the seventh largest corporation in our country: it does over 10 billion US dollars of business a year, and employs some 180,000 people. The second was Cinépolis, which is Mexico's biggest cineplex chain. Total it has over 600 theaters, with 5,000 screens, and employs more than 25,000 people in 17 countries.

GMR:

How did you break into such big companies?

Victor:

A friend at university provided a reference to Coke for me, and I sent in a resume. They gave me a call and asked if I wanted to start as a trainee—I jumped at the chance, even though at the time trainees only made about US$250 per month.

After 4 or 5 months, they promoted me to analyst—which consisted of not very interesting work on projects. It had nothing to do with my education and what I wanted as a career: I was really hoping I could work in marketing.

I kept my head down and worked crazy hours, showing my commitment: I was just very persistent, and delivered everything on time, whatever I had to do. My boss was happy with me, and helped me get into my dream department: media & advertising.

Here I got promoted to an executive and spent about a year as the youngest manager of about 200 people; I kept working amazingly hard, meeting all the deadlines, writing all the reports, perfect attendance—the model employee.

Then the woman who was my direct boss got promoted, and took me with her; and suddenly I am like an executive chief in the advertising department, at the age of 24! It was a super-happy time of my life: I got to deal with crowds of clients, I made big-money deals, I kept getting promoted.

GMR:

Now that you're a major DCI player—a big part of the management team at DCI's teacher-training college, SCIM—what kind of advice would you give to readers who work in a large company like Coke, and who want to achieve the kind of success you did?

Victor:

I have a very strong opinion about this. The most common thing that happens to people in big corporations is that they start to get *selfish:* very selfish.

In reality, you're just working for a bigger company that belongs to other people; but we start feeling like we *own* our position; and we *own* our department; and our budget is *our* money.

You begin to feel super-powerful in this big bubble, like you are the best person in the whole company.

And so I think the first most important advice I could give to our readers in large corporations is to always remember that you are *replaceable:* those big companies don't really need you at all.

GMR:

But how does that help you get ahead in the company?

Victor:

When you give some careful thought to how much your position in a big corporation depends on the people around you—when you realize how fragile you are, and how dependent on others you really are—then automatically you start caring more for the coworkers around you. You break out of your selfishness; and when we reach out to help the other people around us, automatically we are planting seeds.

These *more conscious* seeds will move us ahead in the company, and keep us there.

I'm even talking about not being selfish with your boss: with the person who is on top of you in the company. Normally, we want our boss's position; we are jealous of them, we feel angry when someone else gets promoted instead of us. The whole corporate environment tends to increase these intense feelings of competition.

When you finally understand though that things come from mental seeds—when you understand The Pen—a big breakthrough you make is to see that one of the best ways to become a boss in a large company is to *do your best to help your own boss.*

Make them successful! We talk a lot about making our own staff successful, but this goes as well for the people above us in a company.

And if you really want to get ahead in big corporation fast, the very best seed-planting you can do is with the people that you are competing with, inside of the company.

GMR:

Can you explain a little more what you mean by this?

Victor:

You know, when we do the 4 Steps, we need to choose a seed-planting partner: Planting seeds is like bouncing a basketball, and to plant a seed we need to "bounce" it off of another person—we need to *do something nice* for someone else.

Choosing our seed-planting partner carefully is a huge part of how powerful our seeds are going to be. For example, if we want to plant a seed for good health and we only have so much resources, then rather than buying a lot of medicine for just a single person, we could put that same money towards hiring a doctor to work for a week or two in a poor community.

As far as the people we compete with, we get one level of seeds if we help someone who is a friend, or a family member. We get a higher level of seeds if we help someone we don't know personally. But the very highest level of seeds—for getting promoted in a big company like Coca Cola—would be to *help someone that maybe we don't like:* somebody who is competing with us for the same position in the company.

GMR:

Victor, now that you're a Seed System expert, could you put that into a 4-Step format for us?

Victor:

Sure; here you go—

Step #1
Say what you want:

I would like to get promoted to a higher position in this corporation.

Step #2
Choose a seed-planting partner:

Is there someone else around me in this company who would love to get a promotion?

Step #3

Help your seed-planting partner:

Do your best to show your seed-planting partner in a good light; keep an eye out for good things they're doing, and praise them to other people, especially their boss. (This doesn't mean by the way that you should lie or exaggerate about what they're doing: if you try, you'll find a lot of real things your friend is doing that you can praise about them.)

Step #4

Do your Coffee Meditation:

When you put your head down on your pillow at night, think through all the things you've been doing to help your friend get a promotion, and celebrate your good deeds to yourself, quietly. Remember as well to think up some new sneaky plans for things you can do this next week, to help them get a promotion—even if it's the promotion you wanted for yourself. *Especially* if it's the promotion you wanted for yourself!

GMR:

Good! A solid, compassionate plan that always works, to get promoted! But, having been in a big company myself for many years, I have to ask: Is the promotion going to make you happy? Will it be enough?

Victor:

Well now, *getting* a promotion is one thing, with its own mental seeds; and *being happy* with your promotion is another thing—which I learned the hard way at Coke.

As an important executive in the advertising department at Coca Cola, and in my next position with Cinépolis, I was living high. Big cars, expensive trips, and fancy lunches out with media execs and suppliers— where by the way I was expected to drink alcohol with them constantly. Pretty soon, all that started to affect me. I began to get more and more emotionally unstable, and then within six months I was fired—I was out on the streets, without a job at all. And then later I went into a period of deep depression.

Zazi Abarca:
As Victor's wife, this was the most difficult time in my life. You see, I had met him very young—when we were just 14 years old. We started out as friends, but when we started dating at 19 I realized that I felt different about him: that I wanted to spend my life with him. So we married very young, at 21—in fact, our 22nd wedding anniversary is coming up soon.

Within the year after our wedding we had our first child, a boy, and then our second, who's a girl. So you can imagine how hard it was on us—just into our early 20's, trying to raise two kids, and then suddenly we have no income, and my husband is stuck deep into an extended bout with depression.

GMR:
How did Victor break out of these years of depression? What did you do to help him?

Zazi:
I think the first thing we have to say about breaking Victor out of depression is that—even with the seeds—really beating depression takes a lot of hard work, and a lot of determination. Depression is I think a deep seed, maybe because the result of that seed is also in the mind—not an outside thing like money, or a new house.

So I think the first advice I would give to people trying to help someone break out of an extended period of depression is to never give up. It's the same advice that I would give people who are working hard to bring up their children, and who have trouble with that. The most important thing is to understand that the seeds *are* going to work; that some things, even with seeds, *take time;* and that the hard work is worth it.

That is, we have a certain responsibility to our wife or husband, and to our kids: we have chosen to get married; we have chosen to have children; we have chosen to make a family. And as a wife or husband, and as a mother or a father, we have made a commitment to do our best to make these other people happy—to help them have a happy life, for their whole life. If a mother, and a wife, gives up on the children and husband, then who else is going to make that kind of commitment? Who is going to help them?

My dad, you know—by occupation, he was a general in the army. And I would say about these tough periods with Victor and my kids, I kept thinking: "I will *never* surrender."

This is one of the main reasons, I think, why our marriage and our family have survived, and grown, and become a success—along with the successful advertising business we have built together since then. It is all founded on the commitment that all of us in the family have made to each other, to help the others be happy.

GMR:

Do you guys have a 4-step formula that you would offer to other couples or families that are struggling to get through an extended period where someone in the family is fighting with serious depression?

Victor:

Yes, here is the classic, ancient 4-step approach to long-term depression. For Step #4, Zazi and I have added some special techniques that we have found especially useful!

Step #1

Say what you want:

We want to see this member of our family fight free of this depression that's been staying with them.

Step #2

Choose a seed-planting partner:

This is the most important step here. When a person is depressed, or we have someone in our family who is fighting depression, we are very likely to be *selfish*: the same problem that we had with working in a big corporation.

That is, a depressed person is always caught up with how *they* feel, and what *they* need. It's the same if this person is part of our family: We are always thinking, *my* family member needs help; *our* family has a special problem.

But even in the hardest moments—especially in the hardest moments—we need to remember that the only way to plant a seed to change things is to *help someone else who is feeling depressed: to help another family that is fighting depression.* And so we need to choose another person who is sad, to be our seed-planting partner; and since that's so, so difficult for a depressed person to do on their own, we need as a family to help our family member to turn their attention towards someone else's needs, if only for an hour or two in a week.

Step #3

Help your seed-planting partner:

Recognizing that we may not be the perfect person to help someone else with their depression, nonetheless we need to reach out to this other person, even just once a week, for an hour, to give them the best comfort we can. Maybe all we can do is just bring them a flower, or share a new favorite song with them. That's enough; with good Coffee Meditation, even tiny seeds make huge results.

Step #4

Do your Coffee Meditation:

When you put your head on the pillow to go to sleep, think about the person you're helping; and plan some more cool things you can do to help them in the coming week.

Our special Coffee Meditation trick has three steps:

(1) As you start to wind down towards bedtime—say when you start to brush your teeth before bed—**turn off** your electronics: no phone, no texting, no laptop. This already puts you in the mood for Coffee Meditation.

(2) Buy a fluorescent sticker, like the kind you get for your

Success: 5 Goals, 5 Continents   265

kids, say of a teddy bear or a silly cat or whatever you like. It should be the kind that glows in the dark after you turn the lights out. Attach this sticker to the ceiling over your bed! When you and your spouse get into bed, you'll be staring up in the dark at this silly kid's toy, and it will remind you to do your Coffee Meditation and be happy about the good things you've done this week for someone else who is fighting depression.

(3) In the dark, as you fall asleep, help each other remember, and talk to each other, about the good seeds you've each been planting to help these other people who are sad or depressed.

And always remember to keep up your determination—never surrender. Even with seeds, depression is not going to go away easy, or fast: but in time, the seeds always work. Keep planting!

GMR:

Thanks for that special trick to make seeds grow fast! I have to ask one last question that I can't help asking. When you were talking about working in that huge corporation, Coca Cola; and then you were talking about your love for your kids; didn't you feel strange working in a big company that is making a product that is responsible for obesity and diabetes in millions of young Mexican kids? How do you think any of us can reconcile working in an industry that hurts people?

Victor:

Yes that's a problem! And Geshe Michael, we need to ask the same question about working in the diamond business, which is responsible for so much environmental destruction, and can even finance terrorism and genocide in some of the countries where diamonds are mined! How can we understand what to do here?

GMR:

Ah, now you've put me on the spot! It was my spiritual teacher who first headed me towards the diamond business, and after only a few weeks in the industry, I asked him the same question: "Now that I've seen how this diamond business works—oftentimes with a lot of dishonesty, and also dealing with a product that hurts the earth and many people—I'm thinking I should quit, right away!"

And as usual, my teacher—who was a famous debater in the monastery—gave me what's called "The Sarcasm" in the ancient Asian art of debating. "Yeah, sure, okay then! Just quit! Let those people go on cheating each other; and not paying taxes; and smuggling diamonds; and digging up the earth; and using the money for terrorism. Fine! Just quit!"

Of course I caught his sarcasm, and answered, "Well yes, but even if I stay in the diamond business, how can I—how can just one person—change a huge industry that stretches out across every country in the world?"

"And where does that world come from?" he asked me.

"From seeds," I replied.

"And where does your world come from?" he asked, holding up a pen.

"From my seeds," I answered.

"So change your seeds!" he replied. "And change the diamond business!"

So I have to say that I have tried, for many years, and things are looking up. There is a new system of certificates that helps prove that there was no violence involved in mining certified stones; and that environmental policies were followed.

There is even a more exciting trend, echoed in the original Diamond Cutter *book, towards creating pure diamonds in the lab, where they do no damage to others. This baby industry already creates, for example, inexpensive knives with diamond edges that can never get dull—and affordable wedding dresses covered with hundreds of real (but not* natural*), perfect diamonds.*

Like pens and everything else in my world, these too have come from my seeds. If I keep planting, then inevitably Coca Cola will begin turning their incredible corporate power and brains to producing the very best super-healthy green drinks for making children trim and smart.

If The Pen is true, then whether that happens soon or not is up to us, and not them!

Hope & Humanity

Nour Ibrahim
Africa/Middle East—Damascus, Syria
& Bucharest, Romania

You, your family, and your nation have been through some very difficult times in recent years. Can you tell us a little about it?

Nour Ibrahim:
Yes, we have. I grew up in Damascus, which is the capital city of Syria and is said to be the oldest continually inhabited city in the world, founded over 5,000 years ago. I am the eldest of four children in our family—three girls and one boy.

Financially, we were a middle-class family. Early on in my life I thought I would like to study abroad if I got the chance; but while I was in high school my dad was sick, and I knew it would be too much strain on the family finances if I asked them to help me go overseas.

I decided that getting a scholarship would be the only way to travel, so I worked very hard to be a top student. At a young age then I was appointed an assistant professor at my college—the University of Damascus, specializing in the study of human development.

A few years later I was accepted into a PhD program in Romania, with a major in education sciences—specifically, I studied cultural differences in teaching. Just as I was completing my studies, the civil war in Syria broke out. Since then I have been unable to return to my home, and in time I have become a Romanian citizen.

GMR:

How did you get involved with the Diamond Cutter Institute?

Nour:

After my university studies, I got a job with the UNHCR: the United Nations High Commissioner for Refugees. I was working as a social inclusion counselor, meaning that I would help refugees from the Middle East start their new life, and learn to cope with cultural differences.

One day I attended a DCI program in Bucharest where Geshe Michael talked about the idea of The Pen. It gave me a sudden insight that filled me with my first real hope in many years; and ever since then I have devoted a lot of time and effort to learn all the details of the Seed System. In recent years I have even undertaken the teacher certification program at the Sedona College of International Management (SCIM).

GMR:

Why would the idea of the pen and the dog give you hope, in such a terrible tragedy, where up to half a million people have already lost their lives?

Nour:

You have to try to put yourself in the shoes of those of us who have gone through this horror-filled civil war. Damascus is an incredibly beautiful city, and Syria an incredibly beautiful country, filled with the greatest of ancient architecture, culture, and historical sites. Like most people around the world, we grew up in the middle of our country's beauty without fully appreciating it.

And then suddenly Syria was filled with blood and horror; nobody knew what to do, they could only try to run. I can remember traveling from Romania to Greece in the early days of the war, making visits to the refugee camps and helping people there with whatever I had—food, money, even just a pair of shoes. While I was helping one group of refugees, some of my colleagues not many miles away were rescuing a young woman from a small boat that had just made the very dangerous crossing on the Mediterranean Sea—where almost 20,000 refugees have died in the last six years.

That woman was my sister, and we shared a tearful reunion. Later, she was taken into the home of a wonderful student of the DCI courses in Germany.

In circumstances like this, rare people like myself—who were fortunate enough to have been out of the country during the entire war—feel as if the situation at home is hopeless: We don't really understand how the war happened in the first place, and even when we begin to feel a ray of hope about the future we immediately feel guilty, as if we are forgetting the suffering that our friends and family are still going through at home, every day.

And so what's the connection between The Pen, and the dog, and hope? Maybe the worst feeling a refugee can have is the loss of faith, and the feeling of incomprehension that causes this loss. Why, of all the countries in the world, should my own country become a living hell? What's the sense of it? Why did it happen?

Sometimes I think that only a refugee can really appreciate the teaching of The Pen. The point of this pen, for us, is that *things make sense: there is a reason for the things we see around us.* And if there is a reason, there can be hope.

GMR:

What do you mean by that?

Nour:

When people win the lottery, and suddenly they have a million dollars that they didn't have the day before, nobody cries out, *"Why me???"* It's when tragedies like the war happen to people that they really start to ask where things are coming from.

The war had already forced me to ask that question—*Where is this coming from? Or are things just happening, randomly, without any sense, for no reason at all?* When I heard The Pen, and went deep into the Seed

System, I began to feel that there was a logic to the things that happen to us in our life. Basically, I feel like it proved to me that we get what we give.

And for me, as a refugee, the most important thing about this understanding is **hope**. If watermelon seeds really do make watermelons; and if kindness to others really does make happiness; then we all have a clear path we can take, to overcome tragedies like the Syrian civil war.

GMR:

What does that path look like, for you? And what is a practical way that other people in the world could use the same path for hope, in their own lives?

Nour:

I think that inside of us, we all understand the answer to this question, just by instinct. Still, it would just be useful to have the path spelled out clearly, as a plan of action. Let me try to put it in 4-Step format:

Step #1
Say what you want:

I would like to see everyone in the world to live in hope & safety.

Step #2
Choose a seed-planting partner:

In my case, choosing a seed-planting partner took some time and careful thought. We always need to work backwards from the goal that we want, to find the seed we need to plant, and then backwards from that to choose the person we need to plant the seed with.

GMR:

Can you tell us the process you went through to choose a seed-planting partner, in your specific case?

Nour:

So the specific goals I had in mind were two. First of all, I wanted to see more hope in my world—specifically in my country, with my family and fellow Syrians.

Secondly, I wanted to see my country protected; again, specifically, I wanted to see our ancient Syrian culture survive and thrive.

Since those were my two goals—we can call them "hope & humanity"—I knew I needed to plant two different kinds of seeds. For the hope, I obviously had to do something concrete to provide hope to others. For the protection and preservation, I had to help someone else protect what was dear to them: I had to help give someone else this sense of safety.

So I started a project called "Threads for Wisdom." This project has two parts, to cover the two types of seeds I wanted to plant.

During the entire recent refugee crisis in Europe, over 5 million people have fled the violence in their native countries. About 40% of these refugees are women and children.

So you have millions of women running from their countries; and most of them, like myself, are Muslim. Muslim women are not traditionally encouraged to be out in public, especially working at a job, and so now you have hundreds of thousands of women whose husbands have died or disappeared, with children to feed, and no skills to work to support their family.

With the help of some friends around the world who were also studying the DCI business and personal success principles, I created an entrepreneurship program for these refugee women. We contracted with a trade school here in Romania where the women could come together and learn to use sewing machines, in a safe, quiet, and personal atmosphere.

We fundraised for their school fees and equipment, and in time our women became some of the first refugees in Europe to receive government permission to work in their trade.

We were careful not to be prejudiced in selecting these seed-planting partners; and so in addition to women from Syria, we also have trainees from Iraq, Lebanon, Afghanistan, Iran, Palestine, and Jordan.

Next, my friends and I went "hunting" for countries that needed help preserving their own traditions—which would be the seed for saving our precious, ancient Syrian culture: our human heritage, endangered in embattled Syrian cities like Palmyra, or Aleppo.

We found our first seed-planting partner, amazingly, in far-off Mongolia; the national library there holds, scholars estimate, some 300,000 ancient woodblock manuscripts. Traditionally, the pages of these books are bound together with large sheets of specially-sewn cloth, and so the library has been a natural fit with our refugee women's vocational project. Funding for the work has been coordinated with the ancient literature preservation work headed by John Brady, whose success story was described above in this book.

GMR:

Can you finish up the 4 Steps for us here?

Nour:

Sure. So we had had our first step, our goal: hope & humanity, in the form of more hope in the world, and the preservation of valuable human culture. Our second step then also had two parts: giving hope to these refugee women, and helping to preserve someone else's culture.

I should say that, over the entire course of my life, and as I've learned how the Seed System works, I've come to realize how the key is that—to plant a seed—*we need to help somebody else,* someone *different* from us. My whole life, I've been fascinated by this challenge of creating relationships on both sides of our life.

That is, in my refugee work for the UN especially, I had to be able to relate to officers from affluent backgrounds at the top of the organization, and at the same time get close to the penniless refugees just stepping off their dangerous little boats. With people from home—from Syria—I've had to thread my way through those who support one side in the conflict, and those who support the other side: you can't be a Syrian nowadays without learning to relate at the same moment to people on opposing sides.

This has been a kind of training for my 4-Step projects, since planting a seed always depends upon making a relationship with someone outside of your own group or family or business.

So that has been **Step #3**: actually carrying out our project to help the refugees, and assisting another country that wants to preserve their culture.

Which of course leads us to **Step #4,** Coffee Meditation—where just as I put my head down on my pillow at night, I take a moment to think about the good seeds I've been planting with these projects.

You know, DCI teachers around the world often talk about the 5 most common goals of life: financial independence, good relationships, good health, happy mind, and contributing to making the whole world happy. I feel fortunate that the tragedy in my life has led me to the four seed-planting strategies that I just described; and I think that any of our readers who really want to make a difference in the world—goal #5, the highest goal—can figure out a personal strategy similar to what I just outlined, in my own 4 Steps.

GMR:

We've been asking each of the success stories here if they have any special tricks that they use during this Coffee Meditation at the end of the day. Are there any techniques you use which you'd like to share with us?

Nour:

I can think of three things here that I'd like to share.

First is sort of a clarification about Coffee Meditation. I think many of our readers may come from a culture which feels like my own, on the subject of celebrating our own good deeds.

That is, in Syrian traditions, and in Islamic culture in general, we have a saying: "When the right hand does something, it shouldn't tell the left hand." What this means is that we shouldn't show off the good deeds that we do; we should keep them quiet, and never brag about them—even to ourselves.

And so first of all it took me some time to find a kind of Coffee Meditation where I could truly appreciate myself, and at the same time avoid any feelings of pride. I think that this healthy self-appreciation—without the pride—is a very valuable thing for everyone in the world; especially in a global culture which sometimes encourages feelings of low self-esteem in women or other groups of people.

Second, I have sometimes felt guilty to celebrate good seeds when so many people around me were suffering so terribly: it didn't feel right even to be happy about my good deeds, when others were so sad all day. But

I've come to see how this nightly celebration makes my seeds grow faster and stronger, so I can help even more of these people be happy themselves.

Lastly, I keep a little teddy bear in bed next to my pillow, and when I do my Coffee Meditation at night, it's like I'm sharing with him my little successes in trying to be a good person. That's an easy thing that all of us can do to help us remember Step #4.

Creativity, Beauty & Health

Uta Scharf
Europe—Berlin, Germany

GMR:

So far in these success stories, we've seen a wide range of goals that people have for their lives: a home of their own; a marriage; a new business; safety for their country. Your life is an example of an entire different set of goals—starting with creativity. Let's talk about your career in the rarified world of high-end art, and then your ideas about creativity and the Seed System. How did you get started?

Uta Scharf:

I grew up in northern Germany, as the eldest of four children. My father was an engineer, and my mother was interested in art; but it was my grandfather who was a painter, a musician, and a ship engineer, all at once. I completed an MA in the Berlin University of the Arts, and was also a ballet dancer—which we'll talk more about later on. I got a job in an art gallery to help support myself, and it was there that I met my future husband.

As it turned out, his family had been collecting very high-end art for four generations, and had assembled one of the most famous art collections in the world. We're talking about pieces by great masters like Picasso, Matisse, and Cezanne; and emphasizing what we would call seminal works—those that triggered major new trends in the world of art.

GMR:

How did that meeting transition into your career as a dealer of fine art?

Uta:

My husband, and my father-in-law, educated me in this level of art. The family name of Scharf is quite famous in the art world, and so it was natural and easy for us to use our home in New York City as a setting for showing expensive, one-of-a-kind pieces to exceptional clients from around the world. We did very well and eventually I worked my way up to the position of president of the company.

GMR:

Of course that was before you had learned anything about the Seed System; but that same system would say that you must have already been attracted to planting the seeds for success, even if you didn't know exactly how they worked, or do the planting consciously.

Uta:

Yes, that's right. Now that I've been through my certification at DCI's Sedona College of International Management, I can look back and say that my crazy success in those days was what we jokingly like to call "bird poop success."

GMR:

What's that mean!??

Uta:

Sometimes a beautiful flower grows up in the middle of your garden, but it's a species that you never planted. What happens is that birds find a big bunch of those flowers somewhere else, and eat too many of the seeds at one time, and can't digest them all. They get diarrhea while they're flying over your garden, and you get a little perfect package of seeds and fertilizer dropped down to grow in your garden, all by itself.

And that's true of many of these amazing, unexpected successes that people can suddenly experience early on in their life: they did plant the seeds, by helping someone else, but they didn't know the Seed System and they didn't plant consciously. That's what happened to me, shooting up suddenly into the highest levels of the global art business.

At the same time, this kind of sudden success most often becomes very frustrating later, because when those bird-poop seeds start to wear out, we go crazy trying to figure out how to repeat our earlier success. We see lots of young musicians and artists and even businesspeople like that—unable to repeat their first grand achievements, and suffering intensely from the frustration that follows.

GMR:

Knowing the result that you experienced, though, and knowing the Seed System so well now—teaching it in fact around the world—do you have a feeling for what kind of seed triggered your great success? Can you share with us any conjectures you might have about the very nature of creativity?

Uta:

I can, and it's surprising and deep. Over my years of experience with important art pieces—because of the extraordinary opportunity I was given, at the top, by the Scharf family (although after some years, my husband and I divorced)—I have come to believe that there is a clear distinction between "normal" creativity, where people create what we might call "normal" art or music or literature, and what I would call "transcendent" creativity.

What lasts in the art world, and what costs a lot of money, is exactly this transcendent kind of art. Here, the artist has made a conscious effort to transcend their own life—their personal story. They have an urge—whether it be conscious or not—to make their art into a universal language that everyone else can relate to and understand. This universal artistic language then transcends all normal cultures and tongues.

That is, the artist wants to speak to every person on the planet, regardless of where they come from—to communicate directly with their heart, their soul. This elevated desire is the essence of a great master of art and, in my opinion, it plants the seeds for artistic creativity which is truly great.

GMR:

So far in these success stories, we've been challenging people to put such thoughts into a concrete 4-Step Plan that others could put into practice in their own life. Will you give it a try?

Uta:

Sure, that's what DCI teachers are for! So here are the four steps that a person seeking transcendent creativity—an incredible level of creativity—could undertake:

Step #1
Say what you want:

I want to reach a level of creativity where I can produce new things which are truly great, whether it be in art, music, literature, or commerce.

Step #2
Choose your seed-planting partner:

A normal seed-planting partner here would be someone else who seeks to be creative. But in this "transcendent" version of creativity, our seed partner can be the consumer of the product of our creativity: the person who sees the painting, or hears the song, or uses the amazing new commercial product that we've created—whether it's a new kind of electronics, a special new car, or anything of the kind. The important thing is that we feel the strong motivation to please and inspire this person with our creation.

Step #3

Actually undertake to create something of high beauty or function which would elevate another person. By the way, we don't necessarily have to *succeed* in actually elevating or inspiring them, every time—we just have to try, with sincerity and honest effort. As usual with mental seeds, it is our sincere intention which is 90% of the power of each seed.

Step #4

Be very sure to do your Coffee Meditation each night as you lay your head on your pillow: be happy that you tried to contribute to the happiness and uplifting of others.

GMR:

If you don't mind, I'd like to cover two other kinds of success with you, since you're such a good example of both. First of all, you have a wonderful, beautiful personal appearance that you've kept up for many years. What's your secret?

Uta:

Seeds, of course!

GMR:

So what seeds do you plant, on a daily basis, to keep up such a beautiful face?

Uta:

First of all I have to say that, as we all know, inner beauty is the important thing, and not our outer appearance. That having been said, we can think of outer beauty like a flower: if we carried around a beautiful flower in our hand all day, or attached one to our clothing, it would provide a basic kind of pleasure and happiness to other people around us, all day long. I think if we think of personal beauty in this way—almost as a gift to others—then it can become a meaningful thing.

So on a conventional level, I have a very simple beauty routine. I don't buy those very expensive skin creams—I've tried both in my life, and to be honest I can't see a huge difference between a $3 jar of cream and a $300 one. I have also tried treatments like botox but I don't like the tight feeling you get in your face from them, and the fact that they don't last very long! So I don't do those either.

I think my exercise and nutrition habits play a huge part: years ago, I was invited to visit a special spa in India, where we got all kinds of ayurvedic treatments. But what stayed with me from that trip was the vegetarian food: up until then, I had eaten meat, but at the spa I was forced to eat vegetarian, and found to my surprise that it was especially delicious, and left me feeling light.

This is reflected in our faces, I think. I can say the same for alcohol: in the world of high-end art, we are constantly meeting clients for lunch, or attending black-tie openings at museums. And everywhere you go, there is expensive wine or champagne to drink. I got caught in that culture for a while, and I quickly saw how destructive alcohol is for your face and your health—so now I avoid it.

Finally, there is the ultimate cause of beauty—the seed. This is to maintain a cheerful and pleasant disposition all day, despite the challenges that inevitably pop up hour to hour. Anger is an especially negative seed that the ancient wisdom says eats away good seeds inside of us, and makes our face quickly age and wrinkle.

Earlier in my life I had a bit of a temper—getting mad at my computer or things not working out the way I had intended them to, for example. In recent years, now that I understand the deeper causes for beauty, I consider keeping my patience as just as important for my face as a light daily application of cream. And it has worked!

GMR:

You are also really physically fit and trim—I remember seeing you do some full splits in a recent yoga class, when younger people around you couldn't even get close.

Uta:

Well first of all, as far as surface causes, my parents encouraged me and my siblings to attend a tough gymnastics school—Olympic level, in fact—from a young age. Later I found out they just wanted to keep us busy after school so we wouldn't be out on the streets learning bad habits! At some point in this school, my teachers noticed that I had an aptitude for ballet movements, and ultimately I ended up spending some years in a very well respected ballet school in Berlin—just about the time I was beginning to get into fine art.

Of course, we can't keep up a professional level of ballet for many years, but the habits I learned stayed with me. First of all though I'd like to say that, as ballet performers for places like the German Opera, we were expected to stay impossibly thin, and so we had to diet almost constantly. As a result, many of us developed eating disorders—on the weekend after a performance, we would head out and buy a cake and actually eat the whole thing in one sitting.

And so I came to hate dieting, and I never do it any more. I eat healthy food, I eat what I want; I have a non-complicated health routine of fresh water, fresh food, and exercise—such as a very regular yoga practice.

GMR:

What would you credit as the deeper seeds that help the good food and exercise work for you?

Uta:

Now that's the real secret! I've seen people come to a yoga class and instead of getting trim, they leave with a neck injury that stays with them for years. And I've seen people who don't eat that much, but the food seems to stick on them as fat, almost immediately.

I personally feel that these things prove that there must be secret, "deeper" seeds to staying healthy and slender; and I try to plant those seeds on a daily basis. Again, it's all in the motivation.

GMR:

So give us one more 4-Step Plan, your secret one, please!

Uta:

Sure, here is a version of a 4-Step Plan to stay trim & healthy, in your body. I have customized it, according to my own experience, to add the seeds for great personal energy. I've found that it's one thing to look slender and fit; but it's another thing to have tons of personal energy to get things done in your life, whenever you want to. And so we want to plant both.

Step #1
Say what you want:

I want to look trim; I want to have a super-healthy body; and

I also want to have tons of energy all day long.

Step #2

Choose your seed-planting partner:

To get *both* a healthy body and all-day energy, you're going to have to do the seed-planting from two different angles; and that's going to require two different seed-planting partners.

As far as the healthy body, choose another person in your life who you can help get into a regular, daily exercise routine, and into healthy (preferably vegetarian) eating. You can assist them by doing your exercise together a few times a week, and sharing new dishes with them that you eat together, and which they learn how to cook. Helping them pick up a daily green-drink routine here is a very very easy and powerful seed you can plant.

As for the energy, your seed partner could be the same person, assuming they have trouble feeling enough energy throughout the day. Or, it could be another person who has this challenge with low energy.

Step #3

Here's where I have a special trick for you. I mean, you can have good blood work every time your doctor checks it, but at the same time you feel sad, you have no energy. Health and energy are definitely different things.

But when we have these two together, it also energizes the people around us. We become a living example, and then just by being near us, people feel inspired to live a healthy and compassionate life—which is just about the definition of living your life by the Seed System.

The "to do" in this case, then, would be *to make yourself your own seed-planting partner*. That is, you still need to spend an hour a week helping someone else eat and exercise well, and that's your intention-seed: to help them.

But above and beyond that, your intention is to get this 4-Step System going for your own super-healthy body and your own abundant energy, every day. Your intention is to be a living advertisement and inspiration to others to try the same 4 Steps for their own trim, healthy, energetic self. So every day, when you go through your own yoga routine, for example, you are very consciously remembering that you are doing it, yes, so you can be fit and trim; but more importantly because that will make you a good example—one which inspires others to do the same. This in itself is a powerful Step #3.

And just as a side-note, my yoga sessions took a big jump when I decided I would do them every day, whether I had time to go to the yoga studio or not. I made a promise to myself that on those many days when I didn't have time to go to a class, I would still do my yoga in my home—and I do. The ready availability of yoga videos on the internet means that there are hundreds of choices there, if you still want a guided class.

Step #4

Do your Coffee Meditation:

When you put your head down on your pillow, put in a good fight with your mind! Almost all of us tend to think worry thoughts as we go to sleep—I guess it's because, by definition, we are tired at that moment, so all of our problems seem bigger.

This is especially true if we wake up during the night. So what I've learned is that we have to catch ourselves when we're doing Problem Meditation instead of Coffee Meditation. And then we have to wrestle with our mind to bring it back to some good news about the help we have given others this week. I've found personally that *the morning hours*—say, at breakfast—are a much better time to worry about our problems. The pleasant breakfast and sunlight coming through the window seem to team up to make our problems manageable, at that time of day.

Don't let thinking about problems while you're going to sleep wreck your Coffee Meditation. By the way, this wrestling match with our own mind at night—when it wants to think about problems—is pretty much the essence of all ancient meditation techniques: good meditation is building up our "meditation muscle" by confronting our habit of worrying, and forcing it over to healthy thoughts about the good we are doing for others—the good seeds we are planting.

GMR:

Wow, I was just going to ask you about your personal tricks to get a good Coffee Meditation, and there you gave them to us already!

Uta:

Yes, although I have to add that—like Nour, whose success story we just read above—I carry around a little teddy bear with me wherever I travel; and when I see his smile waiting for me in bed, I remember it's time to do my Coffee Meditation. I really recommend it!

The financial

independence to be able

to help others

Seiji Arao Takahashi
a citizen of the world

GMR:

There, we've seen the Seed System working for people in countries from every major part of the world. But there's a new kind of citizenship nowadays—people who have been able to move around to different countries their whole life, and pick up the very best of each culture they've lived in, and share it with others. Seiji Arao Takahashi is one of these people. Seiji, can you give us some background about why we would think of you as a "citizen of the world"?

Seiji Arao Takahashi:

Well, first of all, my great-grandparents on both sides moved to Mexico from Japan during the first world war; so genetically I am Japanese, but we have lived here in Mexico for about a hundred years, and I grew up speaking both Japanese and Spanish.

My parents though were intent that I should have an international education, and so from kindergarten up to high school I attended schools where the medium was French. During my BA studies though, which I did with a major in entrepreneurship at Tech de Monterey (which in Mexico has a status similar to that of Harvard Business School in the US), I spent a year in Sweden on a scholarship exchange.

For my MA degree, which I did in environmental economics, I attended university in Australia. After that, I was hired as a consultant by DCI's Sedona College of International Management, and have assisted in establishing and administering academic programs here for the past three years, serving students from over 20 countries.

I also work as one of the ten primary translators in SCIM's School of Ancient Languages, and am currently responsible for translating a text about the Seed System that was written in Sanskrit about a thousand years ago. The manuscript itself currently survives only in Tibetan.

GMR:

So let's count those up. We can call you a citizen of the world, then, because intellectually you are part Japanese, part Mexican, part French, Swedish, Australian, Tibetan, Indian, and American, right?

Seiji:

Well yes, I guess you could put it that way!

GMR:

Anybody with that much inside of them from so many different cultures must have sort of a global view about life. How have those cultures informed your career goals?

Seiji:

I think the more time you spend around people from many different cultures, the more you get this desire to bring those people together—to devote some of your energy to making this world a place where everybody appreciates the precious differences between us: the delicious spice of life, you could say.

GMR:

Have you tried to carry out this viewpoint in your actual life, and work?

Seiji:

Well yes, exactly. Being inside of so many different cultures sort of automatically inspired me to reach out and help different kinds of people.

GMR:

What's an example?

Seiji:

Well, for example, I've also always had a big interest in the native cultures of Mexico. As I was growing up, I got involved in social work to help indigenous Mexican peoples like the Maya, the Huichol, and the Purepecha. In one project, I tried to help with an NGO where we made an attempt to market Huichol art, in order to preserve their culture and give them employment at the same time.

GMR:

The way you say it—"we made an attempt"—makes it sound like maybe the effort didn't work out that well.

Seiji:

Well yes, you see. I began to feel that there was an inherent problem in this whole attempt to help these native cultures. We would put together an NGO and get to work, but we never had enough money to do a good job. So we would take a leave from the NGO to go work for a "real" company for a while; save some money; and then come back to do our social work.

And so it always seemed like two bad choices: either you help people and don't make enough money to live on yourself, to keep helping; or you let go of helping other people and work where you can put together some money, and then come back to helping people. It seemed like we couldn't do both at the same time.

GMR:

And the way you say that, it sounds like you found a solution to this problem. What was it?

Seiji:

Well, that's exactly it. One day I had an opportunity to go to a DCI talk, where I heard about the Seed System. And I decided to give it a try, in a real and practical way. A friend of mine was giving lectures about this system around the city, and I put together actually all the savings I had at the time and donated it, to help him keep giving his talks.

It was a classic 4-Step approach, with all the steps done carefully, by the book. Two weeks later, I was awarded my scholarship to go to Australia, where I spent four years and completed my master's degree.

After that success with the Seed System, I started to use the 4 Steps on a regular basis.

GMR:

How has that manifested recently?

Seiji:

Well, as I've said, I was trying to solve this puzzle—like, how could I plant the perfect seeds to have a great income, and at the same time devote myself to helping people from different cultures like those I've had the good fortune to live in, in my life so far. How could I make my dream come true?

I designed a 4-Step Plan for this, which is sort of the first and the fifth of the five goals that we talk about in DCI; that is, I wanted financial independence (Goal #1); and at the same time I wanted to contribute in some way to the happiness of people around the whole world (Goal #5).

I carried out my plan, and I can say it succeeded: I was one of the first people chosen to work in the administration of SCIM. And so here I am; over the first three years I have worked my way up to assistant professor, and I have literally helped with the training of about a hundred DCI speakers, who have spread out across the world to help people in every part of the world. My dream has, truly, come true.

GMR:

As we've gone through these success stories, we've been asking each successful person to put their success into the format of an actual 4-Step Plan that our readers could try out for themselves. Can you express this plan in plain language, for us to use ourselves?

Seiji:

Sure; here we go—

Step #1

Say what you want:

I want to do what I'm passionate about—I want to make a real difference in this world—but at the same time I want to have a great income. I don't want to sacrifice my income to do what I'm passionate about; and I don't want to sacrifice my passion to get a good income.

Step #2:

Choose a seed-planting partner:

Identify people around you who would like to be financially independent, and still do what they're passionate about, at the same time.

Step #3:

Actually *do* something once a week, for an hour, to help this seed partner achieve these two goals, together.

Here, I'm going to make the same suggestion that we saw back in Uta's success story, from Germany. She talked about a two-prong approach to planting these seeds.

So let's say this seed partner is very similar to Seiji (they're *supposed* to be, to be a seed partner), and they want to find a job where they can make good money and at the same time do something to contribute to people from different cultures and countries around the world—let's say this is their *passion*.

First of all then, obviously, I could meet with them once a week for coffee, for about an hour, and discuss with them new ideas and resources I've come up with to help them get this dream job. The more sincere I am about helping them this way, then the more seeds I'm going to plant to be able myself to have financial independence and my dream job at the same time.

But secondly, there's another very important strategy I can use, and that's what DCI calls a "living example." To put it very simply, sometimes the best way we can help other people be successful is *to become successful ourselves.* That is, you can talk all day about how to become financially successful and still do what you love the most, but *the best way to convince other people that it's going to be possible is to **do it yourself, first!***

Step #3 in this scenario then is—yes—go ahead with your coffee-shop consultations with this seed partner; but in the same moment make sure that you walk into the coffee shop as a person *who has already reached the goal, themselves, of making a great salary and at the same time living out their passion—of actually helping people from different cultures and countries all over the world.*

Your seed partner—and everybody else—can "smell" whether you yourself have actually used this 4-Step Plan that you're asking them to try. And there's no better advertisement for a success method than a person who's a success because of it. So use both these strategies, at the same time, for your Step #3 here.

Step #4

For the fourth step, of course, it's *crucial* to remember, every night, to take joy in all the good things you're doing for making this other person successful. I've learned that *you can never skip* your pillow-time Coffee Meditation; this is the secret weapon for success!

GMR:

On the subject of this Step #4—since it's the most absolutely crucial step to success with the Four Steps—we've been asking each success story to share with us their own secret tip for a great Coffee Meditation. Do you have one for us?

Seiji:
Absolutely. Now you have to remember that I grew up in Mexico, where we have an attitude about recognizing our own good deeds which is very similar to what we heard from Nour before, from Islamic culture. Here in our Mexican Catholic culture, we are also encouraged, from a very young age, not to get feelings of pride about our good deeds. And I really do think that's a good thing, because we all know that it would ruin a good seed to think to yourself, "I'm just the best good-seed planter in all of Mexico. Nobody is as nice and as moral as me!"

Having said that, what I myself have learned—and I can say many of my DCI colleagues around the world have learned the same thing—that there is a big difference between pride about your good deeds, and celebrating your good deeds. Celebration doesn't compare itself to other people; rather, celebration just looks at the sweet things we've done for others today—as well as the sweet things we've seen others do for others today—and *enjoys the good in the world.*

This is the real essence of Coffee Meditation, and if you can steer your bedtime thoughts to this sweet place, I can personally say that it makes a huge difference in your life.

On a practical level, I have one more suggestion for Coffee Meditation. Since I do have friends that I've made over the course of my life in different countries and different cultures, I really enjoy making my Coffee Meditation a collaboration whenever I get a chance.

That is, I choose a person from another time zone, across the world, and I make an agreement with them that we call each other when we're in bed and ready to think about the good things we've done and seen others do, today. That means each of us is going to get a chance to think about good seeds twice a day—at bedtime in the two different time zones—and that really makes those seeds grow much, much faster and stronger.

Give it a try!

*A word about my
own success*

Geshe Michael Roach

This whole book—*The Diamond Cutter*—started out, twenty years ago, as a way of describing the success I had achieved by using the Seed System, and sharing with others how they could do the same. Of course it's one of the most joyful things in anybody's life when we hear from others that we have helped them be happy and successful, and I've enjoyed this pleasure countless times since the book first came out.

It's not my goal in this 20th anniversary edition then to talk more about myself, but I would like to add a few words here, at the end, to describe my own feelings and experiences now—twenty years later—just as encouragement for you. If the Seed System really works, then we want to be sure that it worked for the person who helped get it going in modern times.

And right here, right now, I just want to tell you that this system has been an incredible success, in my own life. Without seeming arrogant, but at the same time wanting to be honest, I can say that I am the happiest person I know.

In terms of the 5 goals that most people in the world would like to achieve in their life, I have first of all had considerable financial success and security (Goal #1). This began with my income from Andin International Diamond Corporation—the success described in the original *Diamond Cutter* book—which by the way eventually reached $US250 million in annual sales and was purchased by super-investor Warren Buffett, one of the world's four or five wealthiest people, in 2009.

As Seiji pointed out in his success story, my own financial share of this success allowed me to found and fund many very successful charitable projects, such as the 30-year effort to preserve ancient spiritual literature described in John Brady's success story.

As far as relationships (Goal #2), I have used the 4 Steps to create some five or six very successful corporations which are still going after many years, and where my colleagues have become close family members who love and support each other year after year, decade upon decade. My own personal relationship at home—with my lifelong love Veronica—is also very precious and beautiful.

As for health (Goal #3), I am now 70 years old and still do yoga almost every day of the week—sometimes with ballet exercises thrown in—and continue with a personal travel schedule that sends me to 20 countries of the world every year: the airplane companies love me! I do thousands of pages of translation from ancient texts, and new books and training manuals, every year; and I lead about 200 translation sessions, as well as a few hundred management training classes, annually. The 4 Steps, as Uta pointed out, have given me the energy that all of us want to have, for the whole length of our life.

One thing I haven't figured out though is how to plant the mental seeds for hair, so in the second ten years of *The Diamond Cutter* I've kept the same bald spot that I had during the first ten years. But I'm working on it; still checking all the ancient books, to find out which seeds to plant!!

Mentally and spiritually, I feel extremely happy and content (Goal #4)—and I can say that almost every day I feel new inspiration and creativity pouring into my brain. I know almost all of us, as we reach older age, feel that our mind is slipping a bit each year; but I can honestly say that by constantly working on my 4-Step Plans, my mind to me seems sharper and deeper as each year passes—a real pleasure to be inside of.

As for the final goal, I have had the pleasure and the honor—along

with my dear and devoted colleagues such as DCI vice-presidents Scott
& Orit Vacek, and my personal assistant for 25 years, Elizabeth van der
Pas (each of whom literally makes my life possible)—to spend my days,
every day, trying to help people all over the world have a happy and
successful life. And looking back, I can honestly say (as *The Diamond
Cutter* promises us) that I have made beautiful and precious use of my life.

All of this is because of the Seed System—the 4 Steps that you've
heard about here in all these pages of success stories. I think you'd be
crazy not to at least give this method a try! Design yourself a tiny 4-Step
Experiment, and then give it 5 or 6 weeks to see if it works! You have
nothing to lose, and everything to gain. For example, you could give this
a try:

Step #1

Say what you want:

I would like to increase my income by 10%.

Step #2

Choose a seed-planting partner:

Someone else you know who wants a larger income.

Step #3

Help them, once a week, for an hour, for free:

Take them to a coffee shop, and talk together about things
they might try to get that income boost they are looking for.

Step #4

**This is the most important step: do not ignore it, put real daily
energy into it!**

When you put your head down on your pillow at night to go
to sleep, give just a few minutes' thought to what you are already
doing to help your seed partner, and what you plan to do this
coming week to continue helping them.

You **will** be a success!

About the Author

Geshe Michael Roach was born in Los Angeles. He is an honors graduate of Princeton University and received the Presidential Scholar Medallion from the President of the United States at the White House. He has also been awarded an honorary PhD for lifetime achievement in the Congress of Mexico; and is a recipient of the McConnell Scholarship Prize awarded by the Woodrow Wilson School of International Affairs.

Geshe Michael is one of the founders of Andin International Diamond Corporation of New York City, which became the world's largest diamond jewelry company and was sold to super-investor Warren Buffett in 2009.

Michael is also the first American ever to be awarded the degree of *Geshe,* or Master of Buddhism, from a traditional Tibetan Buddhist monastery. At Princeton, in 1987, with the help of the Hewlett Packard Foundation, he founded the original version of the Asian Legacy Library, which has located and digitalized millions of pages of ancient Asian manuscripts, and provided them online free of charge.

In 1993, Michael also founded the Asian Classics Institute, for in-depth studies of this ancient Asian tradition of wisdom. In 2003 he established the Diamond Mountain Retreat Center, for bringing the tradition of quiet creative retreats to the United States. In 2010 he started the Diamond Cutter Institute, for personal and business success trainings; DCI currently leads programs each year for 30,000 people in more than 20 countries. In 2016, Michael founded the Sedona College of International Management for training DCI teachers.

In 2000, Michael published *The Diamond Cutter: The Buddha on Managing Your Business & Your Life.* This quickly became a global bestseller and has been translated into more than 30 languages. He has authored more than 80 other works, and has translated and published over 10,000 pages of ancient Asian literature.

Resources for Going Deeper

BOOKS

(ORDER THEM ONLINE AT AMAZON,
BARNES & NOBLE, AND OTHER MAJOR DISTRIBUTORS,
OR AT THE DIAMOND CUTTER PRESS WEBSITE:
www.DiamondCutterPress.com)

The following books are all written by Geshe Michael Roach and are available in 35 languages. For information about your language, contact Diamond Cutter Press at *info@diamondcutterpress.com*

❖ To start a business, or to reach financial freedom:
   The Diamond Cutter: The Buddha on Managing Your Business & Your Life

❖ To run a business, or to be a successful manager:
   Karmic Management:
   What Goes Around Comes Around, in Your Business and Your Life

❖ To find or improve a relationship: *The Karma of Love*

❖ To fix your health, keep it good, increase energy: *How Yoga Works*

❖ To apply seeds to the state of the world:
   China Love You: the Death of Global Competition

❖ For serious study of the Yoga Sutra: *The Essential Yoga Sutra*

❖ For practical tips on how to do yoga: *The Tibetan Book of Yoga*

❖ For peace & spiritual development: *The Garden: A Parable*

❖ About the history of the ancient wisdom tradition:
   King of the Dharma: the Illustrated Life of Je Tsongkapa

❖ General advice for life:
  The 20 Biggest Mistakes You Can Make in Your Life, and How Not To!

❖ New ideas about science and understanding the universe:
  A Better History of Time:
  Impossible Solutions to the Biggest Questions of Science

MEDITATION TRAINING & RETREATS
Asian Classics Institute at *asianclassicsinstitute.org*
Diamond Mountain Retreat Center at *diamondmountain.org*
Three Jewels NYC at *threejewels.org*
Yoga Studies Institute at *yogastudiesinstitute.org*

FREE ONLINE COURSES FOR SPIRITUAL DEVELOPMENT
Asian Classics Institute at *asianclassicsinstitute.org* and *acidharma.org*

ABOUT 5,000 FREE TALKS BY GESHE MICHAEL
Check out *theknowledgebase.com*

SUCCESS TRAININGS

Geshe Michael and the Diamond Cutter Institute offer professional trainings in success and personal development throughout the year to more than 30,000 people in about 20 countries. For more information on attending or requesting a program, see *diamondcutterinstitute.com* or write *info@diamondcutterinstitute.com*

DCI TEACHER TRAINING COURSES

Come become a teacher for DCI!
Three academic sessions per year,
at the Sedona College of International Management,
See *sedonacollegeinternational.com*
or write *info@sedonacollegeinternational.com*

BUSINESS RETREATS AND CONFERENCES

DCI also organizes business retreats and conferences at the Bear Springs Retreat and Conference Center. This is an extraordinarily beautiful, natural site in the mountains of Arizona, with 30 comfortable retreat cottages for group or individual use. Contact us if you'd like to schedule an event at the center; *info@diamondcutterinstitute.com*